Manhattan - Elwood Public Library
Condition: W9-AAU-389
Date/Initials: 7/17/15 NB

ABOUT LITTLE HEATHENS

"I found myself in another world, being brought back to my childhood with my brothers. Great memories, great book. I want more!"

—Linda Young in Lexington, Kentucky

"Are you sure you kids weren't part of my banshee family...really good stuff...and I swear we did a lot of the same crazy stuff."

—Annette Ardolf in Burnsville, Minnesota

"I caught myself waxing nostalgic for the days of my youth."

—Dale Dodds in Rochester, Minnesota

"Marvelous, hilarious, well written tales."

—Laura Vitt in Marietta, Georgia

AUG 22 2013

LITTLE HEATHENS

LITTLE HEATHENS

BY

RON BAY, JR.

TATE PUBLISHING
AND ENTERPRISES, LLC

MANHATTAN-ELWOOD
PUBLIC LIBRARY DISTRICT

Little Heathens
Copyright © 2013 by Ron Bay, Jr.. All rights reserved.

No part of this publication may be reproduced, stored in a retrieval system or transmitted in any way by any means, electronic, mechanical, photocopy, recording or otherwise without the prior permission of the author except as provided by USA copyright law.

Scripture quotations taken from the *New American Standard Bible*®, Copyright © 1960, 1962, 1963, 1968, 1971, 1972, 1973, 1975, 1977, 1995 by The Lockman Foundation. Used by permission.

The opinions expressed by the author are not necessarily those of Tate Publishing, LLC.

Published by Tate Publishing & Enterprises, LLC
127 E. Trade Center Terrace | Mustang, Oklahoma 73064 USA
1.888.361.9473 | www.tatepublishing.com

Tate Publishing is committed to excellence in the publishing industry. The company reflects the philosophy established by the founders, based on Psalm 68:11,
"The Lord gave the word and great was the company of those who published it."

Book design copyright © 2013 by Tate Publishing, LLC. All rights reserved.
Cover design by Samson Lim
Interior design by Mary Jean Archival

Published in the United States of America

ISBN: 978-1-62510-203-4
1. Family & Relationships / Siblings
2. Family & Relationships / Life Stages / School Age
13.02.27

3 8001 00112 2575

To God be the glory. For blessing me with my parents and siblings who made these stories possible. For my wife and sons, for my daughters in-law and grandchildren. For my ability to remember my wonderful childhood.

CONTENTS

FOREWORD

Over the years, I've had numerous conversations with friends and coworkers regarding our school days, childhood, our growing-up times. Inevitably, I would end up telling a story about my brother, sisters, and myself and some of the predicaments in which we found ourselves. The reactions were varied: uncontrolled laughter, blank stares of disbelief, and even the occasional walking away while shaking their head (after reading this book, you too may find some of these stories leading you to shake your head; I certainly do, and I was there).

Another phenomenon would occur whenever the four of us were together, and we began reminiscing and reliving our adventures. On one such occasion, we were at a restaurant following a major family event (in this case a funeral), and the entire family—nephews, nieces, aunts, and uncles—were seated at a large table. The tenor within the restaurant was the normal buzz of people eating dinner and chatting when all of a sudden we began telling our tales. The people at our table were soon cracking up with laughter as each tale was told. As the hilarity increased, so did the volume. Soon, those around were seen bending their ears to catch a little of the stories, and they too would be seen smiling and chuckling to themselves (it may have been the stories, but could have been the spectacle that we'd become). All of these were common reactions to our family adventures.

Not all of those that I've spoken to over the years had fond memories of their childhood. I've never understood that feeling. I absolutely had a wonderful childhood from the time I can remember all the way through high school. Whether I was playing in the neighborhood or going to school, it all seemed like one grand adventure. For this reason and those listed above, I decided to share these stories with a broader audience. I find great joy in bringing the same to others.

This is a story of four little kids growing up together in an era when life was a little more innocent and kids entertained themselves, if they were going to be entertained. We were mischievous, ornery, fun-loving, high-energy kids, not unlike most other kids. As my wife would sit and listen to these stories being told, she would often remark, "You guys were little heathens." Thus the title of this book.

I LOVE THIS NEIGHBORHOOD

A favorite family movie is *The Burbs*, and one of the memorable lines in the movie was uttered by Corey Feldman, "Man, I love this neighborhood." I know why I love *The Burbs* so much: it reminds me a lot of the neighborhood where my siblings and I grew up, and I share the sentiment with Corey Feldman's character, Ricky. We had wacky neighbors (and we were wacky neighbors), strange houses, conspiracy theories, teenagers, and toddlers and plenty of adventure to relish. If you haven't seen the movie, you should rent it and enjoy, and if you do, you will get a feeling of déjà vu (having read the narrative I am about to elucidate).

Ours was a typical middle-class neighborhood: cookie-cutter houses with about ten feet between them, one tree along the curb, surrounded by a freeway behind us, and two major roads running alongside and in front of our street. All of the above were off-limits to us kids, but you know how that goes. One really interesting feature of our block was that all of the houses were interconnected by a cinder block wall that stood approximately five and a half feet high (I know the height because Dad could barely look over the fence, and he stands six feet two). You might think that this wall gave every house on the block plenty of privacy, but you would be wrong, considering the four of us. The wall was plenty high enough for normal kids (I said normal kids), but we somehow found a way to get up on top of the wall. In order to climb the wall, you had to jump as high as you could, grab a hold of the top (sometimes, the top brick came loose and would cause you to fall back and try again), and push yourself up with your feet, digging in on the cinder blocks (stubbing one's toe was common, and scrapes and cuts on the arms and upper body were inevitable). For little sister Kathy, who was too small to climb up alone, one of the older kids would reach down and pull her up to the top of the wall. Once on top of the wall, we would make our way in either direction, from one end of the block to the other. Can you imagine the neighbor's musings? The neighbor man, casually relaxing in his lawn chair, turns to his wife, "Honey, there are four kids walking on top of our wall! I wonder who they are and where they're going." His wife, just as nonchalant as her husband, replies, "Dear, I believe those are the Bay kids from the other side of the block. They've recently been appearing on the wall." "Well, why are they all barefoot?" he wants to know. Venturing a guess she responds, "I don't know for sure, but I don't believe I've ever seen them with shoes on. Should we tell their parents?" Not wanting to be bothered he answers flippantly, "No, maybe we'll get lucky and they'll fall off and break something."

We became pretty adept at traversing the top of the wall, which was wider than our foot, but not by much. Because of this, you had to travel single file, one kid behind the other. Occasionally, a neighbor would yell at us, "Hey, you kids get off the wall!" (Why, the nerve!) and the turning around part became a little dicey (we did pass each other on the wall, but that took the best of our balance and dexterity to pull it off and normally didn't happen unless the front person had encountered something that they were afraid of and the ones behind hadn't yet figured it out). Vicki was usually in the lead and on one such occasion offered this to the rest of us following single file behind her, "Turn around and go back. The neighbor is yelling at me. Hurry up!"

During those times when we did lose our balance and fall, we would be back up on the wall within seconds of hitting the ground, especially if there was a dog in the yard. It might take me thirty seconds to climb the wall on a normal day, but if there was a dog in the yard bolting toward me, barking, with slobber dripping out of its mouth, I could scale that wall in five seconds flat (dogs scared me). There was a section of the wall that was impeded by a large bush in one of the neighbor's yards. The branches were lying across the top of the wall, and getting past them required much balance and the mobility of a mountain goat.

The wall became a problem for us when we were playing any game when there was a ball involved (the ball had a tendency to leave our yard and land in the neighbor's). What to do? It was obvious we had to get the ball, but how? In addition to the wall, there was a bigger problem with retrieving our ball: each of our neighbors on all three sides had dogs! The neighbor to our right had three Chihuahua dogs. These were not your normal Chihuahua dogs; they were huge, vicious, long-toothed, some type of hybrid breed of Chihuahua dog. Timmy and I were scared to go over there and get our ball (it never occurred to us to walk around to the front of the house, ring the doorbell, and ask for our ball). Simultaneously, we came up with the same plan (send Kathy over the wall!). But how would we convince her? Initially I tried to bribe her and said, "Kathy, I have some candy I'll give you (I don't mess around), if you'll go get our ball next door." Timmy chimed in and begged her, "Pwease, pwease, pwease Kathy, would you go get ow bawh?" Kathy would not fall for either ploy and responded, "No. I don't want to." Besides, ahn't theh dogs next doah?" I've been known to lie and said, "Kathy, those are little Chihuahua dogs that couldn't hurt a flea. I'll give you all of my candy. Please?" "Okay" was her response and I had to assume it was that final bribe that put her over the edge.

I know what you're thinking: what a cruel thing to do to your little sister. I never felt guilty about it until the event was over; besides, we didn't have a choice. Timmy and I got Kathy up on the wall, and we could see our ball across the neighbor's yard. No dogs in sight. As we slowly lifted Kathy down, we told her to hurry up before the dogs were the wiser. As she grabbed the ball and headed back to the wall, out of nowhere, the three amigos,

I mean Chihuahuas, bolted toward her. As Kathy tried to get up on the wall, the dogs were jumping all over her, biting her bottom and pulling down her pants. Up on the wall, Timmy and I were pretty helpful. "Kathy, thwow the bawh ovah the fence," Timmy offered. I followed up with this encouragement, "Kathy, don't worry, those dogs aren't hurting you. Timmy and I will pull you up, but you have to throw the ball over the fence first." The only words out of Kathy at this point were, "Waaahhh!"

We finally got Kathy to throw the ball back into our yard, lifted her over the fence, pulled her pants up, told her not to tell Mom, and then went to the tree in the front yard to pull a switch for the discipline that surely would come. In all future endeavors involving balls in neighbor's yards, Kathy was not involved.

The neighbor behind us had a dog too. This dog was a bit larger than the Chihuahuas and was much more aggressive and faster. He was black and white (a cocker spaniel), had very thick fur, and his bite was worse than his bark. When the ball went over the wall into this dog's yard, we had to work on our strategy. You couldn't just climb down the wall into the backyard because before your foot hit the ground, this dog was all over you, tearing you to pieces. He was a smart dog (adept at undercover work and counterespionage), always hiding behind bushes, beside the house, wherever he could conduct his surveillance. It didn't matter what time of day it was, you could not get a foot down and that dog was right there, no bark, just *wooosh*! He was there. We weren't about to let any dog outsmart us however. Our strategic battle plan was brilliant. If the ball was on the east end of the yard for example, one of us would go to the west end of the yard and begin the climb down. This time we had him fooled. While the decoy was on the west end, the other kid was on the east end where the ball was located. The decoy never intended to set foot in the yard, but the strategy was effective. The dog ran over to the kid on the west end, and in the meantime, the other kid would quickly jump down, grab the ball, and be back up on the wall before the dog knew what hit him. Then we would sit on the wall, stick our tongues out, and make fun of the dog. If nothing else could be said about us, we were smarter than a dog, at least on this occasion.

The neighbor on our other flank also had a dog; her name was Trixie. There were indeed times when we lost a ball over the wall into their backyard, but the ordeal of climbing the wall and somehow outsmarting the dog didn't apply here for two reasons: Trixie was not very aggressive (the one dog in the world that I wasn't scared of), and all we had to do was yell over the fence and the ball would miraculously come flying back into our yard. I really don't think the neighbors were being helpful or kind, it was more that they didn't want us in their backyard. The odd thing was we really wanted to be in their backyard because it was far more interesting than ours. They had a large tree in the middle of the yard, and someone had built a neat tree house in the top of it. They also had a fenced-in pigeon house where they raised pigeons. We did make it into their yard if only for a little while (until the parents figured out it was us back there and then sent us home) and had some fun times. One memory that stands out from their backyard was not fun at all, but a very dark experience for me. It was this experience that took away some of my innocence. It involved the pigeons in the pigeon coop.

One day, David and his brothers allowed me into their backyard, unbeknownst to their parents, but soon after, they disappeared and I was alone. As I looked around, my eyes became attracted to the pigeon coop, and curiosity got the best of me. The coop was made of chicken wire (not pigeon wire) nailed around a wooden frame, and in order to get inside, there was a door that was latched and always kept shut. Once past the latched door, I was inside the coop. I saw adult pigeons and they pretty much ignored me (cooh, cooh). I also saw some baby pigeons, referred to as squab, and decided to have a closer look. I picked up one of the babies and noticed how soft and fluffy it felt. It seemed pretty helpless as I held it in my hands. Suddenly, I began to squeeze it. I'm not sure why other than I must have had a hidden and severe mean streak in me. As I placed the baby pigeon back where I found it, I noticed it was no longer moving. I had murdered a baby pigeon! I was shaken and distraught. This was much different than killing a slug or ant. This was a living being, a warm-blooded creature. I don't believe that I intended to kill the bird, but I did nevertheless. As I was trying to figure out what to do next, David appeared around the corner and headed my way. I panicked, but only briefly. My initial reaction was to lie (I was an expert liar, although I was usually found out eventually). As David approached me, I quickly said, "David, one of your pigeons is dead." Caught off guard he said, "What happened?"

I was already gone. He never got an answer. This event weighed on my psyche for quite some time, at least until I got my first BB gun and shot birds, squirrels, rabbits, frogs, snakes, my brother, and other assorted victims.

As I mentioned earlier, there were plenty of kids in the neighborhood ranging from toddler age to teenage. On our left were the brothers: David, Ronnie (my age), and Bobby. On our right was Patty, who was my age. Next to Patty's house were my best friend Russell and his sister Sandy. Two houses down from Russells, were the brothers Mark (my age), Matt, and Mitch. Moving across the street was Neal, an only boy and Vicki's age. Next to Neal, coming back the other direction was the Z family with Ronnie and his sisters. The next house had the only pool in the neighborhood (of which we were only invited to swim once; go figure), owned by a family with a boy Mark (my age) and his sister (Kathy's age). Next door to Mark were David T. (my age and my nemesis) and his older sister. There was a family up the block that we called the Seven Kids for obvious reasons, but we didn't have much interaction with them. One time, we found out something had happened at the Seven Kids' house and ran home excitedly to tell Mom. Vicki said excitedly, "Mommy, The Seven Kids aren't The Seven Kids anymore!" Mom was incredulous and said, "I'm sorry, what did you say?" Timmy chimed in, "They ahn't seven kids anymoah!" Mom even more confused, "I don't understand. How can they no longer be The Seven Kids?" "They have eight kids now," I replied in a matter of fact way.

It took us a while to change our lingo, but finally the Eight Kids rolled off our tongues as easily as the Seven Kids had. Most of the kids mentioned above were within a few years of age as the four of us, with a couple of teenage girls as the exception.

The San Gabriel Freeway ran behind our house, and during the time we lived there, it was under construction. All we had to do was walk around the block, cross the street, and the construction site with all of its possibilities was just waiting for us to explore. There were large mounds of dirt, giant concrete boulders and pipes (I'll never forget the smell of those pipes, kind of a wet, clay smell that I have run across over the years, and each time I have, I remember crawling through the pipes at the construction site), and a trailer where the foreman worked. The opportunities for mischief were endless.

The giant mounds of dirt provided a place to ride our bikes (it seems that the street wasn't quite exciting enough). The mounds were so high that it was difficult to ride to the top, so we would walk our bikes up and fly down the hills. Coming to a stop upon reaching the bottom had to be maneuvered with the utmost care.

The best thing the dirt mounds gave us was a never-ending supply of dirt clods. Dirt clods were not good for anything other than throwing: at cars on the freeway (to be explored in a moment), at other kids, and at each other. Dirt clod fights were common. Most of the dirt clods were just that, dirt. However, some of them had other substances mixed in with the dirt; in this case, rocks. It is one thing to get hit by a dirt clod, but quite another to get hit by a rock clod. In a typical exchange, Timmy—upon being hit with said rock clod—tearfully exclaimed, "Hey, youh diht clod had a wock in it! That huhts! I'm tewhing Mommy." To which I replied in mock defiance, "Go ahead and tell. I'll tell Mommy that you were at the construction site and we'll both be in trouble."

That was a mistake on my part as I had forgotten that getting us both into trouble didn't faze Timmy.

We actually had a dirt clod war one day. There was an empty field near our house, and we discovered that in addition to the normal dirt clods, this particular field had large clumps of grass. If you grabbed the grass by the handful and pulled it out of the ground, you not only got the roots, but a large clump of dirt. The grass made a good handle with which to throw, and these clumps became our hand grenades and sometimes were used as mortars (actually more of a catapult). If there were a bunch of kids involved in the war, you not only had to watch for the dirt clods that were thrown, sometimes at point-blank range, but you also had large clumps of grass and dirt raining down out of the sky. We didn't have army helmets.

I mentioned earlier throwing dirt clods at cars on the freeway. The one kid in the neighborhood that everyone's mother made off-limits (the one other than me) was Brad C. One day, Brad and I decided to climb up on that big mound of dirt at the construction site overlooking the freeway and play. Once on top of the dirt pile, we looked down at the cars on the freeway, looked at the dirt clods at our feet in great supply, and looked at each other. Soon, one dirt clod after another flew through the air and exploded around passing cars, the drivers unaware of the danger surrounding them. If we hit a car, shouts of glee erupted, and the dirt-clod throwing would increase in intensity. When we finally hit one car, the vehicle came to an immediate stop and we ran. As we got down to street level, we talked about the incident. In an anxious tone Brad asked, "Do you think we'll get caught?" I answered assuredly, "How could we? The cars can't get off the freeway until the next exit, and how would they know it was us?"

As we walked down the sidewalk, a car pulled up beside us on the street. We turned to look and recognized the car we had hit (it still had a large dirt spot on the windshield). It may be hard to believe, but the driver of this particular vehicle just happened to be an off-duty policeman. As he loaded us in the car, he pressed us for our vitals: "Where do you boys live?" the policeman asked. Brad, more concerned with wiping the dirt off his hands, replied, "I don't know." Once again I lied (to a policeman!) and said, "Santa Monica?"

As the policeman drove away from my house in his unmarked car, I made my way out to the tree in the front yard to peruse the branches for the ideal switch. This was going to be a doozy of a whipping.

We had a lot of fun at the construction site where we weren't supposed to be, but the thing that intrigued us most was the foreman's trailer. We would see the workers entering and leaving the trailer throughout the day, and the curiosity got the best of us. We just had to know what was in that trailer. We noticed that everyone went home sometime in the late afternoon.

One day, we decided to make our move. After the construction workers went home, we snuck up to the trailer and climbed up onto the makeshift porch. We tried the door, but it was locked. That small detail did not deter us however. There was a window next to the porch, and lo and behold, it was unlocked. We slid it open, and one by one, we climbed into the trailer. It was pretty neat inside the trailer. There were separate rooms with desks, and on the desks were large blueprints and some pencils and pens lying around. We didn't stay in the trailer long (a slight fear of getting caught caused us to overlook a few things we could have destroyed), but my guess is that when the foreman came back to the trailer and saw what we'd done to his blueprints and toilet, he probably wasn't much fun to be around for a few days.

Next to the foreman's trailer was an enclosed area with a chain-link fence and gate. Completely covering the fence was some very thick ivy, so that if you were in the enclosed area, you could not be seen from the street. This was a great hiding place. One day, it became more than that. One of the older boys had obtained some cigarettes and was egging us on to try one. For some reason he looked directly at me when he said, "Are you guys scaredy-cats? I bet you won't smoke one. You're chicken!" Trying to be brave I came off cocky when I replied, "My dad smokes Camel no filters. I'm not scared. Give me one." (As if my dad smoking them had anything to do with me.) In my support Timmy offered up, "Yeah."

I didn't even know how to light a cigarette, let alone smoke one. The older kid lit the cigarette and handed it to me. I took one puff, and the second the smoke hit my lungs, I thought that I would die. My lungs burned, the world started spinning round and round, I turned green (or so I was told), and within a minute or two, whatever I had for breakfast ended up at my feet. It took me awhile to get my bearings, amidst all the laughter from the other kids, and I finally managed to stagger my way home. The dentist would have been proud of me that day as I think I must have brushed my teeth ten times to make sure no one knew. I bribed Timmy to keep quiet; he liked candy as much as Kathy.

Speaking of freeways, Kathy, and candy, there was an incident on the San Gabriel Freeway that is still talked about today. The fact that we were banned from "playing on the freeway" made total sense (of course, at the time, we had to ask "how come?") and is probably why we were destined to end up there anyway. One day, Mom called me into the house and peppered me with this: "Ronnie, where is your sister?" she asked. Being a bit of a smart aleck I replied, "Which one?" Beginning to be irritated, Mom was a little more forceful, "You know which one. You were supposed to be watching Kathy. Where is she?" By now I was becoming exasperated with the line of questioning and replied, "Am I my sister's keeper? (I really didn't say that, although it does fit). I don't know where she is." Timmy, always helpful, added,

"David P. said he was taking heh to his gwandma's to get candy and ice cweam." Mom now turned her attention to Timmy, to my relief, and questioned him, "Where did they go? Where did he take her?" Timmy answered, "He said they weh going to his gwandma's and they weh wahking on the fweeway." Once again, Mom turned to me with instructions, "Ronnie, you go get your sister and bring her back home. Now!" Mom didn't seem too worried about *me* being on the freeway.

Now David P., our next-door neighbor, was often times a little bit off (in the way that Jack Nicholson in *The Shining* was a little bit off). He had to take medicine to remain calm, if you know what I mean. We didn't quite know the clinical term, but today, I think he might be considered mentally challenged. All I know is, when he wasn't taking his medicines, we tended to play on the other side of the block. Just to give you a little insight as to David's possibilities: one day, Kathy came home missing her ponytail. Mom saw the new hairdo and demanded of Kathy, "Kathy, what happened to your pony tail!? All that's left of it is a rubber band!" Kathy, not knowing what else to say told the truth, "David cut it off." (Maybe David thought we were in a game of cowboys and Indians and he was just claiming the white girl's scalp).

David, after the incident, was seen around the neighborhood with Kathy's ponytail attached to his belt. Anyway, David apparently convinced Kathy to go with him to his grandma's house to get candy and ice cream (I indicated earlier that candy was Kathy's kryptonite). It was news to me that I was supposed to be watching her, but then again, I was known to have selective hearing. I got on my bike and headed to the freeway, and I saw two figures walking on the shoulder of the freeway, about a half mile ahead. I rode real fast and caught up with them. As I jumped off my bike and grabbed Kathy's arm: "Kathy, Mommy said you have to come home. I came to get you, so get on my bike and I will ride you home." Kathy was intent on the candy and tersely replied "No!" Not to be deterred, I insisted, "Kathy, Mommy said you have to come home! Stop pulling and come with me." She too was insistent and adamantly replied, "I want candy and ice cweam."

David and Kathy were pulling one way and I was pulling the other (a little tug-of-war by the side of the road, or better yet, Kathy was the wishbone and David and I wanted to see who would get their wish). Cars were flying by at seventy plus miles per hour, and the tugging and pulling spilled out into traffic. A woman in a passing car was heard to exclaim, "Honey, those kids are going to get killed!" Her husband, not near as concerned, said, "I wonder what they're doing on the freeway?" His wife, in a moment of introspection said, "Probably looking for ice cream and candy."

At this point, I gave up and turned around to head back home. I wasn't sure what to tell Mom, but figured I might as well tell the truth this time. As I pulled into the driveway, a black-and-white police car was leaving (I waved at the policemen). When I got in the front door, Kathy was bawling, and Mom was staring at me with a mean look and a switch already in hand (at least I didn't have to go get my own switch).

On the other side of the freeway (since the freeway was off-limits, it should have been our outer boundary) was the San Gabriel River. I'm not sure why it was called a river as it never had much water in it. We called it the riverbed. In years past, this river was subject to flash flooding, but since then, dams were built along the way to control the flow of water. Most of the time, it was fairly dry with patches of water and long stretches of mud (in the movie *Terminator 2*, there is a scene where the bad Terminator, T-1000, played by Robert Patrick, is in a semi-truck, chasing the good Terminator, played by Arnold Schwarzenegger, who is on a really nice motorcycle. They end up driving off the streets and down into the riverbed). The sides of the riverbed were made of concrete and slanted down from the top to the river bottom (about a twenty-foot drop). That being the case, it didn't stop our imaginations from running wild. While we played in the riverbed, we imagined a huge wall of water crushing down on us at a moment's notice and always kept one eye upstream, just in case. The setup was perfect for riding our bikes. The riverbed was often strewn with assorted trash and junk; old tires, bicycles, and auto parts were common. Our main purposes for being there? We were forbidden to be there, and we thought it would be a good idea to catch tadpoles.

Our backyard was a typical backyard with grass and bushes, a brick patio with trellis and ivy, and on one side of the house was a parcel of dirt. In one corner of the yard was a section for Mom's cactus garden. We often played what we called "trucks" in the backyard. It included trucks, cars, earth-moving equipment, whatever other toys we had on hand. I had the best truck money could buy: the big, yellow, Tonka dump truck. That truck was so well built that you could basically stand inside of it and use it as a skateboard, or, in some cases, stick your little sister inside of it and push her around the driveway. Timmy had a dump truck too, but it was made of plastic and wasn't as sturdy as the metal Tonka truck. We would take all of our trucks, cars, etc., out in the yard and lie down in the grass and drive them (always with the accompanying car or truck noise made with our mouths) from one point to another. At that angle, the grass blades could be trees, or other growth. In order to have roads, we dug up the grass and into the dirt with a handy stick or small shovel, making trenches that intersected throughout the backyard (Dad didn't like our roads in his yard). We all had fairly active imaginations and wondered how we could make trucks more realistic, more like real life. One thing that appealed to us was to take the water hose and fill up the trenches in the backyard with water (you know, like a flood or river), and our cars and trucks would navigate through mud and water. It sure was realistic.

The effect we liked the most, however, was accomplished alongside the house where there was a large patch of dirt. We had one next to our house (eventually, Dad had sand dumped there, which eliminated most of the fun) and so did the neighbor. We were playing trucks next door, and we decided to create the same atmosphere that we saw every day at the construction site. During dry spells, and there were plenty of those in LA, the dirt patch would turn to a thick layer of dust on the surface and hard-packed dirt underneath. Timmy and I were playing and I came up with an idea. "Timmy, go get Dad's driveway broom out of the garage." Being the big brother, I could direct Timmy and he would comply, at least in these formative years. Timmy curiously questioned, "Okay. Ah we going to pway twucks?" "Yes, we are" I responded.

Timmy took the broom and swished and stirred that dirt (he looked like a video of the janitor at school in fast motion) until a large cloud of dust arose between the two houses (fire trucks were called in, but sent home shortly thereafter). It was great! We were coughing and sneezing and making truck noises, and we repeated the activity each time the dust would settle.

On one occasion, the dust got so bad that we had to get the hose out and spray water to dissipate the cloud. It had to be like the construction site, remember? When we came into the house at the end of the day, Mom was treated to a couple of possibilities: either we would be covered in mud from head to toe or every pore of our body would be caked in dust (those lines around the neck [a dirt necklace] and under the arm where we sweated the most would be extremely grimy). Either way, Mom wasn't too happy. "Who tracked mud into this house?" was her question to no one in particular. Of course, the answer from the four of us, in unison, was "Not me."

My best friend in the neighborhood was Russell. He was a year older than me and lived two houses down. Even though Russell liked me, I'm not sure his mother did. I think I know why as the following was a typical daily exchange: I would first appear on Russell's doorstep at 7:00 a.m. on a Saturday morning and push the doorbell. "Ding dong" the chimes would ring. Answering the door was Russell's mom and with a forced smile, and as pleasantly as she could, she greeted me, "Good morning, Ronnie." Not waiting for a question I blurted out, "Can Russell come out to play?" As patiently as she could, she answered, "Russell is still asleep. Come back later when he wakes up." "Okay," I replied. I waited about as long as I could and at 7:10 a.m. rang the doorbell. "Ding dong." Russell's mom appeared once again, still in night gown and house slippers, and this time she wasn't so patient and the smile was nowhere to be seen. "Ronnie, Russell's still asleep! You will have to come back later. How about waiting a couple of hours this time?" With head down I replied "Okay" and left the front porch of Russell's house a little deflated.

My disappointment only lasted a couple of seconds and I proceeded to the next couple of houses down the street and rang the doorbell. Mark was the next friend on my list and at 7:15 a.m. I rang his doorbell, "Ding dong." Mark's mom answered the door, also in night gown and slippers, and greeted me, "Mark is asleep. You will have to come back later." I quickly moved down the brother list and said, "How about Matt? Can he play?" Her reply was similar, "No, Matt is still in bed. Come back later." I pushed my luck with the third brother, "Is Mitch awake? Can he play?" Mark's mom was becoming quite agitated and said, "Ronnie, go home!"

I made my way around the rest of the neighborhood with much the same results. By the time I had tried all of the other boys' houses, Russell had awakened from his beauty sleep and was ready to play. Russell's backyard was one place that we played that did not have public access. He had a gate alongside his house, and it was always locked from the inside. I couldn't just pop in; I had to wait for an invitation. Once behind the gate, we played catch with a baseball or played army men (Russell had the only GI Joe doll in the neighborhood. My dad wouldn't let us have one because "boys don't play with dolls." The term *action figures* had yet to be coined). Timmy would finally figure out where I was and come knocking. (I have to admit that there were times we heard Timmy yelling for us, and we hid and wouldn't answer him. I was rotten.) From the other side of the gate we heard Timmy, "Wonnie, wet me in! I want to pway too." Showing off in front of Russell I played the tough guy, "Go home. You can't play with us." (I really was a mean brother). Then Timmy pulled out his trump card, "Wet me in oah I'm tewhing." I was defiant and feigned nonchalance, "Go ahead and tell. I don't care." (I really did care and knew what would probably happen next, but couldn't lose face in front of Russell).

Timmy started to cry and ran back home, tears flowing all the way. Not long afterward, Timmy came back and said, "Daddy said you have to wet me in to pway." I called his bluff, and he went away crying again. The next thing I knew, the voice I heard on the other side of the gate was not Timmy's; this voice was a little deeper and more authoritative. Needless to say, the gate was opened, and Timmy was allowed to play with Russell and me in *his* backyard.

In addition to the doll-sized GI Joe, we also had army men made of the plastic variety. These men were colored an army green, naturally, and stood about three to four inches in height. They came in a bag of one hundred, purchased at the five-and-ten-cent store. Within the bag were a variety of army men in different poses. Some were standing at attention with rifle on arm, some were shooting a rifle from a kneeling position, some were firing a rifle lying on their stomach with rifle on a tripod, etc. Similar to our games of cowboys and Indians, when we shot at each other, we had to take the other guy's word as to whether or not we had been killed or wounded.

Oftentimes, we took out entire units with a bomb or hand grenade. We would load the men into the backs of our trucks and transport them from the sandbox to the grass in the yard, a definite change of terrain. Because the men were green, it was easy to camouflage them in the grass and bushes (and easy to lose and later find chopped up in the lawnmower). Snipers could fire at your unit at a moment's notice. When we really got bored, we would light the men on fire and watch them melt. Of course, once we did that, we could no longer play army with a bunch of melted troops.

Russell's mom was not one to mince words when lunchtime rolled around as she called from the back door, "Ronnie and Timmy, you need to go home now. Russell has to eat lunch." We thought that there might be an invitation to lunch and I said, "Can we just wait out here in the backyard until he's finished eating?" "Russell's done playing for the day. He has to take a nap." We thought the nap thing was pretty funny (although it was obvious by the look on his face that Russell didn't), "He has to take a nap. Ha, Ha."

As we returned home from Russell's, we ate lunch and then took our naps. Only, we didn't take naps, Mom just assumed we did. As she tiptoed out of the room and locked the door (from the outside, so we couldn't get out), we waited a few minutes and then climbed up on the bunk beds and slowly and quietly climbed out of the bedroom window.

Outside of the two front bedrooms were two ledges, presumably for flower boxes, and under the ledges were some flowering bushes that we named the "bee bushes" because they always had bees buzzing around them. Once out the window, the next step was the ledge. From the ledge, you had to jump over the bee bush to get to the yard. We must not have been destined to be in the Olympics in the long jump competition because we seldom made it over the bush; rather, we landed in the bush

(Dad was not overly impressed when returning home to find his landscaping looking like a tornado had gone through).

You might be asking yourself this question, "Did Mom ever figure out that the boys were not napping in their beds?" I'm glad you asked. As Mom was out front watering her flowers, Ronnie rode by on his bike. Shortly afterward, Timmy rode by on his bike. As if nothing was amiss Timmy gleefully said, "Hi Mommy" as he rode by. Not realizing what had just happened Mom replied, "Hi Timmy."

In *The Burbs*, there was one house in the cul-de-sac that drew the ire of the rest of the neighbors: the Klopek house. It wasn't like the rest of the neighborhood houses: perfectly manicured lawns, immaculate landscaping, well-maintained structure, the typical suburban house. No, the Klopek house was in dire need of paint, with dead bushes around the front porch, rotted boards on the front steps going up to the door, and when someone stepped in the grassless front yard, the wind began to blow and the feeling was eerie. The neighbors all suspected nefarious activities going on inside.

In our neighborhood, we had two such houses. The first house we called the "witch house." The house was green stucco with the landscaping completely overgrown on all sides to the point that you could barely see the door and windows. The front porch was a concrete platform style with five or six steps and no railing. The landscaping had to be stepped around to get to the front door. *No one was ever seen entering or leaving!* (There was probably a little old lady living alone by herself that her family never came to see anymore; we could have brought her cookies.) This is one house in the neighborhood that was bypassed on Halloween night (we had to be pretty intimidated to miss a chance for more candy). Once in a while, we got brave. Approaching the house, but only as close as the sidewalk, Vicki offered this challenge, "I dare you to go ring the doorbell." I came back with the typical little kid retort, "I dare *you* to go ring the doorbell." Vicki subtly countered with, "I dared you first." It was a standoff until I came up with an idea, "Let's send Kathy. Where did she go, she was standing right here?" Timmy had silently been watching and listening when, trying to appear brave, he offered, "I'uh go do it, if you give me some candy." With Kathy and Timmy around, it was always a good idea to have plenty of candy around for the often-needed bribe.

Timmy eased up onto the witch's front porch, and as he pressed the bell, Vicki and I were already halfway down the street. As the two of us were attempting to set new land speed records in an effort to get out of there, Vicki could be heard, "Rrrruuunnnn!" As Timmy's finger touched the doorbell of the mysterious house, he scrambled off the front porch, not too far behind us, yelling all the way, "Witch, witch, witch!"

If the witch did come to the door, we never saw her, what with the huge amount of landscaping surrounding the house and the long distance between her and where we eventually stopped running.

The second house was on the corner of the block and was more weird than scary. There was a huge pine tree in the front yard, but the really weird thing, just like the Klopek house, there wasn't any grass in the yard, only dirt. Plenty of red ants, no grass. To add to that oddity, the owner of the house must have been a big record collector, because strung throughout the dirt yard were broken pieces of vinyl records: the 45 rpm variety (maybe the broken records were an anti-Beatle backlash that was a result of John stating the Beatles were more popular than Jesus). There must have been a thousand records broken up in that yard. Other than collecting red ants, we stayed away from that house.

Sometimes in LA, it would rain and rain some more (I know, "It Never Rains in Southern California"; Albert Hammond and Mike Hazelwood didn't know what they were talking about), a heavy downpour that lasted all day. Now you might think that a day like that, full of rain, would keep the four of us indoors playing games, like hide the thimble or Fish. Not the Bay kids. We put on our raincoats and rain boots (bright yellow in color) and headed out the door before Mom knew what had happened. I think she would have been okay with it, but we didn't wait to ask.

The gutters were flowing with water, deep enough that the water overflowed our boots. Debris floated by as the four of us, single file, walked completely around the block in the gutter, sloshing through the water, rain pouring down. We were having a ball. As we finally arrived back at the house, the rain had intensified, and thunder and lightning had commenced to make a racket. I was scared of the crack and boom that the thunder made. Getting ready to step on the front porch, a loud crack and boom was heard, the kind that comes out of nowhere and startles you. I looked back and noticed Timmy, standing in the yard with a funny look on his face. "Timmy, what's wrong? You look like you've seen a ghost." Timmy, a bit disoriented, mumbled, "I was stwuck by wightning."

Of course, I didn't believe him until he showed me a hole in his raincoat, a ragged hole with black around the edges. I became a believer after being shown the evidence. Mom, however, was not convinced and attributed the hole to Timmy playing with matches or one of Dad's cigarettes. Timmy maintains the story to this day, although not everyone in the family is convinced.

After the rain stopped, we went back outside and back to the gutters. The gutters were still flowing with water, and we decided to make a lake in the street. We scoured the garage for old newspapers (there were plenty of newspapers stacked in bundles being saved for the next paper drive). Piling the newspapers in the gutter, we forced the flow of water out into the street. We had succeeded in damming up the gutter and forming a lake in the street. As the neighborhood parents arrived home from work for the evening, their cars were flooded up to the door, some of the cars engines temporarily dying out in the street. A neighbor man mumbled to himself, "Weatherman got it wrong again. I heard nothing about a flash flood."

Search parties were standing by, just in case.

~

Our backyard was a fun place for us kids. Dad tried real hard to make it as fun as he could. He bought us a swimming pool, the kind with wire sides that was about two and a half feet deep. Dad wouldn't just leave us to play, but would stand next to the pool and toss us one at a time into the pool, water splashing everywhere. Some of the neighbor kids got in line and Dad threw them in as well. ("One for the money, two for the show, three to get ready, and four to go," Dad would say as he swung us back and forth, holding on to an arm and leg and then releasing us into the pool.) The second we landed in the pool, we would cough and choke and immediately climb out, run to the back of the line, and impatiently wait for the next toss. Dad was a real trooper and didn't quit until we all tired out or the water running out of the pool (due to us climbing out over and over and bending the sides of the pool so that they wouldn't stay upright anymore) caused the fun to be over.

If the broken-down pool wasn't available, we learned how to have just as much fun with the water hose. We would each take turns controlling the hose. We didn't have a spray nozzle on the end of the hose, but we learned to use our thumb as a self-made sprayer, and it worked pretty well. If we wanted to shut the water flow off, we just crimped the hose and it worked perfectly. As one of us had the hose, the other kids would run by as fast as they could while the kid on the hose would squirt us as much as they could. We would then circle back around to be squirted again. When we got thirsty, the water from the hose seemed to be colder and tastier than the water from the faucet in the house.

Some houses in the neighborhood had water sprinklers in their yards, and we would sometimes run through the sprinklers; the fact that we weren't invited didn't matter to us. Some sprinklers were circular, some were a back-and-forth arc motion, but the favorite one sounded like this: *tcchh*, *tcchh*, *tcchh*. As it went from one end of the yard to the other, it would make this sound as it returned to its original point. This sprinkler was so fast in its operation that the timing of running through it had to be just right. More often than not, the running through yard sprinklers was not seeing how wet we could get, but more a contest of running through the sprinkler and seeing who could stay dry.

Other than Mark A's pool across the street, which was not on our list of frequently visited places, the only other pool to swim in was the public pool at the high school. The high school was across Orr and Day Road, the road that was off-limits to us, except when we walked back and forth to school and when we went to the swimming pool. Mom would give us each a quarter for admission and send us out the door with towel in hand (we walked fast during the summer months; the asphalt was pretty hot on the bottom of our feet).

When we arrived at the school and paid our money, we were handed a mesh bag with a number on it to hold our clothes. On the bag was a pin that we attached to our swimming suit, which identified the particular mesh bag belonging to us (similar to a coat check program at a fancy restaurant).

Once inside the pool area, there were two pools to swim in: the shallow pool (the water was a maximum four feet deep) and the deep pool which was twelve feet deep and had a high diving board and two low diving boards. Of course, we were directed to the kiddy pool, but our eyes focused on the big pool the entire time. I figured that the big pool held much more excitement and decided to sneak my way over there. I headed straight for the high dive, conspicuous as I stood in line. One of the lifeguards spotted me and asked me, "Hey kid, what are you doing here at the deep end?" Not seeing any problem with what I was doing, I answered him, "I'm going to jump off the high dive." Bursting my bubble he then said, "You can't come over here until you prove you can swim." I asked him, "How do I do that?"

The lifeguard sent me back to the shallow pool, and the other lifeguard there told me that in order to get from the shallow pool to the deep pool, I would have to swim across the shallow pool and back in order to qualify. (She figured that by giving me this seemingly unattainable challenge, I would go away and not bother her anymore.) You should have seen the look on her face as I jumped in and started swimming, first across and then back to her chair (she even began cheering me on when she saw how determined I was). Before I could get too excited, the lifeguards all began blowing their whistles. All of the kids were told to get out of the pool. As we sat out on the cement, the lifeguards began to throw bucketfuls of chlorine into the pool (that many kids swimming in the pool for that long may have caused the water to become a little tainted, so to speak). The kids were then instructed to sit around the edge of the pool and kick our feet. Kicking our feet over and over stirred the water and allowed the chlorine to dissipate in the water. Even when that was done, we still had to wait thirty minutes before re-entering the pool. We hated to hear those whistles.

The next thing I knew, I was standing on top of the high dive, ready to take the plunge (be careful what you wish for, I soon realized). The smile on my face, while on the way down, was one of triumph mixed with terror, but once I hit the water and swam to the edge of the pool, I couldn't get back to the top of the diving board fast enough.

We even swam on days when the temperature was questionable for swimming (our purple lips and knocking knees may have been an indication that it was probably not a good day to swim). The four of us were little fish, and swimming would be a way of life for us the entire time we were growing up. I remember the feelings and sounds while lying on the cement next to the pool, arms folded under my forehead, breathing heavy while resting from all of the swimming, the water dripping from my nose to the cement, the smell of the wet cement and the sounds of the kids laughing and playing in the water. After a short respite, back into the water, swimming, diving for rocks or pennies on the bottom of the pool, even in the deep end. We would challenge each other to swim all the way to the bottom and touch the drain. We loved that pool.

One day, Dad decided to build a playhouse, primarily for Vicki, but the rest of us knew that we would share in the finished product. Dad didn't mess around; two-by-fours were nailed together, and the frame looked pretty close to a real house and almost as big. That thing was huge! After the frame was built, Dad added a door, and cardboard sheets were tacked to the frame, completing the roof and sides. Vicki was pretty impressed and started to set up house, all the while telling Timmy and me to stay away (Kathy was welcome since she was a girl, and it was a playhouse for girls). What Dad didn't foresee—well, maybe he did, and Vicki and Kathy weren't ready for—was two boys being told that the playhouse was off-limits and how they reacted to that prohibition.

We began to jump onto the side and roof of the playhouse from our perch on top of the wall surrounding the backyard. Vicki would yell at us and threaten to tell Dad, but she knew better than to leave the playhouse unattended while she ran in the house to tell. It didn't matter one way or the other. Timmy and I climbed up and over, around and through that house. We climbed through the window, swung from the rafters (yes, monkeys in the zoo do come to mind); man, was that fun. Within a few short moments, we had completely torn that house to smithereens. There wasn't a piece of cardboard left; the only thing standing was the wooden frame. It wasn't long before Timmy and I were in the bedroom, facing the fury of Dad's doubled-up belt. In a few days, the playhouse was torn down, and we moved on to destroy other things.

Most of the kids in the neighborhood were in the same age range, preschool through grade school, but there were two or three teenage girls across the street. They pretty much ignored the younger kids; although during the summer, when they ran around in short shorts or bikinis, all the boys didn't ignore them. They seemed to be involved in what most teenage girls were involved with: boys and cars. Neither of those interested me, but they did have one other interest that I absolutely loved: music. In 1964, the Beatles had six number 1 hits including "I Want to Hold Your Hand," "She Loves You," "Can't Buy Me Love," "Love Me Do," "A Hard Day's Night," and "I Feel Fine."

During the summer, while the parents were away at work, the teenagers let their hair down, so to speak, and turned the volume up on their mom and dad's stereo. It wasn't enough to just play the music; the windows and doors had to be opened, the stereo turned up full blast, with the girls dancing around in the living room of the house. We decided that it would be fun to be the Beatles on the front porch of the girls' house. Four of us chose which Beatle we would be (I was Paul) and made guitars out of sticks and cardboard, even a whisk broom worked as guitar. With the music blaring out of the windows, we stood on the front porch, pretending that we were singing and moving with the music, just like the Beatles. The Beatles were all the rage in my neighborhood and in America. It was the Beatles who took me away from my dad's music—Johnny Cash, Hank Williams, Merle Haggard—and turned me into a rock and roller.

Two years later, however, the bloom fell off the rose. John Lennon made his famous "more popular than Jesus" remark, and all the admiration and adoration turned into rage. Kids gathered on street corners and took their Beatle records and trading cards and tore them up and threw them on the ground. On the corner across the street from my house I noticed some commotion amidst a group of kids and queried, "Hey, what are you guys doing?" One kid said, "Tearing up Beatle's stuff." I hadn't heard any of the news stories and ignorantly asked, "How come?" Another kid, not believing my lack of knowledge, said, "They said they were bigger than God." Well, that was all I needed to hear and I joined in the fray, "They did? I can't believe it. I hate those guys." I joined in on the tearing and stomping of records, playing cards, and magazines.

A few years later, I returned to the Beatles, but by that time they had disbanded and moved on to Yoko (John), raising sheep (Paul), gazing at navels and chanting (George), and drinking oneself into a stupor (Ringo).

The neighborhood was one of intrigue, excitement, adventure, and all-around fun. I have to say that I couldn't have asked for a better childhood than I experienced in the neighborhood where I grew up. I could probably fill a few more chapters with stories that might make your eyes grow to the size of saucers, so I think I will. "Man, I loved that neighborhood!"

THE PLAYERS

This is a good time in the narrative to introduce "The Players" (the Bay family). A few anecdotes for each family member will allow you to get a little background and color so that the remaining stories have more depth and texture.

MOM

She was the sweetest, most laid-back person that you could ever meet: my mom. Low maintenance would be an understatement. She was often singing and almost always in a good mood, and with the four of us and Dad to deal with, it's a wonder. When I think of Mom, her smell, her touch, the clothes she wore, the best way to describe her would be warm, sweet, and pretty. I remember the ritual of putting us kids to bed. We each had to be tucked in and given a good-night kiss. Mom would come in, often in her nightgown, and lovingly tuck us in, making sure the covers were nice and tight around us, and when she kissed us good night, I can still recall the sweet smell of her perfume (Jungle Gardenia if I remember correctly). If for some reason the tuck-in was delayed or forgotten, we would yell out from our bedroom for Mom to come and tuck us in. We couldn't go to sleep without it. On such rare occasions you could hear me, "Mommy, come and tuck me in. Please!" Then Timmy, "Mommy, you fohgot to kiss me good night." From the other room Vicki's voice could be heard, "Mommy, you didn't give me a good night kiss tonight." Finally, Kathy, who let us speak for her, would chime in, "Yeah!"

I remember the way that she would wake us up in the morning, and it was quite a contrast to the way that Dad did it. Mom would be singing her favorite morning tune, the Everly Brothers' "Wake Up, Little Susie," and come swishing into the room. She would softly touch us to make sure we opened our eyes, and even though we didn't want to wake up, her voice was so soft and cheerful, it was almost painless. Dad had a less subtle approach; he would kick or pound the door open, all the while yelling, "You kids get up!" Apparently, he felt that every moment of sleep past 7:00 a.m. on a Saturday was wasted time that could be used for, well, something else, anything but sleep.

It's been said that as little boys become attracted to the opposite sex, they often choose someone that reminds them of their mother. Growing up, I was attracted to two actresses that were very popular in movies at the time: Debbie Reynolds (*The Unsinkable Molly Brown*) and Doris Day (*The Thrill of It All*). I suppose that the conventional wisdom was true in this case as these two movie stars did remind me of my mother, although I never thought of it at the time. They were both pretty: check. They were both either blond or brownish blond in hair color: check. They were both wonderful singers: check. Mom was always singing the popular tunes heard on the radio at the time, and I credit her with my eventual love of music.

Mom was a great cook, and we always seemed to have plenty of food on the table. For our birthdays, we each got to choose our favorite dish and dessert. I always chose spaghetti and meatballs with marinara sauce. Her meatballs were the best. My dessert was lemon meringue pie. The other kids always chose something really good too, like tacos. Mom's tacos were the best in the world, and the recipe has been passed on to my brother and me, always pleasing those lucky enough to try them.

I mentioned earlier that Mom was laid-back, and after reading the stories in this book, you might agree that she was to the point of being invisible. It was almost as if what we did or where we went really didn't matter much. Not much seemed to faze her. Vicki, in a typical exchange, "Hey, Mommy, we're going out to play on the freeway." It was almost as if what Vicki had said didn't register. Mom's response was, "Okay. Just remember to be home for supper."

A memory of Mom that is etched in my mind and speaks to her laid-back nature goes like this. After supper, while all the rest of us had retired into the living room to watch *The Red Skelton Show*, *The Wonderful World of Disney*, or some other family show, Mom would stay in the kitchen, doing the dishes and putting them away, storing leftovers in the refrigerator, and generally cleaning up. While this was going on, a copper tea kettle was on the stove, soon to release its steam pressure with a loud, irritating whistle. Mom would take her cup of hot water, a couple of tea bags, and a magazine or newspaper and proceed to the nearest couch or chair, usually out of earshot of the television group, and proceed to relax for the next couple of hours prior to going to bed. Mom knew relaxation. Mom knew laid-back. In the midst of the chaos of raising the four of us, Mom could still find her own time and her own world.

Of course, in these earlier times, there wasn't the paranoia surrounding the safety of kids (or near as many perverts running amok), but even with that said, Mom didn't have a very watchful eye. Maybe she just trusted us (did I also mention that she may have been a little naïve). That's my mom.

KATHY (THE BABY SISTER)

Kathy, unlike Vicki, wasn't much of a rough and tumble kid (except, of course, the time she was the tail end of the whip in Crack the Whip and was snapped off and went sailing through the air, landing in the bushes in front of the Z house), preferring to sit in her room in front of a dressing table mirror and play with makeup, jewelry, and other girlie things. She could do this for hours, by herself, in such a silent way that no one would know where she was or if she was gone. She would be in her room playing, and the only sound emanating from the room was a faint whisper as she talked to herself and her dolls. In many ways, she was the model child. As long as no one bothered her (too bad she was so much fun to bother), she pretty much stayed to herself, a low maintenance type of kid.

One time, while playing dress-up in front of the mirror, she decided to make earrings out of some loose pearls (not real pearls, the plastic bead kind). As she tried to balance the bead on the edge of her earlobe, it fell into her ear. When she tried to retrieve the pearl from the inside of her ear, it wouldn't come out. It was too deep in her ear; her finger would not reach. At this point, the usually silent Kathy became a little distressed, and she ran to find Mom (By the way, Kathy could not pronounce her *r*'s). This is what Mom heard her say, "Mommy, theah's a pull in my eah!" Making sure to clarify what she had heard, Mom said "There's what in your which?" Kathy was getting a little panicky and raised her voice, "Theah's a pull in my eah!" Mom was becoming exasperated with the inability to communicate and responded, "Kathy, I don't understand what you're saying. I can't help you if you aren't making sense."

By this time, Dad had wandered in and obviously became concerned. Dad interjected himself into the conversation, "Maxine, what's wrong with Kathy?" "Theah's a pull in her eah" imitating Kathy's diction. Dad's response was the same as Mom's earlier one, "A what in her which?"

Now the tension, tears, frustrations, and anger had all escalated. Mom and Dad finally figured out (maybe the fact that Kathy kept pointing to her ear and crying gave them a clue) that there was something inside Kathy's ear, and she couldn't get it out. They finally took a flashlight and tried to shine a little light on the subject, literally. Even with the flashlight and tweezers and amidst the intermittent bawling, the pearl wasn't going anywhere. So off to the doctor they went. The doctor questioned Mom as to why Kathy was brought in, "So, Mrs. Bay, what brings you here today?" Again, Mom stayed with Kathy's vernacular in her answer, "Kathy has a pull in her eah." The doc, as everyone else had been, was stupefied and said, "She has what in her which?" Mom, showing her laid back personality, giggled in her response and said, "Kathy has a pearl in her ear." The doctor reciprocated, "Is it valuable?"

Mom seemed more entertained than worried, much to Kathy's chagrin. Being the baby, she felt like Mom should have been a little more concerned, if only for appearances. Even after this traumatic experience, Kathy continued to play with jewelry; although when it came to earrings, she would only use the clip-on kind.

Kathy hated to be teased (and to this day still does; shhh!). Now this is the classic chicken or egg question: did she hate to be teased because we teased her so much, or did we tease her so much because she hated to be teased? Being the baby sister, I have to lean toward the former explanation. This may explain why she played by herself so often. The old joke, "It hurts when I do this," twisted a bit, would apply here: "Hey, Doc, every time I play with my brothers and sisters I get teased mercilessly," Kathy conjectured. The doctor replied, "Don't play with your brothers and sisters."

By now, most of you are feeling a bit sorry for Kathy, what with the mean brothers and sister, but don't be so hasty in your sympathy. Like a possum playing dead, Kathy developed the perfect defense mechanism in order to lash out at her would-be attackers. She perfected what policemen and criminals alike call the snitch. No matter what the teasing entailed or how she was "accidentally" hurt or slighted, nothing was ever kept a secret, and all slights were reported to Mom. We were brought to our knees, begging, promising all that we owned, if she just wouldn't tell, but to no avail. After "accidentally" knocking Kathy to the ground and bloodying her lip, I tried to forestall the inevitable punishment to come by pleading, "Kathy, Kathy, please don't tell. You're not hurt. I'm sorry, I'm sorry. Stop crying. Please, please, please (James Brown anyone?) don't tell." Her response wasn't encouraging, "Waaaahhhh!" Now I was desperate and I threw in the inevitable bribes, "Kathy, if you stop crying, I'll give you all my money, all future Christmas presents, and my baseball card collection." Even with my prized possession baseball cards thrown in she wasn't biting, "No! I don't want youh baseball cahd collection."

At this point, I had to walk away and hope she would forget the incident. She never did. Three days could have passed since the offense was committed, and I would delude myself into thinking that I was in the clear. We would be playing in the bedroom, Mom would walk in to see what we were up to, and Kathy would give me a devilish side glance and burst out crying. My spirits would go from the extremes of contented bliss to the pits of despair. She had done it again. Payback was brutal. You might think that Kathy had found a way to slow down the teasing, but for whatever reason, Timmy, Vicki, and I were slow learners.

We weren't a churchgoing family, but Mom, in order to get a little peace and quiet, would drop us off at the local church Vacation Bible School. That led to some of the caring adults inviting us back to church. One sweet lady volunteering at VBS must have felt sorry for us and asked, "You kids want to come back to church on Sunday?" Our representative Vicki avoided the question by answering, "If Mommy and Daddy will let us." The nice lady was persistent in her questioning, "When you children go home, ask your mother if you can come back on Sunday."

We asked, and Mom said, "Sure, why not. You kids feel free to go. Be careful crossing Orr and Day Road."

The next incident is still in debate among family members as to the exact details. One version goes like this:

Mom and the four of us kids arrived at the church on Sunday morning. We were dressed in our best clothes, girls in dresses and guys with hair slicked down and combed. The usher took us to a row on the left hand side of the auditorium toward the back of the church. After we took our places, the organ started up, everyone took their hymnbooks, and the service began. Being the active children that we were, we had trouble sitting still (surprise, surprise), and Kathy, in her cute little dress, began to lean over the back of the pew in front of her. Suddenly, we heard giggling and laughter coming from the pew behind us. Kathy was still leaning over and fidgeting when Mom looked her way and finally noticed that under Kathy's dress there wasn't any underwear, only a bare bottom. Mom, quite embarrassed, immediately ushered the four of us out the back of the church, into the car, and straight home. On the way out of church and toward the car Mom glared at Kathy and asked, "Kathy, how did you go to church without your underwear? Who dressed you?" Kathy, being completely honest, as most kids are, gave Mom this response, "You did."

The other version goes like this:

The four of us decided we were going to church one Sunday. We dressed ourselves in our best clothes, girls in dresses and boys with slicked down and combed hair. We proceeded to head out the door and walk to the church, single file up the street, across Orr and Day Road and about a half mile to the church. After attending services, we all headed back home, and Mom discovered that Kathy wasn't wearing any underwear. Mom glared at Kathy and asked, "Kathy, how did you go to church without your underwear? Who dressed you?" Kathy, being completely honest, as most kids are, gave Mom this response, "You did."

Now, which one is more believable: Mom taking us to church, or the four of us just deciding that we needed to go to church and heading out? As we begin shuffling out the front door on Sunday morning Vicki says, "Good-bye, Mommy. We're going to church." Proud of her little angels, Mom replies, "You kids look so nice. Be careful crossing Orr and Day Road."

The second scenario, although the least plausible, was probably the correct scenario. One thing is for certain: Kathy went to church one Sunday without her underwear. She is still teased about it to this day. That's my baby sister.

(One side note: in all of the "going to church" stories, Dad is never mentioned. Dad, at this point in his life, felt that if he happened to walk into a church building, thunder would clap, lightning would, and the roof of the building would collapse, killing only him. His strategy was to avoid God and postpone the inevitable; only later in his life would God catch up to him.)

TIMMY (THE LITTLE BROTHER)

Even at a very young age, Timmy was a brilliant military tactician, and if he had been utilized as a consultant during the Vietnam war, we would have won. He utilized two classic military maneuvers when dealing with his siblings: the hit-and-run tactic and the siege. The purpose of the hit-and-run maneuver is self explanatory and Timmy used it to his benefit from time to time, but being slower than his older sister and about the same speed as myself, he used it sparingly, and only when he had a decent escape route planned out in advance. This leads to the next maneuver. Once he hit and ran, he often found a safe haven in which to bunker down. An example of such a place, one that we could not penetrate, was the inside of Mom's car with the doors all locked. His strategy at this point was to wait us out. The classical siege maneuver perfected.

When employing these tactics, he very rarely made mistakes, and through repetition and constant drilling, he became a master.

Before Timmy attacked, he spent plenty of time in surveillance, and all of his escape routes were well planned out. When he attacked, he usually came out of nowhere (sneak attack versus frontal attack) and would hit you from behind, sometimes in the back or maybe the kidney (I'm convinced that I suffer kidney stones today due to one of these vicious attacks to the kidney), and then immediately, he would run. Of course, after first catching my breath, I would begin the chase. Timmy might head straight for the station wagon, which offered him three options.

The first option was to stay on one side of the car and, as I moved toward him, continue moving away from me, utilizing the width and length of the car to his advantage. This tactic worked for a while, but as I got angrier and raised the threat level, he decided that this wasn't the safest place to be.

The second option was to crawl underneath the automobile and lay flat on his stomach as close to the center as possible, just out of reach of his assailant. He had the advantage in this position, with his head on a swivel, he could see my feet as I moved around the car, trying to figure out how to get to him or get him to leave. I was at a real disadvantage with him under the car. If I tried to reach under and grab him, he would move to the other side of the car, just out of reach. If I got down and crawled under the car after him, he would just slide out the other side and run away. This was extremely frustrating.

The third option was to jump inside the car and lock all of the doors. This allowed Timmy to not only be safe, but from this position, he could taunt me by sticking out his tongue and laughing, honking the horn, looking smug and satisfied. While he was inside doing this, I was outside, yelling and threatening. With the car window rolled up I realized that I would have to raise the decibel level, so while pounding on the car window I shouted, "Unlock the door! I'm going to kill you!" Even though I could barely hear his reply, I could see him sticking out his tongue (a common practice of his) and heard this, "Twy to get me. Ha-ha-ha, ha-ha-ha!" (As was Kathy, Timmy was unable to pronounce his "R's" and in addition could not pronounce his "L's" either.)

Obviously from Timmy's view of things, it would be highly illogical and foolish to unlock the door, when the result of doing so might be your death. I can't describe to you how frustrated I would get, just out of reach of my revenge, but unable to satisfy my urge to beat Timmy into a pulp.

Another escape route that Timmy frequently used was the large pine tree in the front yard. This tree was about forty feet in height, and the branches were perfectly positioned for climbing. Timmy wasn't that fast of a runner, but due to the sneak attack and me subsequently catching my breath after being punched, he usually had enough of a head start to stay just out of reach. Once I realized he was headed up the pine tree, I followed in close pursuit, but with him just out of reach. Once he got to the top of the tree, he would sit and wait, gathering up ammunition as he sat. As I climbed up the tree, all of a sudden pinecones would come raining down on my head, one at a time. I was helpless (now I understood why the military strategy of seeking the high ground was so important). Not only did I not have any ammunition, but even if I did, I couldn't throw it through the branches, up to the top of the tree. I soon climbed back down to the ground and saw plenty of ammunition on the ground around the base of the tree. I wore myself out trying to hit Timmy, sitting at the top of his tree, raining down pinecones on my head. Again with the taunting, he used the classic lines, "You can't hit me, nyah, nyah, nyah, nyah, nyah, nyah!" I was exasperated to the point of boiling and responded with, "I hate you! When you come down from that tree, I'm going to pound your brains out!"

I couldn't hit him (I had a pretty good arm and plenty of ammunition, but to no avail). He was perfectly positioned and had the upper hand.

Timmy had other escape routes: locking himself in the garage, locking himself in the bathroom, hiding underneath his bed, etc. He was brilliant in his tactics, and as I said earlier, he rarely made a mistake. So once he had executed the hit-and-run tactic, the next maneuver was the siege, and he was the master. With Timmy in the car, tree, bathroom, garage, etc., it would seem that all I had to do was wait him out. That is a correct assumption, but in this game, the one with the most patience would survive to fight another day. I have been described in many terms, but *patient* is not one of them. All Timmy had to do was wait; I would move on to other interests, and once he had surveyed the scene, for hours if necessary, he would silently exit the car/tree/garage and show up as if nothing had ever happened. Rarely did he pay the price. His military tactics and maneuvers were impeccable and saved him many a beating.

Timmy was skilled at taunting and utilized a variety of techniques; it didn't matter which sibling was the tauntee. His taunts were designed to create frustration and anger, and in this, he succeeded: often. One such occasion was while playing games, specifically Monopoly. At the beginning of the game, everyone got the same amount of money, and then as the game proceeded, you either added to your stash or began to run out. At the most crucial point of the game, when money was tight and the next time you landed on an opponent's hotel you may have to go bankrupt, Timmy reached underneath the game board and pulled out a crisp new, $500 bill. We assumed that he had cheated, but he swore that he put it under there at the beginning of the game (no one ever saw him do this, so we all believe that he cheated). It's not even the fact that he had the bill that irked us, but how he kept waving it in our faces and laughing. The suspect bill allowed him to bankrupt the remaining players and win the game.

He would also taunt us with treats, for example a candy bar, that he pulled out of thin air and made sure everyone saw that he had it, all the time grinning and giggling that he had it and we didn't. (He would hold the candy up in the air and wave it around, in effect saying, "Look what I have and you don't.") We could have all had candy bars the previous day, but somehow, all of ours were eaten and Timmy still had his. (On November 25, he would still be pulling out hidden Halloween candy, while all of ours had been eaten by November 1). He would then proceed to eat it in front of all of us, not even having the dignity of going off in a corner to enjoy his prize.

His biggest taunt, however, was nothing more than a whistle. This wasn't a normal whistle (Timmy wasn't a normal kid), and he fashioned it in a way that drove everyone within earshot near to suicide. The whistle was a learned thing, and he practiced it until it became an art form. It was high pitched and loud, and once he had it going and realized how much he was irritating us, he would ramp it up. If you tried to walk away to alleviate the frustration, he would just follow you, whistling all the time: Timmy, getting as close as he could without touching you would start up with, "Phweet, phweet, phweet, phweet!" At about the fourth phweet I had taken about all I could. "Aaaaaaggggghhhhh! I'm going to kill that kid!"

If I tried to get permission to knock him senseless, the old "I'm not touching him" defense would come into play (he wasn't, in fact, touching me, but a thousand paper cuts would have been preferable to his insufferable whistling). I had no recourse except to run away. And I did.

Timmy was not near as intense as I was when playing competitive sports (this is not to say that he wasn't a good athlete; he turned out to be a great athlete, better than me). Our first year together in baseball (we played together on the Al and Jerry's Liquor Store team), I recall an incident that reveals his attitude and demeanor as much as any other. He, being a southpaw, was the obvious pick to play first base. In one of our first games, I was pitching, with Timmy on first base, when an infield popup came his way. It was a routine play, but for some reason, Timmy muffed it (the sun was in his eyes, his glove was too big, a squirrel was running through the stands and distracted him). He stuck his glove in the air, but the ball landed at his feet. Everyone began shouting, "Pick up the ball, throw to second, throw to third, throw to home, don't just stand there, do something!" Then the coaches chimed in, "Pick up the ball, throw to second, throw to third, throw to home, don't just stand there, do something!"

With all of the excitement going on, Timmy's reaction was a little bit odd; he just stood there, with a funny little smile plastered on his face, while all of the opposing players ran to home plate. The coaches went berserk, I went berserk, but Timmy couldn't be moved. At that moment, he just couldn't be flustered (he would be a great guy to share a foxhole with). That's my little brother.

VICKI (THE BIG SISTER)

As mentioned earlier, Kathy and Vicki were complete opposites as kids; Vicki was the prototypical tomboy. She was faster and tougher than any other kid in the neighborhood, including all the boys. Not only was she physically superior, she was also the smartest kid in the neighborhood, and many of the ideas that we came up with originated with her. She was also smart enough to come up with the ideas and not actually implement them, leaving the implementation to me, with the origination of the idea not being traceable back to her (kind of like a slick politician or mobster, Vicki's fingerprints could not be found). After all, how do you explain the fact that I was held accountable for baby sister wandering off with David P., down the freeway, off to grandma's house to get candy and ice cream? Where was the older sister in all of this? Why did I have to go to the freeway and bring Kathy back? Why did I get the whipping? Where is the justice?

Timmy, the taunter, wasn't all that fast of a runner, but he only had to be fast enough to stay ahead of his pursuer and in my case, he almost always got away to his strategically placed hiding places.

(This reminds me of the joke about the two guys and the bear. Two guys in the woods see a grizzly bear coming toward them, and one guy starts to run. The other guy says, "You can't outrun a bear." The second guy says, "I don't have to outrun the bear, I just have to outrun you.")

In the case of Vicki, not so fast my friend, or Timmy's not so fast, my friend. It didn't matter if Timmy got a head start or not, Vicki, like a bolt of lightning, left Timmy in the position that he didn't know what hit him, figuratively only, because once Vicki caught him, Timmy surely did know what hit him. Down on the ground Timmy would go, face in the dirt. On his back, straddling him like a horse, Vicki would rain down upon him, blow after blow, Timmy's crying only interrupted by the individual blows, briefly knocking the air out of him (the sound coming out of Timmy was like the sound made when you talk into an oscillating fan). Timmy may not have been the brightest kid around, but he learned to limit his taunting of Vicki and reserved most of his taunting for me.

When it came time for all of us to take our monthly, er, evening bath, Mom came up with a brilliant plan: have the girls bathe together and have the boys bathe together. The reason could have been environmental, limiting our use of the precious natural resource known as water, but was more likely a desire to save time (four separate baths the way we took them could have taken a few hours) and so it was. Vicki, being the smart one, came up with a really fun idea for the bathtub experience.

For her and Kathy's entertainment, prior to adding water, Vicki obtained some dishwashing liquid from the kitchen and proceeded to squirt a layer on the bottom of the bathtub. With or without water, this created an extremely slick surface (the Olympic bobsledding team would be envious) that made for an altogether great time. Vicki and Kathy, sliding back and forth, round and round the bathtub (either the tub was extremely large, not likely, or we were really skinny kids). Mom and Dad had to wonder about all the giggling coming from the bathroom: Dad, from his living room perch in front of the television, sent a yell toward the bathroom, "What are you two doing in there? Hurry up and take your bath." With the door shut, Vicki wasn't about to get in a hurry and responded, "We're just now preparing to draw our bath." "Yeah, weah pwepawing to dwaw ouh bath," little sister chimed in. Dad raised the intensity, "Well hurry up. Your brothers have to take their baths next, and you've already been in there thirty minutes."

Once again, Vicki was the mastermind behind a great time had by all, as Timmy and I repeated the "bobsled in the bathtub" when it was our turn to go (after both groups had finished, the bathtub was so clean, you could eat out of it).

In junior high school, Vicki had the ultimate stage in which to show off her physical attributes. Each year, there was a series of competitions within the school where the ultimate prize was the President's Physical Fitness Award. This included competition in sit-ups, pushups, and running events that test strength, quickness, and endurance. Vicki had won the competition and was awarded the prize (at this point in my athletic career, she accomplished something that I never did). This was the peak of her tomboy life as she began to change gears once she reached high school.

You can see how much I admire my older sister by the things I've written, and I would say that the feeling is reciprocal. However, it wasn't always that way. There was a time when the tension and angst between us was felt by all that knew us. She was two, and I was a baby. There was an immediate dislike on her part (once she got to know me a little more, she warmed up to me), and she wasn't shy about making it known.

Her first attempt to welcome me to the family (or quickly eliminate the threat) was to take the container of baby powder and liberally pour it into my face ("Take that, you roly-poly little tub of lard!"). I survived that attack with only a slight case of "dry lung" to show for it.

Her next attack also centered on the oft-repeated diaper-changing ritual. Long before disposable diapers, cloth diapers were all the rage, and in order for the diapers to remain on the infant, diaper pins were used. They looked like a normal safety pin, but had the added plastic decoration on the end: pink for girls and blue for boys. Vicki decided that she would attempt acupuncture on her brother (presumably to alleviate his diaper rash) and poked me numerous times with said diaper pins. ("Bleed, baby boy, bleed!") I eventually recovered from this serious attack, after a blood transfusion, and lived to tell about it.

Even though I was a little tyke, I did get my revenge. One of Vicki's special possessions was a box of Sun-Maid raisins. She carried the box around in her little purse and would from time to time reach in and grab a couple of raisins to eat. One day, plotting my revenge for the diaper pins and powder, I noticed Vicki setting her purse aside and going off into another room. I saw my opening and stole the raisins, eating every last one of them. ("Take that, big sister.") That's my big sister.

DAD

In the movie *The Wizard of Oz*, the key players all had something they thought was missing from their lives that they spent the entire movie trying to find. For the Cowardly Lion, it was courage. In one scene from the famous movie, the Lion, in a thunderous oratory, describes what courage is all about, and cites some well-known examples of courage, including the magnificent elephant and the sphinx. One line from his oration sums it up; "what makes the muskrat guard his musk?" At the end of his oration, the Lion asks this question of the rest of the crew, "what have they got that I ain't got?" Their answer: courage.

Rather than seeking the advice of the Wizard, the Lion could very well have collaborated with my dad. Dad had enough courage for both of them. He wasn't afraid of anything or anyone. When Dad was around, we all felt safe and secure. If we ran into trouble in the neighborhood or school, we always knew that as long as we were in the right, Dad would be on our side (just like the muskrat guarding his musk).

At six foot two and 185 pounds, he was physically intimidating with not an ounce of fat on him. In a similar way to John Wayne's many characters (Dad always reminded us of John Wayne), Dad didn't take any guff, and most people didn't mess with him. When other kids in the neighborhood came over to our house to play, you could see the respect they had for Dad, and this led to me walking around with a little more cockiness than normal. I was proud of my dad.

I remember the time when David T. and I got into it, which wasn't that unusual, as we were always getting into it. He had a habit, much like my brother, of hitting and running. His normal escape was to hop on his bicycle, a nice red Schwinn, and pedal as fast as he could to his house, and before he even got to the front door, he would leap off of his bike and continue running through the door, the bicycle rolling to a stop somewhere near the house. Once inside the house, he would stand behind the screen door and call me names and make faces. Of course, I would be at the edge of his yard yelling epithets back at him.

This particular day, I must have gotten to him really good because the next thing I knew, his sister came running out the front door and chased me down the street. I know what you're thinking, but I must explain the reason I was running. I was eight years old and David's sister was eighteen, so even though she was technically a girl, the age difference more than made up for that fact.

She eventually caught me and proceeded to pound me into submission. I did what any normal kid would do: I ran into the house bawling and went straight for Dad. Like John Wayne, Dad was concerned about justice, and this obviously wasn't a fair fight. Now he couldn't go over to the T's house and challenge the teenage sister to a fight, so he did the honorable thing. Dad stood in the middle of the street and called out Mr. T. Wow! Everyone in the neighborhood came out of their houses to see what would happen next. Dad angrily yelled toward the T house across the street, "Hey, T., get your cowardly —- out here on the street. Your brat little kid can't stand up for himself, so he sends his teenage sister to beat up an eight year old boy!" Not a peep came back from Mr. T., only silence. Dad was more incensed and increased his volume, "Hey, T. Stop hiding in your house. Get your —- out here and let's settle this like men." Again, silence.

Finally, after a few more angry shouts, Dad grew tired, gave up, and went back home, but the message was sent and the victory was won. I walked around the neighborhood like a prince for weeks. My dad was the greatest! All the other boys were not only impressed, but envious just the same. It's the kind of scenario that all boys dream of. "My dad's tougher than your dad." "My dad can beat up your dad." We all thought it, and we all said it at one time or another. Now whenever I got involved in one of these back-and-forths, I had credibility.

Dad loved kids. He truly enjoyed having us around. I believe it was an entertainment kind of thing. He thought we were funny, and he loved to tease us. Once, when we were grilling out on the back patio, Dad decided to make homemade ice cream. The ice cream maker was the hand crank kind and required rock salt and ice to create the temperature necessary to turn the cream, vanilla, and sugar into ice cream. Why rock salt? Dad knew that the rock salt, due to its chemical makeup, caused the ice to be colder than normal (he didn't know it scientifically, but intuitively and experientially). It was the perfect additive to the process of making homemade ice cream.

Dad decided to have some fun with us; one, because we entertained him, and two, because he wanted us out of his hair while he simultaneously ran the grill and cranked the ice cream maker. He turned to the four of us and said, "Kids, come over here. We're going to play a game." We excitedly said, "Okay" and ran to the patio.

Dad explained to us that the rock salt made the ice colder and the game was this: each of us would have a handful of ice and rock salt and then run around the backyard; the winner would be the person that held on to the ice the longest without dropping it. We were pretty naïve, so off we went, running around the backyard with ice and rock salt in our hands. Dad, meanwhile, stood at the grill with a mischievous smile on his face while we ran around in circles with ice in our hands, thinking we were having fun.

When Dad went to buy the ice, he took all four of us with him. In that era, there weren't bags of ice cubes to buy at the local convenience store, so we had to buy blocks of ice, and then Dad would use an ice pick to break up the ice into useable pieces. To buy the ice, a couple of quarters were inserted into a big metal ice machine, and a number of seconds would pass before a large block of ice would come tumbling loudly out of a chute into a large holding pan. With ice tongs, the ice would be grabbed and loaded into the back of the station wagon. Dad, again wanting to have fun with us, would insert the quarters into the machine, and during the seconds before the ice came out, he would bang on the side of the metal machine and say, "Ice man, if you're in there, send out the ice. Hurry up, we're waiting out here."

He banged a few more times and out came the ice. We believed that there really was a man inside the machine and that he responded to Dad's instructions. Like I said, we were extremely naïve.

Whenever we were good (sometime between seldom and never), Dad would load us up in the family car and take us to the Rexall drugstore for ice cream. Unlike today's pharmacies, such as Walgreen and CVS, the Rexall drugstore sold ice cream and had a long bar with stools where a person could sit and order food and drinks. The ice cream was the hard dip kind, and the cherry flavor had little cherry bits that tasted oh so good. After we devoured our ice cream, we would hop back in the station wagon and head home. Sometimes, Dad would have one of us sit on his lap and he would let us "drive." We would have both hands on the steering wheel, rotating it back and forth while he controlled the brake and accelerator pedals (and just out of our detection, he would also have a couple of fingers on the steering wheel, just in case we got a little carried away). In those days, the cars didn't have power steering, so the steering wheel could be moved back and forth without really moving the vehicle. Nevertheless, we felt like we were driving and Dad was the hero once again.

Due to his truck-driving job, Dad was often gone over the road, sometimes for a few weeks at a time, but when he got home, he made up for it by playing with us. Often, we would play on the floor inside the house, kind of wrestling around and jumping on Dad. He would pretend he was a horse, and we would ride on his back. I can still feel his shoulders going up and down as he walked. We had to hold on tight or we would fall off. Sometimes, he would stop short and we would go flying over his head, but he would catch us to make sure we weren't hurt, at least not too badly. Another horse move was the buck, which also challenged our ability to hang on, clutching tightly his white T-shirt. There were times when he would ride all four of us on his back (I have a strange feeling that this may have contributed to his recurring back problems). Another of his games was to have us sit on his foot with our arms wrapped around his leg and then he would walk around the house (sometimes, a kid on each leg). We would hold on as tight as we could, giggling the entire time.

As Mom had made going to bed an enjoyable experience, what with all of the hugging and kissing going on, so too, Dad made going to bed a fun experience for us. We played a game where Dad was the horse and we were the riders, and he would individually give us a ride to bed. At one point in the evening we would hear Dad say, "Okay kids, it's time to go to bed." Vicki would ask for all of us, "Daddy, would you give us rides to bed?" "Yeah, can we have horsie rides?" I added. Timmy too made his feelings known, "I want to wide a hohse to bed." Kathy, not to be missed exclaimed, "I want to wide too." Dad, always willing to have fun with us, directed us to the couch, "Okay. All of you go over to the couch and get in line."

We would stand on the couch while Dad would sit on the edge with his back to us. We would then climb up on his back: broad, wide, strong shoulders ready to be grasped tightly. We would wrap our skinny arms around his thick neck and our skinny legs around his waist, and he would interlock his arms behind our knees and then proceed to gallop around the house, us bobbing up and down all the while. It felt like we were riding a horse. Dad would gallop through the kitchen, down the hall, and into our bedroom, depositing us one at a time into our beds. It was fun waiting for Timmy to come riding into the room while I was lying in bed, my heart still pounding from the experience. All of us wanted to ride again, but after the four of us, the old gray mare had had enough. Once deposited, Mom would arrive with hugs and kisses for all. How could a person not sleep well after that kind of special treatment?

Dad was really into pretending, and we usually bought into whatever he was trying to sell us. We would be on the floor playing, when all of a sudden Dad would say, "I'm blacking out." He would pretend that he couldn't see, and with outstretched arms, he would reach out for the nearest thing or person he could grab. He then would act like he was passing out and lie across us on the floor while we struggled to get out from under him. When we tried to get him to move, he stayed in character and appeared to be passed out, all the while, cracking up on the inside. Even when we tickled him, he wouldn't move. Underneath him Kathy could barely get out, "Daddy, wake up. I can't bweathe." When it became Vicki's turn, she too had to ask, "Daddy, get up please. You're squishing my stomach."

Eventually, the game went a little too far, and when one of us began to cry, Mom got involved, and the blackout game came to an end. It was one game that Dad revisited many times.

Many of the games we played as children could be traced back to Dad. He taught us so much of what we knew about playing. He taught me more about baseball than any coach I ever had and spent countless hours in the backyard, allowing me to break windows while learning to pitch the baseball. He set up the pool in the yard and spent entire afternoons tossing us into the pool, one at a time, including half the neighborhood kids. He taught us how to ride our bicycles. He built a playhouse for the girls and stilts and slingshots for Timmy and me. He taught us how to play King's Base. He taught us how to stand on our heads, and once we started, we stayed entertained for hours. He told us stories about his childhood and sometimes about ghosts (*The Man with the Golden Arm*). We couldn't have asked for a better dad. Many parents think that in order to show love to their children they have to buy them things. Dad gave us the most precious gift that he could give: himself. That's my dad.

RONNIE

If you read this entire book, there is enough information in here to draw some pretty accurate conclusions as to who I am and what makes me tick. In case you need additional anecdotes, here are a few more stories.

I was an extremely active kid, not liking to sit still, always looking for the next adventure or excitement. I suppose I felt incarcerated and needed to escape. I escaped at Disneyland when I was two years old. I escaped my clothes in the Z's backyard. I escaped the neighborhood numerous times, only to return. When I was an infant, Mom placed me in a playpen in order to constrain me. I would have nothing of it. The playpen had wheels, and by shaking it back and forth, I learned that I could move it across the hardwood floor. One day, Mom must have been in the kitchen and I was in the family room in my playpen jail. I began to move vigorously to and fro, and the playpen started scooting across the floor. As I increased my movement, the playpen reciprocated. Finally, I arrived at the television on the other side of the room. Curiosity got the best of me, and I began to fiddle with the dials on the television. Mom recalls first a very loud sound emanating from the television and, immediately following, a very loud sound emanating from me. My first experience with a television, and it wasn't at all rewarding.

I was curious about many things, and at that young age, hadn't learned the proper dos and don'ts that would serve me well later in life. Crawling around the floor as a baby, there were plenty of things to get into. I would crawl for a while, stop, sit up, and chew my fingers. Then I would begin crawling again. I finally arrived on the other side of the room and just happened to be sitting in front of an electrical outlet. That electrical outlet sure looked interesting. Electrical outlet, wet fingers. I wonder what happened next. The sound that emanated from me when I turned the television sound up full blast was nothing compared to the sound I made after sticking my wet fingers into the outlet. A shocking experience to say the least.

The next two stories tell a little bit about my sensitivity. The first involved my eighth birthday. Mom must've thought that I had been good lately (it had to have been some strange time travel sort of thing where Mom missed out on much of my past year because she was transported to Greece during the time of the apostle Paul), and she decided to throw a birthday party for me. I felt honored. She invited most of the boys from the neighborhood, which increased my chances of getting presents, and so I didn't care if some of them were mortal enemies. She spent an entire day decorating the back patio with balloons and streamers. She baked a birthday cake and had ice cream; she went all out. Everything was going along fine until it came time for the game where two contestants passed oranges to each other, without hands, using only their chins. At this point, the boys suddenly became rowdy and began throwing oranges at each other, knocking down balloons, and basically destroying Mom's decorations. Mom began to cry, and because Mom began to cry, so did I. The guests were asked to go home, and it was the last time I had a birthday party.

Another day, I was over at Neal's house and noticed his dad loading up the car with fishing equipment as well as food and beverages. I asked Neal what was going on, and he said that his dad was taking him fishing. I almost invited myself when Neal said, "Do you want to come with us?" Was he kidding? I ran home as fast as I could and gave the news to Dad, who seemed a little surprised that anyone would ask me, but acted excited for me just the same. Dad got a fishing pole, tackle box, and pack lunch all ready for me and sent me back down the street with wishes for a great day of fun. As I arrived at Neal's house, the car was all packed up and Neal rolled the window down to tell me that I couldn't go anymore, they were taking one of the other neighbor boys instead. My heart sank as I went from euphoria to extreme disappointment. As they drove away, I stood there with my fishing pole and cried. I cried all the way home. I could not be consoled. That was me.

DISCIPLINE AND PUBLIC PLACES

Mom and Dad were quite different in their disciplinary methods and techniques. Mom was a little more subtle, whereas Dad was direct, swift, and his punishments had an air of finality about them. They both agreed that corporal punishment was not only acceptable but desired (if you knew us the way they did, you would completely understand). One big difference between them was their weapon of choice. Mom had a tendency to choose a variety of disciplinary tools, a smorgasbord as it were. Depending on her mood and the situation at hand, she would vary between switches, yardsticks, wooden spoons, taco turner, her hand, a bar of soap, whatever was within reach at the moment. Dad, on the other hand, stuck mainly with the big, fat, leather belt around his waist, with an occasional foot or hand thrown in for good measure.

Mom's favorite disciplinary tool had to be the switch. It must have come from her childhood (I do remember a lot of trees surrounding Grandma and Grandpa's house). The odd thing about the switch was that Mom would order us to go get our own switch! Imagine Che Guevara yelling at a political prisoner: "Manuel!" "Si, senor" is Manuel's timid response. "Run out back and get me a Dragunov SVD sniper rifle. I need to shoot you in a firing squad later on this afternoon."

Unlike Manuel, we had the ability to keep on going and never come back. For some reason, we never did. Maybe the food was better at home than in Cuba.

When choosing a switch, it was important to take your time and choose wisely. It couldn't be too thick (that might break a bone) or too thin (paper cuts hurt the most), so you would try to find one that would break after the first blow (removing the leaves as you walked to your destiny had a degrading air about it). If the switch happened to break, Mom would rarely have you go pull another one off the tree, and by that time, the other kids would be doing something worse than what you did to get into trouble in the first place, creating a diversion of sorts. I was known to hide switches that I had recently obtained by breaking them apart and hiding them either under or behind the couch. Unfortunately, Mom would just get a wooden spoon or yardstick and proceed with the whipping anyway.

One time, and who knows where I heard it (wink, wink), I said the word sh—within earshot of Mom, or one of the others told on me, I'm not really sure. I am sure of the punishment however. Mom called me into the bathroom and proceeded to unwrap a brand new bar of Ivory soap (you know, the one that was 99 and 44/100 percent pure). Pure what, no one is really sure, but one thing I do know, it tasted so bad that I could only handle a few seconds of it in my mouth, and the next thing I knew, breakfast and lunch were leaving my stomach at a rapid pace. I think Mom must have decided that this form of punishment wasn't worth the cleanup, so I never had to eat soap again.

Mom was really a pushover, and the punishments were few and far between, at least compared to what was deserved (eventually, due to our size and exasperation, Mom referred all major corporal punishment to Dad). Besides, sometimes Mom would just cry and that was the worst punishment of all. Dad, on the other hand, was not such a pushover.

Since Dad was on the road a lot when we were small, he had to make his presence felt when he was around, and he did. If we were getting out of line too badly, just the mention of his name would make us straighten up and fly right. I don't really believe that he enjoyed spanking us, but he was a perfectionist in all that he did. Oftentimes, when something around the house was broken or gone, he would line up the four of us for interrogation, and it would sound something like this: "Okay, kids, which one of you burned down the garage?" Vicki, being the oldest and bravest, answered first, "Not me."

I too said, "Not me."

"Not me" was Timmy's response as well and Kathy just muttered "Okay." (She was little and sometimes didn't have a lot to say.) By this time Dad was becoming a little perturbed and asked one more time, "So none of you burned down the garage? Well, I'm going to have to spank all of you unless someone confesses." The silence at this point was deafening.

It was an odd thing that happened once the spanking was complete. As we were all lying in our rooms, bawling our eyes out, Dad would say something along these lines, "You kids stop that crying or I'll give you all something to cry about!"

Is it just me or did he not just give us something to cry about, which is why we were all crying? Sometimes, parents can say some pretty dumb things. Like the famous "Do you want me to spank you?" Well, of course we do. In fact, we would like a spanking at least once per day, just for good measure.

The sibling that was normally guilty was Timmy. He was a pretty smart kid, not wanting to suffer alone (maybe it was his idea of bonding between the siblings). The funny thing was, not long after the spanking, Timmy would confess, but by that time the spanking was complete, Dad was watching football and drinking a Schlitz, Mom was sitting on the couch reading a magazine and drinking some hot tea, and the rest of us had already cried ourselves to sleep.

Like I said earlier, Dad wasn't subtle about our punishment and would always tip his hand right before the punishment was delivered. After we were sent to our rooms to await our fates (the door was closed for privacy reasons and/or we were hoping that by closing the door, maybe Dad would forget we were in there and the punishment would be averted, kind of like a possum playing dead), the silence of the room and muffled conversation of Mom telling Dad all of the horrible things we had done, just waiting, knowing what was coming next, was horrible. Suddenly the door would open, swoosh, and in came Dad. The split second his hand began to move toward his belt, we knew we were done for. I would immediately start crying (I was afraid of everything and would cry at the drop of a hat), and Timmy would curl up in the corner of his bed against the wall, trying to limit the swinging space for the belt as well as protecting the vital areas of his body.

The actual spanking was something to behold, resembling some form of Aztec mating dance. Dad would grab us by the left hand with his left hand, us trying to fall to the floor all the while (we tried to limit exposure to our rear ends and legs, but Dad would have none of it). His right hand would have the belt, doubled up, and as he reached back to take a swing, we would lunge our lower half forward to the point that if Dad let go of our left hand, we would completely fall over (picture someone trying to do the limbo dance with the bar at about three feet high). As he kept swinging, we would keep lunging forward, and this would cause us to go in circles. Sometimes, he would swing and miss (good lunging on our part) and that would only make him try harder (he must have had a set number of swats in mind, so whether he missed or not really didn't matter). One mistake we always seemed to make was trying to block the belt with our right hand. Not only did it not stop the belt, it really hurt.

Dad was a yeller. He yelled quite often, expecting that we would be more attentive. If the yelling didn't work over time, he would then resort to a foot in the rear (Timmy comes to mind on this one) or to the dreaded belt. The yelling normally worked. He wouldn't use foul language often, but if he had to yell more than once or twice, the obscenities would sometimes spill out. Dad was often hard to read as he had a tendency to tease us kids. If he was teasing us and we thought he was serious, that usually didn't lead to any problems, but if he was serious and we thought he was teasing (and this happened often), then watch out.

Not all of his yelling was intended to stifle or prevent further activities, some was meant to encourage. At all of our sporting events, it was known by all, that the number one encourager of all the parents was our dad. Everyone knew it; teammates, opposing players, coaches, even umpires. An exchange on the bench between innings sounded thus as I said, "Jimmy, which one is your father?" Jimmy pointed and said, "See, up in the stands with the blue shirt and red hat? Which one's your dad?" Sarcastically I replied, "Just listen. No, really, see where your dad is amongst all the other fans? Look to the left of that, way down the stands, down in the corner sitting by himself, wearing the gray jacket. That's my dad."

Throughout the course of the contest, all of us were encouraged in some way. Dad knew many of the umpires and referees by first name, and they seemed to know him by first name as well. It seemed he knew much more about the game than either the coaches or the officials. It isn't a stretch to say that when I was playing left field (300 feet away), I could hear my dad's encouragements. "Hey, ump! Can't you see that the ball was an inch over the inside part of the plate. That's a strike in my book! You need to borrow someone's glasses? Come on!" The umpire, not wanting to react too obviously as it might encourage further outbursts, said under his breath, "Yes. I'm sure that you can see the plate and ball much better than I can from where you're sitting, down the right field line, one hundred feet away, at an angle, than I can squatting down, two feet behind the catcher. Yes, Mr. Bay, you obviously have superior vision."

That's why, at the end of a long day of playing, when it was time to call all of us kids home, if Mom couldn't get any reaction, Dad would take his turn (simply yelling at the top of his lungs each of our names in order of birth usually was enough). Not only did we come home immediately, but a few neighbor kids and a dog or two showed up for supper with the rest of us.

ꟷ

We didn't often go out in public as a family (you can understand why), but when we did and Dad was with us, he had a routine that he followed. Somewhere between the car and the building (restaurant, store, etc.), he would line up the four of us and with finger pointed in our direction, he would let us know that we were not to touch anything, say anything, breathe loudly; we weren't allowed to look anywhere but straight ahead. Or else. Now why was this necessary? (See title of book.) The result of this lineup was a well-behaved group of kids. We knew that whatever we were promised if we got out of line would surely happen, and the whole time we were in the restaurant, we behaved wonderfully. A lady sitting at an adjacent table turned to Mom, "Your kids are so well behaved. They haven't said a word the entire time. You've done such a wonderful job." Surprised at the comments from the lady, Mom replied, "They are little angels, aren't they?"

Dad wasn't always along, in fact he was rarely along, and when he wasn't, the "cattle dog" role fell to Mom. The results were often quite different. One of our favorite outings was the grocery store. Once we hit the front door, the four of us would take off running. The produce department held special appeal, and we headed straight for the fresh vegetables (lettuce, green beans, cucumbers, etc.). It wasn't that we had a particular affinity for vegetables, but there was something tucked in among the vegetables that we enjoyed immensely. It seems that when the designers put together the section for fresh produce, they ran some plumbing to the site so that the vegetables could be sprayed with water. It made them look fresh, even if they weren't. So in with the vegetables were spray nozzles like you would screw onto the end of your garden hose. We thought they were put there for our entertainment. We would spray the mirrors above the produce, the produce, each other, other shoppers, but the best thing was drinking the water. There was probably a water fountain five feet away, but for some reason, the water coming out of these sprayers was far superior. The water was cold and tasty, and we drank enough water to satisfy a herd of bison. It wasn't long before somebody noticed these four barefoot, blond-headed urchins playing in the produce, getting water all over the floor, and told the authorities. A concerned store clerk approached Mom and said, "Ma'am, are those your kids over there playing in the produce?" Mom, a bit distracted, answered, "What kids?" "The four little urchins over in the produce section!" was his restrained retort. Mom finally became focused and said, "Oh yes, I guess they are my kids. They must have wandered off." The clerk was now growing frustrated and it came out when he asked, "Do you know what they've been doing the last few minutes? There's water all over the floor; another customer said they saw your little angels spraying the mirrors and each other with the water hoses in the produce. Not only that, they were seen eating grapes!" Mom, at this point a little embarrassed answered meekly, "Eating grapes? I fed them before we came here. Why would they be eating again?"

Our explanation for eating the grapes was really pretty logical. We saw that certain grapes would fall off the bunch from the rest of the grapes and figured that no one would want them because of that, and since no one wanted them, then they were probably free. Luckily for the store, there weren't any other fruits or vegetables to which this logic applied. I can imagine an apple or pear tree in the middle of produce, and on the floor would be the fruit that fell off the tree. The fruit that had fallen and gathered around the base of the tree would also be free. And if there wasn't any on the floor and you "accidentally" bumped the tree and more fruit fell to the floor, that fruit was now also free.

We also liked the shopping carts supplied by the store for the patrons to fill with goods, take to the checkout lane, and then carry out to their cars. Of course, all of these functions had nothing to do with us. We thought the shopping carts were there for us to play with. Three of us would load into the cart (two in the basket and one on the bottom where larger items are usually stored) while the fourth would supply the power. Up and down the store aisles, spinning around the corners, grabbing things off the shelves as we flew past. (On TV during this era was a game show called *Supermarket Sweep*. The premise was to fill your shopping cart with the most valuable items, being timed along the way with the winner being the first one done with the most accumulated value. I believe the four of us could have won some prize money if allowed to compete.) At this point, Mom was done shopping, and even if she wasn't done shopping, she was done shopping. We went home.

Our next trip to the grocery store, we didn't go in with Mom. In fact, we were left in the car (this was in an era when you couldn't arrest someone for leaving their kids in the car). Mom left us in the car for one of two reasons: either she was threatened with arrest the next time any of the four of us were seen in the store, or she was embarrassed that if we were seen in the store, someone would recognize us as her children. I think they are both plausible.

I don't believe for a moment that Mom could have ever imagined what would happen next. Timmy and Kathy were in the front seat and Vicki and I were in the back. Timmy was pretending to drive the car (before power steering, you could turn the wheel back and forth with the car turned off). The rest of us were behaving (ha!). While Timmy was playing with the steering wheel, he grabbed the gear shift and somehow put the car into neutral. The parking lot at the grocery store had a slight grade, and once the car went into neutral, it started to roll backward. Vicki was the first to notice the peril that had suddenly come upon us and yelled, "Timmy, put on the brake! Turn the wheel! Put it in park! Do something!" I was holding on to the seat in front of me when I howled "Aaaaahhhh!" Timmy's response was driven by fear and climbing to the back seat, leaving the scene of the crime, he wailed, "Waaaahhhh!" Kathy was like Timmy as she also screamed, "Waaahhhh!" With all of the crying, yelling and wailing going on, we failed to notice the man running across the parking lot.

The car rolled for a short period and was gaining steam when out of the grocery store came Mom, the basket of groceries, and the carry-out boy (back when there was such a person). The carry-out boy ran toward the car, and as he ran alongside, he opened the door, jumped in, and put on the brakes. As Mom approached the car, she said to the store clerk, the hero of the day, with mixed emotions, "I guess I should thank you."

This time, it was Timmy's turn to go find a switch.

Another enjoyable place for Mom to take us (enjoyable for us anyway) was the department store. We didn't go very often, but when we did, it was quite the adventure. Once inside, we would split up and head out, first to the escalator and then the elevator (our strategy in splitting up was intentional; it made it harder for Mom to catch us). The escalator was not designed for the use that we had in mind. We looked at it not as a way to get from one floor to the other, but more like an amusement park ride. Running up the down escalator, down the up escalator, even sliding down the handrail (today, you might notice a sign on the escalator stating not to slide down the handrail; that public service message comes courtesy of the Bay kids). The elevator was also a good time, but was much slower. The great part about the elevator was the anticipation that went along with not knowing quite what we might find when it stopped and the door opened.

Once we had exhausted the excitement of the escalators and elevator, we moved on to the next item on our agenda. While all of this was happening, the store clerks were having an emergency meeting. The head clerk asked the others, "Did any of you see how many of them there were?" The clerk from accessories was stupefied and answered, "They move too fast, I couldn't keep up with them." "I think there are at least ten of them" the clerk from the shoe department guessed. "It looked more like six to me. A variety of ages, but all blonde headed and barefoot," was offered by the head cashier. The head clerk queried the head cashier, "Where did you see them last?" She replied, "They ran into the ladies' wear department." The head clerk then shared his master plan for catching us, "Here's the plan. You two start at the fitting room and work your way to the front, and then you and I will start at the front and meet the others in the middle. We will catch these little heathens one way or another."

As we hit the ladies' wear department, we decided it might be fun to play hide-and-seek in the ladies' clothes racks. So off we went. There were a few customers surprised as they were sorting through the racks. One customer was startled as she sorted through the knit blouses, "Aaaaahhh! There's a kid in this clothing rack!" Timmy was more startled than the customer and yelled, "Aaaaahhhhh!" and immediately disappeared from sight.

As more customers began to scream, we began to run, but the sweep designed by the clerks worked, and they caught us. Mom wasn't surprised when the clerk brought us over. The head clerk confronted Mom, "Ma'am, did you not see what your kids were doing?" Mom was incredulous, "Of course I couldn't see them. They were hiding in the clothes racks."

Banished from another store and more switches to be retrieved (the tree in our front yard was beginning to look a lot like Charlie Brown's Christmas tree).

Some of our public outings were unsupervised (not much different than the ones that were supervised). There were certain places we were not allowed to go when out roaming the neighborhood, but of course, we went anyway. There was a five-and-dime on the other side of Florence Avenue, a Gemco across the San Gabriel Freeway Bridge and Sam's Liquor Store across Orr and Day Road. These roads were all extremely busy, and the prohibition made much sense (making sense was not a part of our decision-making process).

One day, as I was in our front yard playing, Mom came out and asked me "Ronnie, what did you just throw onto the roof of the house?" I answered nonchalantly, "My rubber knife." "I didn't know you had a rubber knife. Where did you get it?" Mom wanted to know. I was taken aback by the question and thought the answer obvious so I said, "At the five-and-dime, over there across Florence Avenue, where you said we couldn't go." "But you didn't have any money, how did you get it?" was her next question. My lie was, "Uh, I found it?"

It was quickly obvious that the lying wouldn't work, so I had to admit that I stole it.

After the switching, my additional punishment was that I had to climb up on the roof of the house, retrieve the knife, be driven over to the five-and-dime, and tell the sales clerk that I was sorry I had taken the knife without paying for it. It's hard to apologize for something when you truly aren't sorry and you're bawling your eyes out (remember, I cried about everything).

At the Gemco store, across the road from the five-and-dime, we discovered that in addition to all the neat goods for sale (there was even an aboveground pool out in the lawn and garden department full of water), they sold candy by the pound. As customers would fill their bags with the candy of their choice and take it for weighing, inevitably, pieces of candy would fall to the floor. As in the grocery store grape story, in our minds, if they hit the floor, they belonged to us. It didn't take long for the sales clerks to catch on as we were running around the store, touching everything, and eating their candy. They drove us out like sheep. For some reason, they didn't ask for the candy back.

Candy was a pretty big deal for us kids, and we didn't get much around the house. How then to obtain the luscious stuff? We had to have money (the Gemco fall-on-the-floor candy was out of the question now), so we figured out how to get it.

Back in these simpler times, empty pop bottles were actually worth something other than shooting bottle rockets out of (to be explored in a later chapter), and we could usually get three cents to a nickel for each one. So up and down Orr and Day Road, scouring empty lots and trash cans we went. We could usually get an armful in an hour or two. We then crossed Orr and Day Road (yeah, I know) and headed to Sam's Liquor Store (we had some familiarity with Sam's because he sold Schlitz beer). At the front of the store was a shopping basket where empty bottles were returned. We would show Sam our bottles, go put them in the basket, and then he would give us our money. Immediately thereafter, we would head to the candy aisle (Jolly Ranchers, Now and Later, Wax Bottles, etc.) and bring it back to the register and give Sam his money back (a lot of time could have been saved with a bottle for candy barter system).

One of us got the brilliant idea that when Sam was occupied elsewhere, we could go to the basket of returned bottles, grab a handful, and then bring them back to the register as if we had found new ones on the street. The problem with this plan was that we weren't very subtle about it and didn't allow enough time between bottle runs to make it realistic. Sam caught on, and we were banished once again. Dad could still come and buy Schlitz however.

Speaking of candy and treats, in our neighborhood, we had a couple of special opportunities to get treats without having to go to the store: the Good Humor ice cream truck and the bread truck both frequented our neighborhood on a weekly basis. If we were good kids (which was about once every five years or so), we could ask Mom for money when we heard the recognizable melody of the Good Humor truck coming through the neighborhood. Not only did the Good Humor man have popsicles, ice cream sandwiches, fudge bars, and the orange/vanilla bar (dreamsicle), he had cinnamon sticks too. The cinnamon sticks you had to ask for. They were basically toothpicks soaked in cinnamon oil, and when you left them in your mouth for only a short time, the burning sensation was potent. We later learned how to make them ourselves with a little jar of cinnamon oil and some toothpicks. There is an incident that I had with the Good Humor truck that I will share in a later chapter.

The bread truck came through the neighborhood on a regular basis, just like the ice cream truck. Moms in the neighborhood would walk out to the street and buy loaves of bread off the truck. In addition to bread, there were pastries, but what we liked was the back of the truck, which was full of candy. You remember the candy necklaces that ended up all over your fingers and turned your neck different colors? The one candy on the truck that I most cherished was baseball card packs. Inside the baseball card packs was bubble gum, which tasted, at least to me, far better than the Bazooka Joe kind, although with Bazooka Joe bubble gum, you got a comic strip for free. There was one other truck that stopped in the neighborhood on a regular basis that didn't interest me in the least bit, the water truck. It seems that some people in the neighborhood wanted water that you paid extra for instead of the relatively free kind that came out of the faucet.

We made other public appearances seemingly without incident. We visited places such as Dodger Stadium, Angel Stadium, the LA Zoo, the San Diego Zoo, Pacific Ocean Park, the LA County Fair, the Mojave Desert, and I don't believe we were banished from any of them. I did get lost once while we were visiting Disneyland. I don't remember the details, as I was quite small. Mom says I was lost for quite a while. Just realizing that I was not with her, Mom said, "Ronald, have you seen Ronnie anywhere?" Dad, thinking that it was Mom's responsibility to keep an eye on me replied, "No, the last time I saw him was on the teacup ride."

I was two years old. I'm still not sure if Mom and Dad are my real parents. They said they are.

THE HOLIDAYS

Like most American families, my family celebrated all of the usual holidays. I'm not sure if the way we celebrated them would land us in a Norman Rockwell print, but other than a few eccentricities, we were pretty normal. After all, when it comes to family traditions, who's to say what is normal or abnormal. In terms of activities and the time of the year, one of my favorite holidays was Independence Day, or as we always referred to it, the Fourth of July. The sights and sounds of the Fourth: the bands, floats, parades; the smell of smoke in the air, the beautiful explosions of color that lighten up a summer's night; and the red, white, and blue that ribbon the streets of the town, all delight the senses. The neighborhood sounds of pop, pop, pop and whistling rockets as kids run here and there, knowing that what they do on this day and get away with they could never do on any other day, bring a smile to my face. I still love all of these sights and sounds today as I always have, but when I was a kid there were other more important things that I dare not think about doing now. I'm grown-up you see.

JULY 4

I've often heard it said that career criminals start out with smaller crimes, such as stealing and vandalism, and then work their way up to the bigger crimes, such as kidnapping and murder. In a similar way, our Fourth of July activities started out small and ended up with a bang, so to speak.

When we were really small, I can remember the first Fourth of July toy that Dad bought us: black snakes. These were really quite exciting, at least for a kid under age six. They came in little packages and looked like a pencil eraser, only black. Like most other Fourth of July toys, the main ingredient required to make them work was one that we absolutely loved anyway: *fire*! When you applied fire to the snakes, the pencil eraser began to smoke (I liked the smell of the smoke more than any other aspect) and grow and soon looked like a long black snake. What fun! It was easy to tell after each Fourth of July if we had been playing with the snakes because the sidewalk in front of the house would have little black burn marks from one end of the yard to the other (and so would the front porch and patio, even though they were off-limits).

Once we outgrew the snakes, the next toys we indulged in were sparklers. Sparklers were much more exciting than snakes. The sparkler was basically a piece of wire, about nine inches long; that included a fuel, usually charcoal or sulfur (the same as black powder); an oxidizer, potassium nitrate for example; a binder such as sugar or starch, which when coated on the wire and dried, allow the substances to remain; and finally the best part, the aluminum, iron, steel, zinc, or magnesium dust that creates the beautiful, bright, shimmering sparks. The metal flakes heat up until they are incandescent and shine brightly. Once lit, the sparkler would shoot out colorful sparks at a ferocious rate. They were best played with after dark, so that you achieved the full effect of the fire and color.

Each of us would run to Dad with sparkler in hand (Dad had the matches; he probably didn't think it was safe for us to have our own matches), and he would light each of our sparklers. Whereas we would then proceed to run around the yard flailing our arms around in circles, writing our names in the air, and getting as close to each other's faces as we thought we could get away with, squealing and giggling the entire time. When we got really good at it, we graduated to a sparkler in each hand, and then maybe two in each hand (if you tried to hold too many at a time, the sparks would burn your hand). Besides the obvious, in the wrong hands, these little toys had the potential to be quite lethal, only in a less than obvious way. You see, when the sparkler had burned itself out, we had a tendency to throw the remaining wire on the ground and run back to Dad to get our sparkler refill. Unfortunately, the remaining wire was still extremely hot, and as I mentioned in an earlier chapter of the book, we always ran around barefoot, especially during the summertime. A hot sparkler on the bottom of the foot ensured that in addition to squealing and giggling, there was a little screeching and one-legged hopping around to liven up the evening. Dad, with a look of incredulity, turned to Mom and asked, "Honey, what are those kids doing, jumping around the yard and screeching like that?" Mom, oblivious to the reality at hand, "I don't know, dear, I guess they're just having a good time."

As much fun as the sparklers were, we had to move on to something a little more, let us say, raucous. Sparklers were visually stimulating, but did not pack much of a punch when it came to the noise factor. (There was something we used to enjoy akin to the sparkler called the pinwheel, which was nailed to a tree or post and when lit, would whirl around at a high rate of speed, spewing sparks all around. One big drawback with the pinwheel: we couldn't run around the backyard with pinwheels in hand screeching and giggling.)

What was next? Firecrackers! Black Cat firecrackers to be exact. Any other kind would not do as far as we were concerned. The firecrackers came in packages of 500 and were all tied together by the wicks being wrapped around a string running down the middle of the package. Each firecracker had to be untangled from the main string. You could light the entire string at one time and enjoy the cacophonous sound for the short time that it lasted, and we did do that every once in a while, but the best way to enjoy firecrackers was one at a time. You might place them on the ground or in an object (a toad's mouth was always a good place) and light the fuse while quickly backing away and pop! After a few of these lightings, the mind began to wander, and conversations went like this: "Go get one of Daddy's beah cans and wet's see what it sounds wike." I came up with a better idea and offered, "Let's get one of Daddy's beer bottles and see if we can blow it up. Glass is more fun than metal." Vicki came up with another idea and shared it with us. "Let's put a firecracker in the muffler of Daddy's car." As usual, Kathy agreed with all of us. "Okay" she said.

After we had blown up pretty much everything around the house, the next step was to throw them, first in the air and then at each other. There was a certain technique that worked best when throwing a lit firecracker, but I first had to learn my lesson throwing them the wrong way (yes, there is a right and wrong way, and Dad did show me the right way, but as usual, I did not heed his advice, choosing instead to learn the hard way). One time, I lit the firecracker and reached back like I was getting ready to pitch a baseball, and right when my hand came whooshing by my ear on the delivery, the firecracker blew up. Pow! At that exact moment, I remembered my dad's instructions on how to properly throw a firecracker and realized that not listening to his advice had its consequences. Not feeling any sympathy for my pain and anguish, Dad firmly said, "Son, I thought I told you not to throw the firecracker that way!" Barely able to hear him, due to the ringing in my ears, I said, "I'm sorry, did you say something Daddy?"

Mom looked at my swollen fingers and decided that the cure for swollen, burned fingers was butter. Butter? (Mom often resorted to the remedies passed down from generation to generation, like bloodletting, or found in *Poor Richard's Almanac*, remedies that the medical profession had long since debunked). She proceeded to rub butter all over my hand. For some reason, the pain didn't go away and seemed to intensify as the butter began to bubble and pop; in fact, it looked a lot like the grease in the pan when Mom fixed fried chicken.

After we had exhausted all of the firecracker options, the next July 4 toys on our graduating scale were bottle rockets. Bottle rockets were so much more advanced than firecrackers. Not only did they explode, but you could shoot them in the air where they would go one hundred feet or farther, or if shooting them in the air got boring, we would shoot them at each other. They could be shot out of a pop bottle (thus the name), a pipe, conduit, PVC pipe, Dad's car muffler, or just thrown into the air. As we got older, we gathered enough of the town kids together and divided up sides and had some really great bottle rocket wars. I will talk about these events at a later date.

So earlier, I mentioned that criminals start small and work their way up to larger crimes and so it was with the Fourth. Snakes, sparklers, firecrackers, bottle rockets, roman candles, M-80s, dynamite, plastic explosives, you get the idea. As far as the town's fireworks display, I didn't like it, *the loud noises scared me.* On some occasions, rather than drive to the location set aside for the fireworks show, Dad would lift us one by one onto the roof of the house, purportedly for a better view, but I think it was really in hopes that one or all of us would fall off the roof, and well, you get the picture. The neighbors were quite curious as to the four of us up on the roof at night and one man said to his wife, "Honey, look at that family sitting on the roof of their house. The kids are in their pajamas and they're eating popcorn. I wonder what they're up to." His wife was also curious and guessed, "Maybe they think its December and they're on the lookout for Santa Claus and his eight tiny reindeer."

CHRISTMAS

Christmas, to a kid, is the mother of all holidays. Even though it's considered the season of giving, we didn't do much giving, but sure did a lot of getting, thus, the mother of all holidays. In our house, all of the celebration was secular, not much mention of the birth of Jesus Christ. We had Rudolph, Frosty, jingle bells, sleighs, candy canes, icicles, strings of lights on the tree (the lights were different back then: they were much larger, and if one bulb went out, the entire string went dead and Dad would have to replace one bulb at a time to figure out which one was the culprit, and after a few beers, that could be quite the challenge), carols, snow (even though in Los Angeles we never saw any), fudge, ornaments, and the coup de grace: presents!

Before the presents could show up, we first had to have a tree. Dad, being a traditionalist, would bundle us kids up, grab his trusty saw, pile us in the family station wagon, and drive to the nearest grocery store parking lot where he would proceed to examine in minute detail every tree on the lot (except those that were frosted or a different color than green, being a traditionalist after all). There couldn't be a single spot in the tree that had any open space. It had to be perfect in every way. We usually spent a few hours before the right tree was finally decided upon. Once chosen, the perfect tree was tied on the top of the sleigh, I mean station wagon, and we headed home with our prize.

Once in the house, Dad would grab the rusty old red-and-green tree stand with the bent legs made out of some metal compound. After the tree had fallen over a couple of times and Dad had let out a few nontraditional phrases, the tree was ready to be decorated. Mom would begin handing out the icicles first; we got yelled at if we didn't gently toss the icicles, one at a time, spaced just so around the tree (our preferred method was to throw handfuls at a time). If Mom found a lump of icicles in the tree she confronted the four of us with, "Which one of you threw that lump of icicles on the tree?" In unison, Vicki, Kathy, and me shouted out, "Timmy!"

Dad was responsible for the lights and spent quite a bit of time not only unraveling the many strands, but once they were plugged in, replacing bulb after bulb until the entire string was fully lit. Mom continued to hand out decorations, and I have to admit, we had some really pretty ornaments, some of which didn't make it to the next Christmas. The little wire utensil hangers after a few Christmases would straighten out, and when we hung them on the tree, they wouldn't stay, and the really pretty ornament would crash to the floor into tiny little pieces that hurt like crazy when stepped on (barefoot). Just like the icicles, it was very important to space the ornaments evenly around the tree (two red bulbs next to each other would not do). While we decorated, Nat King Cole would be singing Christmas songs in the background. Between the icicles and the ornaments, Mom would wrap strands of garland, gold and silver, around the tree from top to bottom. Finally, Dad would place the Santa on the top of the tree, and all was complete, except for the most important part—presents!

In our family tradition, there were two kinds of presents: those from Mom and Dad, which were wrapped in colorful paper, bows, and ribbons and those from Santa (how Santa usurped Jesus Christ as the focus of the holiday I'll never know, but that's a discussion for a different time), which weren't wrapped and didn't appear until Christmas morning.

Songs played a big role in the Christmas season, and as mentioned earlier, with a secular view, we had songs such as "Jingle Bells," "Rudolph the Red-Nosed Reindeer," and "Frosty the Snowman" to entertain us throughout the holiday. True, we heard "Silent Night" and "Away in a Manger," but because they didn't speak about the celebration, festivities, and presents, they didn't have as much impact. The one song that did have an impact and gave us much pause was "Santa Claus is Coming to Town." The basic gist of this song was that Santa was coming to town and was planning on giving all of the good kids gifts. However, for those kids who weren't good, Bay kids, Santa might reconsider giving gifts, and it was possible that you might be shortchanged. Other than crying and pouting, the prohibitions were fairly generic. We lived in much fear, not knowing for sure whether we were good enough until Christmas morning. The Bay kids were doomed. I like the Jesus story better: he forgives all of our screwups and still gives the ultimate gift. Mom and Dad referred to the lyrics of this song often: "You kids better behave or Santa won't bring you any presents," was heard often and unlike the "boy that cried wolf" story, we believed the threat every time.

Many nights I lay in bed and wondered if I would get anything for Christmas. And yet, I still held out hope.

Unlike many families who open their presents on Christmas Eve, we had to wait until Christmas morning, and the suspense nearly killed us. Dad would always fill our heads with fanciful tales of reindeer landing on the roof while Santa slid down the chimney. Vicki, the one with the most intelligence, was suspicious and asked, "Daddy, we don't have a chimney. How does Santa get into our house?" Dad wasn't one to blow the story, so he ignored Vicki's question and said to the other three, "Anyway kids, do you hear the sound of reindeer on the roof?"

I swear there were nights that as I lie in bed trying to go to sleep on Christmas Eve, I really heard the sound of reindeer on the roof (my guess is that Dad climbed up on the roof and took a stick and scratched around, trying to sound like reindeer), but whatever the reason, I was convinced I heard reindeer up there. I even went to the window and tried to look up the side of the house to see if I could spot them, but I never did. Lying there, I stared at the slats underneath the top bunk where my brother Timmy was, probably staring up at the ceiling, going through the same agony. "I wonder what's in that big package in the corner behind the tree." Over and over, my mind would race. As I mentioned earlier, the suspense and anticipation was agonizing, and needless to say, none of us could make it until daylight. A typical Christmas morning would proceed as follows: one by one each of us would emerge from our bedrooms ever so quietly and meet in the hallway outside Mom and Dad's room. In a low whisper, just outside of Mom and Dad's room, Timmy impatiently stated, "Wet's go open the pwesents." Planning to bypass Mom and Dad on the present opening ritual wasn't an option and Vicki made it plain, "We can't do that; Mommy and Daddy aren't up yet." "What time is it?" I asked. Looking into the living room Vicki could barely make out the time on the large clock (the clock resembled a giant gold pocket watch). "2:00 a.m." she said. Not to give up on the idea, Timmy pushed, "Can we wake them up yet?" Kathy thought that was a good idea and offered, "Okay." Vicki, having that kind of authority within this group, overruled us all and wisely suggested, "We better go back to bed and get up later."

That "going back to bed" would last another couple of hours, and the next time we met in the hallway, we skipped the conversation and headed to the living room, where in the light streaming through the window from the moon (or was it the streetlight?), we would begin to make out all of the presents that Santa had dropped off. Santa's presents were always the biggest and that made them the best. It's funny how kids think (as an adult, I finally realized that the smaller the package, the better).

The weeks leading up to Christmas, we would lie down by the tree and sort out the wrapped gifts and try to figure out what was in each one. The biggest were the best in our minds. We would press the paper to see if there was writing on the box underneath the paper, trying to guess what was inside. One time I thought I could make out some letters if I pushed hard enough and stretched the paper really tight. S-E-T-R-A, I finally had it. Timmy thought I had figured it out and pressed me, "What's it say, Wonnie?" Excitedly I answered, "It's a Setra!" Timmy was confused and asked, "What's a Setwa, Wonnie?" With a little less confidence and a bit confused I replied, "I'm not sure, but that's what it says."

For days, I would walk around the house muttering, "Setra, Setra," pronouncing it a variety of different ways with the accent on the "Set" and then the accent on the "tra." I would pronounce it with a short *e* and then with a long *e*. I tried everything, but I couldn't figure out what Setra was. (Turns out it was the Mousetrap game.)

We shook them, and if they didn't make any noise, we figured they were clothes or gloves or something else of little value (the one exception to this rule were presents from Grandma Nina; she always sent us $2 bills that she had collected during the year). We were looking strictly for toys. Dad was a pretty crafty gift wrapper and would often insert marbles or rocks to throw us off the trail. Well, back to Christmas morning.

After going back to bed numerous times throughout the night, it finally was morning, and we knew then that we could officially wake up Mom and Dad. As one mass of humanity, we would all surround their bed and make as much noise as we could while whispering in hushed tones (after all, we didn't want to be obvious about it). After rubbing the sleep from his eyes, Dad said, "What are you kids doing out of bed, it's only five o'clock in the morning? You kids get back to bed."

And he rolled over to go back to sleep. Vicki, our spokesperson, poked Dad and tried again, "But Daddy, we've already been up twelve times, and we've seen all of Santa's presents."

Timmy was pretty wound up and added, "Yeah Daddy, I saw my new owange dump twuck and I'm weady to go pway with it."

I had seen a different Santa toy and asked Dad, "Can we put up my new tetherball pole right now?"

All Kathy could mutter was, "Dolls."

Mom didn't give Dad the chance to reject our offers and told us all, "Okay kids, but you have to eat your breakfast first." Oh, man!" came out of our mouths in unison.

After breakfast (we ate so fast, it's a wonder any of the food was digested), we all lined up around the foot of the tree and divided up the presents. From: Dad, To: Ronnie; From: Mom, To: Kathy, etc. Mom and Dad always bought things for each other, but we never noticed what they got; if it wasn't a toy, it didn't matter. Vicki and Kathy got the usual girl gifts: dolls, dollhouses, doll clothes, makeup kits, mirrors, etc. Timmy and I got the usual boy gifts: cap guns, army guns, Tonka trucks, Tinkertoys,

Lincoln Logs, etc. Some of the most memorable toys were the big yellow Tonka truck that you could ride on it was so strong, the Davy Crockett outfit with coonskin cap, the tetherball pole set, Tinkertoys, Lincoln Logs, Mousetrap game, Yahtzee game, army helmet with night vision goggles, Erector Set, Pike's Peak Road Race set, electronic football game, and even a spy kit with a compass and other spy gadgets.

Once all of the packaging was ripped apart and thrown around the room and after we searched through all of the paper to make sure a present wasn't hidden among the mess, the cleanup began. After the cleanup was complete, the rest of the day was spent putting the toys together, adding the batteries, crying because the new toy didn't work anymore, shooting a sibling with the new gun I got, watching Dad and Uncle Floyd play with our toys, and various other activities. To top it all off, at the end of the day, we would haul the booty off to our respective rooms and make mental notes as to which toys were our favorites and which ones we would probably never touch again. What a great time! Instead of the "Island of Misfit Toys," our neglected toys ended up in the toy graveyard.

HALLOWEEN

Next to Christmas, we probably loved Halloween the most, and it was for one main reason: we got to eat so much candy that our teeth almost fell out. Halloween had to be invented by the ADA and sponsored by Crest toothpaste. We are talking the large-size grocery bags full of candy. They became so full and heavy that we had to go home midway through the evening to dump out what we had and make room for more.

We started pretty young in the Halloween adventures. I remember my first costume: I was a ghost, not the invisible kind, more in line with Casper, the friendly ghost. Mom took an old white sheet and cut holes where the eyes were supposed to be, threw the sheet over my head, and tied a large rubber band around my neck. The idea was to keep the costume aligned so that I wouldn't run into something in the dark (or the idea was to tighten the rubber band tight enough to cut off the flow of blood to the brain causing permanent, oh, never mind). It didn't work. Throughout the night, the eyeholes ended up where my ears were, and I would run into trees, other kids, werewolves, goblins, and other creatures of the night. Not only would the sheet spin around, it was also so long that I kept tripping over it and falling to the ground. Even with all of that, when I got home at the end of the night with my bag full of candy, the costume mishaps mattered little.

Other costumes were not so memorable, except the really ridiculous plastic masks that came with most of them. These masks were representative of cats, dogs, ghouls, goblins, Snow White, Mickey Mouse, President Johnson, etc., and were made of blow mold plastic and held on your head by a rubber band in the back. They had eyeholes to see out of and either a mouth or nose hole so that you didn't die of suffocation. You couldn't wear these masks very long because your breath would fog up the inside and mix with your slobber, causing a loss of breath at times. You would see kids all over the neighborhood with these masks on top of their heads, gasping for breath. The other drawback to these masks was that the rubber band got tangled up in your hair, and you would lose a bit of it each time you took the mask off.

My favorite costume of all time was being a pirate. Mom would draw a scar on my face and a mustache; put a bandana on my head, scarf around my waist, and a patch on my eye; and voila, I was a pirate. I used the pirate theme over and over throughout the years (even as a teenager, a pirate was acceptable and helped me avoid being made fun of for dressing up as a scarecrow or other lame character).

Once we were decked out, it was time to grab a grocery bag (the big brown paper kind) and head out the front door. Little did we know that the frights would start right off of our front porch. Dad also liked Halloween. As we stepped off the porch onto the driveway, "Wooooooo!" came out from the bush next to the front porch. We hadn't gone ten feet out the front door and Dad was already trying to scare us. It worked. As we all four stopped, shivering from head to toe, hearts beating a hundred beats per minute, Timmy nervously said, "What was that? I'm scawed." Vicki's analysis and logic led her to say, "It sounded like an owl." Brilliant me, not realizing the source of the sound, offered, "Let's go back in the house and get Daddy. He'll protect us." Then we heard another "Woooooo!" only louder this time. At this point, Kathy had gone over the edge and bawled, "Waaaah!"

All of us were so absorbed in our fright that we didn't notice Dad jumping out of the bushes until we heard the "Boo!" I do believe that we all nearly peed our pants that night. The funny thing about it, I remember each of us running, not away from our tormentor, but right into his arms. He got a big kick out of it, and we cried for a while.

With our adrenaline pumping pretty good by now, we were bound and determined to go fill those bags with candy. We really weren't too bright when it came to strategy. Once Dad had scared us, we were very aware of any other thing out there that might scare us, especially goblins. For some reason, we would run from tree to tree, thinking that would prevent the goblins from getting us. (Truth be told; Dad told us that by running from tree to tree, we would evade detection by the goblins. He would watch us running from tree to tree en masse and nearly fall over laughing).] Now, where do you think a goblin would be located, if not in a tree? Of course, none of us really knew what a goblin was, Dad just told us they were scary and they would eat little kids alive if they ever got a hold of you.

Running was the key to staying safe in our quest to fill up the grocery bags with candy. As soon as the door of one house would shut, we would run as fast as we could to the next house

(In between houses was always dark and scary, so running fast took us from lit up front porch, past the dark areas, and back to another lit up front porch). I guess we figured that we could out run any monster or scary creature.

After a long night of knock, knock, ring, ring, "Trick or Treat, smell my feet, give me something good to eat", we ended up back at the house with our treasures. We had a ritual once we all arrived home. We would sprawl out on the living room floor, dump our bags of candy out in front, in a large circle, and begin the trading. There were hard candies, chocolate, bags of candy corn, popcorn balls (which nobody wanted), apples and oranges, (which nobody wanted, and come to think of it, which adult would stoop so low and be so mean as to put fruit in our Halloween bags?), and the name brand candy bars. The trading started with Vicki's offer to me, "I'll give you one Snickers bar for two Baby Ruth's." Since Baby Ruth was one of my favorites, I countered her offer with this, "How about you give me one Snickers bar for two Heath bars?"

The game was to try and unload all of the "bad" candy onto your sibling's pile and get all of the "good" candy on your pile. However, everyone was in tune to the game, even little Kathy. Trying to fool Kathy, I mischievously said, "Kathy, I'll give you this popcorn ball for three Jolly Rancher Apple Stix." Kathy, being much smarter than I had given her credit for, answered, "No!"

After "trading" for the remainder of the night, we ended up taking to our rooms pretty much what we started out with.

Timmy was what you might call a hoarder when it came to candy. He gave up nothing, and even in July of the next year, he was pulling out candy from some hiding place and waving it in your face and tauntingly saying, "Wook what I have, nyah, nyah, nyah." And then, he would proceed to taunt you further with a piercing little whistle that he still utilizes to this day (phweet, phweet!).

In later years, Halloween went from a candy hunt to a hunt for mischief. Oh, we still dressed up in costume and came home with a nominal amount of candy, but the focus had definitely changed, not so much treat and a lot more trick. We would ring doorbells after lighting bags of cow dung, take "for sale" signs out of one person's yard and put them in another's yard a block away, soap car windows (one night, Andy and I soaped a car window not realizing that two little old ladies were still in the car, not until we heard them screaming through the rolled-up windows), egg whatever we thought we could get away with, set off firecrackers, and toilet paper the popular girls' houses. It was as much fun avoiding being caught as it was doing the mischievous deed. We would run in all directions and jump in the ditch when a car would drive by (hiding in a ditch with a police car driving by, so close I could almost touch it, spotlight shooting right over my head, heart beating so hard that I was sure it would wake the neighbors). Man, I could do it again today, except I'm a grown-up, don't you see.

Sometimes, there were Halloween parties to go to, but they were pretty boring for the most part. The only interesting things at the parties, at least as I got older, were the girls, but I was too shy to even talk to them, so I preferred to be out on the streets getting into mischief and other predicaments.

EASTER

Easter, in the same way as Christmas, was hijacked (you ever notice that Santa spelled sideways is Satan), not by Santa, but by a giant bunny rabbit. How a giant bunny rabbit usurped Jesus Christ as the focus of the holiday… that's a story for another time. Anyway, we loved Easter for a couple of reasons: one because there were presents in the morning, mainly candy (come to think of it, Easter took the best of Christmas and Halloween and combined them) and two; the decorating and hunting of the Easter eggs (that's another question; how does a rabbit lay eggs?).

First, Mom would boil three or four dozen eggs. In order to "color" the eggs, all that was needed were the following:

- Food Coloring
- Vinegar
- Water
- Cooking Oil

We each had a coffee cup of water (about a half of a cup) mixed with about twenty drops of food coloring (you could do plain solid colors, combine yellow and blue to get green, or go for the marbled look which we preferred) and a tablespoon of vinegar. With the egg sitting on the spoon, you would dip the egg down into the coloring mixture and wait for a minute or two, or until you achieved the desired effect. If you wanted the marbled look, you added a tablespoon of cooking oil to the other mixture. Coloring the eggs was a really fun event and kept us busy for the entire evening. Conversations during the process were the typical back and forth. "Wook, I made a gween egg, with some wed and bwue mixed in," Timmy proudly declared. Vicki wasn't a fan of his egg and disparaged, "Timmy, that's a dumb looking egg. Look at mine, it's a pretty pink." Kathy was having trouble with the process and turned to Mom, "Mommy, I can't get my egg to wook." I was having a different issue and declared, "My egg's cracked and the yolk is coming out."

The next day, on Easter morning, we would wake up and in the living room would be four Easter baskets with candy: chocolate rabbits (I liked the solid ones, not the hollow ones), chocolate eggs, marshmallow rabbits, and Peeps, (yuck!) and a few minor toys such as coloring books. Not quite the impact of Christmas, but fun nevertheless. As with Christmas, we normally celebrated this religious holiday in a secular manner and didn't include going to church (that was to come years later). After breakfast would come the Easter egg hunt. Mom and Dad would go outside and hide the Easter eggs all over the yard, in bushes, trees, drain pipes, swing sets, trash cans, anywhere and everywhere. Once all the eggs were hidden, we were released to go find them. The search was accompanied by much dialogue. "I found one, there's another one, I found another one! Yee ha!" I was doing well. Vicki too was having much success in her efforts and declared happily, "Here's one, oh, and there's one over there, and another! Woo hoo!" Like his older siblings Timmy seemed to be having fun and let everyone know, "I got one, and theh's one oveh by the cah, and I see one next to the shed! Yippee!" Kathy, however, wasn't very happy and lamented, "I can't find any! They keep taking them away fwom me! Waah! I'm telling."

We would repeat the hide and seek until we got tired of the game. Once we were done hiding and looking for them, what to do with a bunch of hard-boiled eggs (there were those times that the number of eggs found didn't match up to the number hidden, but eventually, the odor would lead us to the missing eggs)? The logical thing to do was throw them over the fence into the neighbor's yard. This was almost as much fun as the Easter egg hunt. The next day, we were playing in the backyard, and eggs came flying back over the fence and landed all around us (a veritable mortar attack from the enemy next door). I guess the neighbor didn't like the free, hard-boiled eggs he found all over his backyard.

There was a community Easter egg hunt, but it wasn't near as fun as our family hunt. Basically, there was a large field in the park where volunteers had placed eggs, out in the open. Hundreds of kids would line up next to each other; someone would blow a whistle, and it boiled (pardon the pun) down to a foot race to the other end of the field. Not much of a hunt, but a great foot race.

TRASH OR TREASURE

(ONE MAN'S CEILING IS ANOTHER MAN'S FLOOR)

In the move, *The Burbs*, there is a scene where Ray, Art, and Mr. Rumsfeld suspect the Klopek's of disposing of dead bodies in their garbage. One night, they observe Hans Klopek stuffing a trash can with what appears to be a body, and they agree to go through the trash the next morning to confirm their suspicions. When they finally wake up, the trash collectors are already there and have dumped the Klopek cans into the back of the trash truck. Mr. Rumsfeld and Art begin to argue with the trash men as to the "ownership" of the trash, with Mr. Rumsfeld, in his underwear, with half a face of shaving cream, and Art, climbing into the back of the truck, throwing all of the trash back onto the street. The trash men get into an argument as to who is responsible to pick up the trash and what right they have to be going through the trash in the first place. At one point, in defense of Mr. Rumsfeld and Art, one of the trash men says to his partner, "The Supreme Court ruled that a person's garbage is public domain the minute it hits the curb." The Bay kids couldn't have said it better, and we were extremely glad that the Supreme Court saw fit to rule in our favor. You see, we were what you might call "trash diggers" (in our minds we were art collectors). We fully believed in the maxim, One man's trash is another man's treasure". Unfortunately, this didn't always sit well with Mom and Dad, well, mainly Mom, since she had to deal with most of the day to day.I'm not sure what got us started on our trash-collecting adventures, but at one time, I was a baseball card collector, and this may have been an early precursor to trash digging. My card collection was very small, and not having much money other than pop bottle returns (my allowance was being saved strictly for the future purchase of a bicycle), I was limited in my ability to expand its size, and I was open to any idea to increase it. One day, a neighbor kid gave me a box of baseball cards, presumably someone decided that they were no longer interested in baseball cards and my collection increased tenfold all at once. Willie Mays, Mickey Mantle, Sandy Koufax, Don Drysdale; I had hit the mother lode! Collecting at my slow pace, I may never have accumulated cards of this value. That got me to thinking, *What if someone else got tired of collecting baseball cards, but didn't have a recipient for their collection*? Where would that collection end up? In the trash! From that day on, I was on a mission. I couldn't walk by a trash can without glancing in and visually going through the entire can, hoping upon hope that I would strike gold. I imagined large boxes full of baseball cards, cards of extreme value that would be mine, *all mine!* I was known to be focused or obsessed, depending on your definition. For weeks, I would go through the neighborhood on trash day and dig through everyone's trash, trying to find the elusive card collection. When digging through other people's trash, you had to be discrete. Sometimes digging through someone else's trash was met with resistance. One man, sitting on his front porch swing smoking a cigarette, was curious as to my activities and asked me, "Hey kid, what are you doing digging through my trash?" I thought nothing of the inquiry and responded, "Looking for baseball cards." I don't think he liked my answer and with raised voice demanded, "What?! Get out of here kid." At this point I thought I would throw some of my newfound legal knowledge his way. "The Supreme Court ruled that a person's garbage is public domain once it hits the curb," I confidently offered.

As the neighbor guy stood up and started in my direction, it dawned on me that the Supreme Court's jurisdiction probably didn't extend to my neighborhood. I moved, rather quickly, on to the next house. I was so focused on the baseball cards, I'm sure I passed on other treasures, to my detriment. Imagine what could have been mine had I not been so obsessed...I mean, focused. After searching for weeks, I came up empty. In a way, I wasn't much different from the man who headed off to California in 1849, purchased hundreds of dollars worth of prospecting equipment, and spent the remainder of his life searching for gold, only to die up in the mountains a lonely and broken man. Because I wasn't one to give up or admit defeat, I switched my focus, partnered with my siblings, and went back to the trash. We were, once again, well ahead of the normal population, recycling long before it became popular.

In order for the four of us to get to Lakeview Elementary School, we had to cross Orr and Day Road, which was strictly off-limits to us with some minor exceptions: going to school and any school function including school carnivals, swimming in the public pool, going to the local Baptist church during VBS, etc. Once we crossed the street, with the assistance of a crossing guard during school time and on our own when school was out, we had to walk past Santa Fe High School. There was a sidewalk that ran parallel with Orr and Day Road, and we made sure to stay on the sidewalk, not venturing too close to the high school. We were afraid of and intimidated by the high school kids. Most of the kids would ignore us, but there were those that liked to make object lessons out of us, specifically me ("Hey, Four Eyes, come here."). So not only did we stay on the sidewalk, we walked at a fairly brisk pace, some might call it a run, until we had gotten a decent distance past the school.

The next landmark was the First Baptist Church (we weren't regular attendees, but Mom did take advantage of the free babysitting during Vacation Bible School) and then a local apartment building. On the outside entrance of the apartment building was a garden of cactus and other plants and next to that was a wall of rock. It wasn't a normal kind of rock, but more like a lava rock, which was not too gentle on the hands and feet. Because the rocks jutted out of the wall at various spots, we saw it as an invitation to climb the wall, so we did. After a few scrapes and abrasions, we reached the top. On the roof, we discovered dried-out starfish and other sea paraphernalia (no explanation as to how they ended up on the roof; could it have been the great flood of the Bible?). After that diversion, we continued on our way and arrived at the school, bloody hands and all.

One year, on the last day of school, we decided to take an alternate route home. Against our better judgment (better judgment was not our strong suit), we decided to take the back way home. This route took us through the playground, where the kickball games took place, past the tennis courts (seven in all), and onto the high school campus. From there, we would wind our way through the school and come out the front entrance, right back on Orr and Day Road. An interesting phenomenon was taking place as we went through the school. For one thing, none of the high school kids were mean. In fact, they seemed overjoyed. They were laughing and kidding around, and they were doing something else that seemed a little odd. As each of them approached a trash can, they would take all of their school supplies: textbooks, notebooks, paper, pencils, erasers, rulers, protractors, glue, etc., and dump the entire lot into the trash can. At first, we were a little shocked, but soon we saw the obvious opportunity staring us in the face. Vicki turned to me and asked, "Do you see what I see?" "I think I do. I see a bunch of really neat stuff being thrown away." "And, are you thinking what I'm thinking?" With a strange gleam in my eye I asked, "How are we going to get it all home?"

There were trash cans lined up all over that school. As we got to each can, the exclamation was always the same, "Hey, look at all of this stuff! Wow!" We went through every single can, and if our arms were full when we got to the next can, we had to decide what was the least valuable and sacrifice it. Back to the can it would go. It would take the four of us to transport all of the valuables back to the house (camels weren't available), and even then, many valuables had to be left behind. We just didn't have enough hands! The look on Mom's face as we struggled through the front door with all of our booty was one of incredulity: "What are you kids doing? And, what are you bringing into the house?" Mom questioned with a slight giggle as she saw all the stuff we had hauled home. We could tell this might be a hard sell and in unison we replied, "But Mommy, this is all really neat stuff!"

It took a while to convince her (four kids whining and nagging have a unique way of bending someone's will), but I think she finally realized the value of all that we had brought home. And it was free! ("Mom, you won't have to buy any school supplies for us until we get into high school.") We took all of the trash, I mean treasures, to our respective rooms and played with it (how you play with school supplies was something only we could conceptualize). It didn't take long for us to tire of the novelty (a trigonometry textbook didn't hold much interest for a grade-schooler), and most of it ended up back in the trash within a few days (the trash man probably had a hard time figuring out how our family always had so much to pick up each week). Up to this point in our lives, the heist at the high school was our biggest score by far.

I mentioned the construction site in another chapter, a place that held much interest and adventure. Some of the things we brought home came from the construction trailer and did not come from the trash. I guess we temporarily borrowed some of the foreman's tools, nothing expensive, just a few blueprints and pencils and books, but we took them all back (in the same way I took the stolen rubber knife back to the dime store).

There were, however, some things at the construction site that would be considered trash and that we considered should be ours.

One thing that you might notice at most construction sites is a large wooden spool (think wooden spool that thread comes on for sewing purposes, only 100× sized). These wooden spools are designed for storing electric cables used on construction projects, but I don't recall ever seeing one that had cable on it, only the empty ones. A large abandoned wooden spool at the construction site just had to come home with us. It may seem like getting this large object from the construction site to our home presented a difficult challenge. Au contraire! We just started rolling it across the street, around the corner, through neighbor's yards, and finally into our backyard.

What did we do with it, you may ask? The large wooden spool was a multipurpose apparatus. If it was laid on its side, it served as a nice table. We could eat our sandwiches on it during lunch. Or maybe put a tablecloth over it and serve tea. If a stray dog wandered into the backyard, it was a great place to climb out of harm's way and taunt the dog (once again, good judgment wasn't our strong suit and even though we didn't think far enough ahead, the dog knew that we eventually had to climb down, and he was patient). The best use of the giant spool, however, was when it was in the upright position and able to be rolled.

We were fans of the circus as kids (big Bozo the Clown enthusiasts), even attending a few, and some of the tricks done in the circus not only entertained us, but if the opportunity ever presented itself, we thought we could duplicate them ourselves. I believe that if we had gained access to a cannon, we would have been shooting each other all over the neighborhood (we settled for the act where one kid lays on the grass with feet in the air, the other kid sits on both feet, and the kid on the ground pushes his legs forward and shoots the other kid into the air. Not quite the cannon, but good enough). Climbing trees and the backyard wall was our way of replicating the high-wire act. Dad even built us a pair of stilts, which were really neat, for walking around the neighborhood (we didn't have the long baggy pants like the stilt walker in the circus, but that did not deter us).

Come to think of it, many of the things we did for entertainment had the ring of the circus in them. For the cannon, we jumped our bicycles off a makeshift ramp. For the trapeze, we would swing as high as we could on the swing set, hoping to go high enough to completely wrap around the top and then, at the highest apex, jump off. Two or three of us on a bicycle replicated the clowns (operative word) piling into a tiny car. The high dive act? Well, how about the local swimming pool high dive, at age seven no less. Tumbling? A daily activity. Yes, we did enjoy the circus.

One circus act had an acrobat walking around on a giant ball. The giant spool was our giant ball. It wasn't quite the same, but served its purpose. Unlike the giant ball, we could only go forward or backward on the spool. Falling off happened often, but did not prevent us from having a ball, or spool in this instance. We got pretty good walking this thing, and at times, the spool was moving at a pretty good clip. As with many of our toys, when Dad came home, he wasn't impressed. Wanting to impress Dad with our newfound treasure I excitedly said to him, "Dad, come out in the backyard and see what we brought home from the construction site!" Although normally fun loving, this time he never left the couch when he answered, "Take it back."

Some of our treasures were found, not around the neighborhood, but much closer to home. Dad was a great source for recycled toys namely beer cans. Lots of beer cans. Dad's beverage of choice was Schlitz. Prior to being canned in aluminum, beer was sold in tin or steel cans. They also didn't have pop tops and had to be opened with a church key which created triangular holes in the top of the can. Recycling wasn't in vogue back then, and all of Dad's beer cans ended up in the trash. We found out that by stepping on these cans, because they were made of steel or tin, the can would bend around the bottom of our shoe and make a new shoe (at one point, one of us must have accidentally stepped on a tin can and liked the effect). Once on our feet, they weren't likely to come off unless we intentionally pulled them off. When walking around with our new shoes, we created a neat, metal-on-cement, clacking sound (these "shoes" were not allowed in the house at all). If all four of us were wearing these shoes at the same time, the sound became irritating to anyone within earshot that wasn't a kid. The neighbors weren't impressed with four kids running around the driveway with metal shoes on. "Honey, what's that horrendous sound coming from the Bay house?" His wife, not knowing for sure, offered, "It sounds like a muffler dragging on the ground underneath a car."

Because Dad cared for us, we seemed to have an endless supply of beer cans, and thus, an endless supply of shoes. Eventually, beer cans would no longer be made from tin; aluminum would be the new material of choice (and pull tabs would replace the church key). Unfortunately for us, aluminum did not work as well as tin for our shoes. When you stepped on aluminum cans, the aluminum did not wrap around your foot, and when you walked, it would fall off. Oh, the good old days!

Dad wasn't the only parent supplying us with recycling opportunities. Sometimes, Mom got in on the act. One sunny day, when we were out looking for fun and adventure (or otherwise going to Mom and saying, "We're bored. There's nothing to do," with Mom replying, "You kids go outside and find something to do"), we decided to look around the garage and see if we could find something to do. In the garage, there was a large box of clothes, probably being saved for Goodwill or some other charitable organization. Digging through the box, we found various pieces of old, worn clothing, from jeans to shorts, cowboy boots, dresses, rubber gloves, long- and short-sleeved shirts, etc. It probably doesn't seem like these old articles of clothing would provide much fun or adventure, but for the Bay kids, it didn't take much to get the mind working on all kinds of possibilities. We decided to wear all of the clothes at the same time. Once again, layering before it became popular!

The picture on the front of the book says it all. I'm the one with the plaid long-sleeve shirt layered with the striped, short sleeved shirt. I'm wearing cowboy boots and jeans with a pair of checked underwear layered over the jeans. If you notice the knees of the jeans, you can see the outline of an extra layer of fabric underneath. On the inside of the jeans, Mom would iron on patches to prevent holes from forming in the knees of the jeans. We spent a lot of time on our knees back then, playing trucks and cars and army men, etc. I hated those iron on patches because they always irritated my skin with each step (today, the jeans wear out in the bottoms from all of the couch potatoing, and instead of iron-on patches, they have strategically placed holes that create a compelling fashion statement). I complained vociferously to Mom not to iron on those patches, but she wouldn't listen. (I suppose the patches were much less expensive than new jeans every few months.)

Kathy has on a long-sleeve, striped shirt with a dress layered on top and a pair of non-matching, white, athletic socks. Timmy has on a regular pair of jeans layered on top with an oversize pair of cutoff jeans, which he has to hold up with both hands due to the size and the fact that he doesn't have a belt. In addition, he is wearing a normal polo shirt. Vicki has on a short-sleeve, flower-decorated shirt layered over with a plaid, long-sleeve shirt. In addition, she is wearing an oversized pair of shorts, white athletic socks, and a pair of yellow rubber gloves, the kind you might wear doing the dishes. This was our fashion show. And we were giddy.

Our most memorable trash-digging adventure happened one Christmas season. As I chronicled in an earlier chapter, the decorating of the family Christmas tree was intricate, detailed, and orderly (globs of icicles thrown on the tree, willy-nilly not withstanding). When the tree was finished, it was a sight to behold. Of course, the presents under the tree held most of our attention and affection, but we loved the tree also. It came as no surprise, when one day, after the festivities had ended, it was time to take the tree to the street (one match would set the tree ablaze so it had to be removed from the house). As we were walking down the street, we noticed that a number of households had put their trees out on the street too. That's when Kathy said, "Those twees ah so pwetty."

Vicki, Timmy, and I agreed; those trees sure were pretty. What a waste to be picked up by the trash truck and taken to the dump. We came up with an outstanding idea: why not take the trees home before the trash truck picked them up? But we had to hurry; the trash truck was on the move. One at a time, trees were dragged down the street, icicles and ornament hangers trailing behind, then, up our driveway, through the gate, and into the backyard. Once in the backyard, they were staged, one by one, to look just like the parking lot of the local grocery store prior to Christmas. Tall trees, short trees, white ones, blue ones, and even green ones. We stood back and looked at our masterpiece, satisfaction written all over our faces. We priced them all and pretended to be tree shoppers. This lasted for a good part of the day until Mom finally glanced out the back window and was overwhelmed with the sheer magnificence of it all. "Aaaaahhhhh! What in the world have you kids done?" Timmy must not have understood her tone and answered, "Do you wike it, Mommy?" She was adamant when she instructed us, "I want all of those trees taken back where you found them. Now!"

Trying to remember which houses had which tree presented a bit of a problem. Our solution? We dragged all of the trees out to the street in front of our house. One neighbor observed, "Honey, look at the Bay place. There must be a dozen Christmas trees piled up in front of their house. I wonder what that's all about." His wife also wondered aloud, "Their house is pretty small. Where did they put all of those trees?"

Even today, occasionally, I will walk by a trash can and wonder what treasures are there, deep down in the recesses of that can? I'll bet that there's a baseball card collection to be found if only I had the time. Don't get me started!

THE GREAT ESCAPE

(HERE WE COME, READY OR NOT)

There was a wonderful movie that came out in 1963 titled *The Great Escape*. It starred Steve McQueen, among many, and was the true story of Allied POWs and their plans to, and eventual escape from, a German prison camp during World War II. Steve McQueen's character was Virgil Hilts, and he was an expert at escaping from the prison, getting caught, and then being brought back to the prison and thrown into solitary confinement (called the cooler). Like the POWs in the movie, we too were often imprisoned, either in our rooms or in the backyard (today it would be called "being grounded"). And like the POWs and Virgil, we too sometimes escaped, only to be brought back and thrown into the cooler. Occasionally we had mass escapes (the climax of the movie was a mass breakout), when the entire family, including Dad, would leave the house, neighborhood, and even our town, and head out on some great adventure or something a little less mundane, but we were together.

> Hilts "The Cooler King," played by Steve McQueen, was me; he was always trying to escape and spent an inordinate amount of time in solitary confinement (one other way I was like Virgil: while in the cooler, Virgil spent most of his time throwing a baseball against the wall and catching it with his ball glove).

Hendley "The Scrounger," played by James Garner, Timmy fits the bill here. He always had something of value that no one else did and used it to his advantage (in Monopoly when all seemed lost and he was down to his last dollar, Timmy would lift up the Monopoly board and voila, a crisp new $500 bill).

MacDonald "Intelligence," played by Gordon Jackson, was Vicki; she was the most intelligent and the brains in the organization.

Danny "Tunnel King," played by Charles Bronson, was Kathy; she was always placed in dangerous situations and in a place no one else wanted to go (sent over the wall to retrieve the ball with three dangerous Chihuahuas lurking somewhere out of sight, for example).

Blythe "The Forger," played by Donald Pleasence, was Mom; she was always a quiet presence in the midst of the turmoil. She loved to read and she loved her tea.

Bartlett "Big X," played by Richard Attenborough, was Dad; he was big and ultimately nothing happened without his permission or blessing.

California is the one state in the union that offers the widest variety of activities for anyone's taste: from the ocean, to the mountains, from Disneyland to Hollywood, the desert and the forests, anything and everything for a typical family to enjoy. At different times, we enjoyed them all.

Even though we weren't the largest family (after all, the eight kids lived right up the street), we made up for it in our energy level, and when going on a trip, logistics was important and needed to be thought through (Dad obviously didn't think it through in much depth, or he wouldn't have taken us anywhere). It would have been difficult to transport us in an average automobile, so Dad invested in a station wagon, a 1959 Chevrolet to be exact. Plenty of room for a family of six, or so it seemed.

We loved that car, not so much because of the ride, but because it had fins on the side, and we would take our Matchbox cars and drive up and down the sides of the station wagon, not in front of Dad of course. One day while washing his new station wagon, Dad muttered to himself, "I just bought this car and there are little scratches up and down the sides of the car. Now I wonder what could have made those scratches. Kids!"

Once we were piled into the car (Dad first had to corral us and that process was similar to herding cats), the arguments started. Vicki, being the oldest, had first dibs, "I get the window." With only one other option left, as far as windows go, I spoke up, "I get the other window."

What remained for the two little ones wasn't really worth fighting over (similar to the Falkland Islands): sit in the middle of the backseat or go to the back of the station wagon and roll around on the hard, plastic surface. Since Timmy didn't want to be anywhere near Dad's reach, he chose the back of the car (the back of the station wagon wasn't designed for people, only cargo, but we made it serve dual purposes). Dad would load whatever supplies were necessary into the back of the wagon, and Timmy would squeeze into whatever space was left. Once everyone was finally in position, the adventure would begin.

One Saturday morning, Dad rounded up the four of us and told us that we were going camping. "Kids, we're going camping this weekend." We were all pretty excited and Vicki said, "Yay! Where are we going?" "Up to Sequoia, up in the mountains," Dad explained. Kathy was excited but didn't understand when she said, "What ah mountains?"

This particular vacation was perfect for Mom, who loved the outdoors, and Dad, who loved driving and adventure, but most of all it was perfect for me because I loved all of it. If I had lived back in the pioneer days of this country, I'm sure I would have been a scout, in the mold of Jim Bridger, a well known mountain man, trapper, scout and guide, who explored the Western United

States in the middle 1800's. I loved seeing and experiencing things that were new to me. I loved to learn. I loved a challenge. This trip was going to be fun.

Dad backed the station wagon into the driveway, and we proceeded to load the supplies: cooler, canvas tent, food, beer (always a staple) as well as blankets, pillows, and other camping paraphernalia, including a Coleman stove. Once loaded up, we headed out onto the street and then Orr and Day Road, then Telegraph Road and onto the San Gabriel River Freeway, eventually reaching State Highway 5, headed north. Approximately 250 miles, the drive would take over five hours and then some, depending on who got sick and how many times we had to stop for throwing up and potty breaks. (Vicki and Timmy usually got sick, Kathy was the potty breaker, and me, well I was the nag: "Are we there yet?") Once on the open freeway, the inevitable squabbling began: Vicki was agitated immediately and whined, "Stop touching me. Get over on your side." I shot back, "You stop touching *me*. Move back over on your side. This line on the seat is my side." Poor Kathy, stuck between us and being shoved from both sides, couldn't win in this situation. "Mommy, Wonnie's touching me." How could I not touch her with Vicki shoving her over on my side? "Tell her to stay on her side," I said. "I don't have any room and I'm smashed up against the door."

It didn't take long for this interaction to begin. We had just left LA and still had a four-hour drive ahead of us. Dad would eventually lose his patience, and when his arm flew back over the seat, he wasn't too concerned which kid he smacked; in fact, I think he was trying to reach all of us at the same time. Sitting next to the window was very advantageous when Dad lost his patience. I usually sat directly behind him (this was a strategic move on my part), and from that position, I was pretty much out of reach. Vicki could scrunch up really tight against the door, leaving Kathy entirely in harm's way (like a cobra, Dad's reach was much farther than it initially appeared). The only thing going for Kathy was the fact that Mom always came to her defense, and when the tears flowed, she got away with almost anything. "Ronald, quit smacking the kids and pay attention to the road. Kathy is crying again." "You kids quit your crying, or I'm going to give you something to cry about," Dad offered back.

That little exchange was pretty common and settled things down for a while. We each withdrew into our own world and pouted, the excitement of the trip far from our minds.

On long trips like this one, we played some games, like Hangman, but once we got into the "every kid for him/herself" mentality, most of the games were in our minds. I played a game where I pretended that every car that came by in the opposite lane was to be eaten. I would open my mouth as the car approached and chomp down (Pacman anyone?), finally swallowing each vehicle. Swallowing a large semitruck was a bit challenging, but I could do it. The goal was to eat every vehicle that went by. It became fairly difficult when we were in heavy traffic, and I have to admit, with some shame, that I missed a few. It was a way to make the time go by a little quicker.

Meanwhile, on the other side of the vehicle, Vicki was playing her own game. In her game, the goal was to jump over all oncoming vehicles with your hand. I know that sounds odd, but it was really quite simple. With the window rolled down, you would hold your hand out the window, fingers together, hand perfectly straight (like a marine saluting an officer), and the force of the wind shear would move your hand up or down depending on the exact angle of your fingertips. As each oncoming vehicle approached, you would tip your fingers down, and then as your hand bottomed out, tip your fingers back up and the wind would quickly bring your hand and arm up and over the vehicle. We all played this game from time to time, and it was much fun.

As we travelled farther and farther from home, the cars, houses, retail establishments, and people began to dissipate, and the scenery slowly became much more interesting. At one point, we started the ascent up into the mountains. Trees, rocks, fields, streams, and animals all started to increase in sightings. My imagination began to be engaged, and as I stared into the woods on the side of the road, I imagined bears, antelope, mountain lions, and deep dark canyons to explore. My heart began to beat faster, and the adrenaline started to flow as this camping trip slowly took shape in my mind. There is something alluring, majestic about the mountains, and although these weren't the Rockies, the Sierra Nevada mountain range was absolutely stunning. Huge mountains, rugged foothills, deep canyons, vast caverns, and the world's largest trees! What more could I ask for?

All of a sudden, the car began to chug, chug, and lurch, lurch and finally gasp and wheeze to a stop. Almost there, the destination so close we could almost touch it, but Dad, in his logistical shortcomings, had also planned a little short on fuel. After a few unintelligible words muttered, off Dad went, walking up the mountain road on a hot summer day. Meanwhile, Mom and the four of us were temporarily stranded alongside the road. What to do? Impatient as usual, I asked Mom, "Are we there yet?" Mom was too tired for conversation and just said, "No." Kathy also wanted to know our position, "When ah we going to be theah?" More patient with Kathy, and understandably so, she answered, "Not yet. It shouldn't be long." Since Timmy was in his own world in the back seat he repeated my earlier question, "Ah we theah yet?" "You kids play a game, take a nap, stare out the window; but don't sing. Daddy will be back in a few minutes, at least I hope so, and we'll be there soon after." Mom had fended off all of our questions and diverted our attention, for the short term.

One hour later, here came Dad, one foot in front of the other, gas can in hand, slowly coming down the mountain road. Dad finally returned to the car and off we went. Looking at Dad, we knew better than to ask our oft repeated "are we there yet?"

We finally reached a place in the mountains near where we were to set up camp, and Dad stopped to ask for some final directions at a ranger station. I couldn't take my eyes off the scenery, my face plastered to the window. Bright sunshine, beautiful clear blue skies with majestic trees of green in the foreground. Wonderful! When Dad exited the car, all of us kids did too; some for a needed potty break and others just to stretch the legs after being in the car for a few hours. As Dad returned to the car with a map in hand, I excitedly approached him: I was so excited to get moving, to the point of hyperventilating. "Daddy, did you see all of the trees? There must be a million of them!" Dad, sarcastically replied, "Yes, son, I see all of the trees; we're in a forest." Breathlessly I asked, "Can we climb them?" Dad burst my bubble with his answer. "No son, the only creatures that climb these trees are squirrels, birds, and students from Stanford."

After driving a few more miles, we arrived at the campsite.

When strolling down Michigan Avenue in Chicago, it's not hard to spot the tourists. They're the ones walking around with their eyes staring up at the buildings, the perfect mark for a panhandler. In a similar way, when we arrived at the campsite, the four of us kids could not take our eyes off the trees. They were huge; nothing like what we'd ever seen. There are actually two different kinds of trees in Sequoia National Park, although most people wouldn't be able to tell the difference. There are redwoods and sequoias. Both types of trees are huge, reaching heights as high as a 31-story building and with bases as wide as 40 feet in diameter. The estimated weight of a mature tree is as much as 2.7 million pounds and they are known to live as long as 3,200 years. Did I tell you that these trees are the tallest in the world? Neat!

After bumping into a few bushes and tripping over some rocks, we finally settled in and began to help Dad set up the camp. It wasn't long before I began to bug, er, question Dad. "Daddy, can we go hiking yet?" Not allowing himself to become distracted he replied, "Not right now. We have to set up camp." I waited a total of five minutes and asked again, "Daddy, can we go hiking now?"

Patiently he answered, which was unusual, “Once we put up the tent, we can all go hiking.”

Unlike the tents of today (that are lightweight, waterproof, easy to put up, and comfortable to sleep in), the tent we were blessed with was canvas. It weighed a ton, leaked like a sieve, did not allow for airflow, making it hot and musty sleeping, and was barely large enough to squeeze in a family of six comfortably (comfortable like sardines in a can). It came with a heavy-duty pole that stood in the middle of the tent and held up the center. Additional poles were set up along the edges of the inside to give the tent some shape. From there, the corners and sides of the tent were stretched out with canvas loops arranged intermittently for the metal tent pegs to hold the tent in place (the pegs were pounded into the ground with a sledgehammer, and when the ground was rocky enough, the tent pegs would bend and not be much good for anything). Strings were tied to the upper edges of the outside, with the other end tied to a tree or other stationary object to keep the tent from collapsing on the occupants (even though all of these measures were put in place, the tent still collapsed on the occupants from time to time).

After the tent was finally secured and in place, the morning was pretty much shot. The hiking trip would have to wait until after lunch. Dad gathered us around and asked, “Are you kids excited about hiking this afternoon?” Vicki was interested in the prospects and answered, “It should be fun. We may see some wildlife.” I on the other hand was so excited, to the point of wetting my pants, that I blurted out, “Let’s hurry up and eat so we won’t miss anything.” Timmy was excited, but a little spooked and asked, “Ah theh beahs out heah?” “Beahs?” Kathy was nervous also. In an effort to calm any fears or concerns, Dad explained, “Don’t worry kids. Bears won’t come anywhere near us here. They like to stay out in the wilderness, away from humans.” Dad surely knew best. At least in our eyes he was an expert on the habits of California wildlife.

The hike was really fun. The mountains offer such a variety that there is never a shortage of visual stimulation and exploration. My favorite part of the adventure was when we traversed the semi-dry riverbed. Giant boulders, trickling waterfalls, silent clear pools of water, downed trees, moss and ferns, and the trees! In one of these silent pools of water, Dad taught us how to skip rocks (on that same pool were strange bugs that scooted across the top of the water, as if ice-skating). Searching for the perfect flat rock to skip across the top of the water took up quite a bit of time, what with so many rocks to choose from. We didn't see much wildlife other than a few chipmunks. Now, why would that be? I think the deer must have had a meeting when they heard we'd arrived in the park: Standing around in a clearing, the deer mob was gathered around the big buck who was addressing them in serious tones, "All of you need to keep your eyes and ears open. These people are dangerous. Stay out of sight at all times." One of the younger bucks scoffed, "But, there are only four little kids and a couple of inept adults. What's the worry?" "Don't underestimate those kids," he replied. "The two adults may look harmless, but the kids have been known to terrorize entire neighborhoods."

Well, the day had been really exciting, and for most families, it would be time to wind down around the campfire, sing a few songs ("Kumbaya," "Clementine," "Oh! Susanna," etc.) and wander off to a peaceful night of slumber. But not our family. The real excitement was about to begin.

Each of us crawled into our sleeping bags, and due to the energy emitted during the day, it didn't take much time for sleep to overtake us (Unfortunately, due to the exertion of the day, or the cool night air, my asthma hit me with a vengeance and I didn't sleep well the entire night). Dad began to saw logs, and other than the snoring, it was a pretty quiet night. Mom was awakened first by a noise outside the tent. It sounded like an animal of some kind milling around the camp. Being the outdoorsman that he wasn't, Dad didn't think to put away all of the food and supplies. Not long after dozing off for the night, Mom nudged Dad and whispered, "Ronald, wake up. I hear something outside." Dad was sawing logs at this point. "ZZZzzzzz….." Mom tried again, nudging him a little harder. "Ronald, get up. Something is outside the tent!" Finally awaking, but not very alert, "Huh?" was all he could muster.

Within a few short minutes, Mom had awakened all of us and directed us to the station wagon. It was pitch-dark outside, and we could barely see our hands in front of our faces. She urged the four of us, "Hurry up, kids. Get to the station wagon and lock all of the doors. We're going to spend the night in the car." "Why the car?" Vicki queried. "We heard something outside the tent. It sounded rather large." Vicki was too smart to be fooled by veiled references and said, "Well, the largest mammal out here in the forest would be the black bear. They can weigh as much as five hundred pounds, but I thought Daddy told us that bears didn't come anywhere near humans." "Vicki, be quiet! You're going to scare the little ones."

Too late, the rest of us had already figured it out (what with all of the whispering going on, the scared sound in Mom's voice, and the fact that we were heading to the station wagon and locking the doors). Dad quickly escorted us in the dark from the tent to the station wagon, and although it was only a few feet, it seemed like a long way. Timmy and Kathy were both scared and let it be known. "Daddy, ah the beahs going to eat us?" Timmy wanted to know. Kathy also shared her fears, "I'm scahed. I want to go home." Dad hustled us to the car rather than stop to answer questions.

Once inside the station wagon, it was hard to go to sleep (in addition to being scared, it was hot and stuffy; we didn't dare roll a window down). A closer look at the car would have revealed six sets of eyes plastered to the windows, straining to catch a glimpse of the bears. It was too dark to see anything, and with the windows rolled up, we couldn't hear anything either. It was a long night in the station wagon.

The next morning, as Dad surveyed the campsite, it became quite evident what the bear or bears had taken. The cooler was gone (in the *land of sky-blue waters*, bears like beer too) and everything in it. A hundred yards down the hill, we found the cooler, empty. The bacon, eggs, and all the rest of the food were gone. Even with this setback, the family was not deterred. We came to the mountains to have fun, and bears or no bears, we were determined to do so.

Dad decided to move camp to a location where more people were around. (This only seemed like a good idea. The problem was that the bears wanted to be where there were more people the same as we did, only for a different reason: more people, more food.) So we moved down the mountain, and this time, for security purposes, Dad parked the station wagon right next to the tent door. That way, if a bear decided to visit again, it was a short jump to the station wagon door.

That day, we did pretty much the same thing as the day before, but there was one special highlight to add. We had a family portrait taken inside the base of a giant sequoia tree! Like I said, those trees are huge. After a few hikes, lunch with whatever we could scrounge up, and some rock skipping, it was time to call it a day. This time we didn't bother with the tent, but started the evening in the car. Mom and Dad, brave souls that they were, had cots inside the tent (I say brave where others might say foolish, crazy, nut jobs, loony tunes, you get the picture). During the night, Mom, being the light sleeper, heard scratching noises on the outside of the tent (with only a thin layer of canvas between me and a bear, the last place I would be was inside that tent) and immediately began to rouse Dad. "Ronald, wake up. The bears are back," Mom whispered. This time, Dad was much more prepared, "Huh?" The four of us kids were sleeping pretty soundly until the car doors flew open and we heard this from Dad, "You kids scoot over. Your mother and I are moving in."

The next morning, Dad decided that we'd had enough fresh air and fun for one trip, and we packed up and headed to Carmel to visit family. We never went back to the Sequoia National Park to camp out. I wonder why?

A great place for a family adventure was the beach, specifically Huntington Beach in LA. The four of us loved the water, and the ocean was a perfect place for exploring and discovery. Dad had us help him load up the station wagon with the supplies: towels, beach toys, Coppertone, and a cooler with sandwiches and drinks (and the ever-present staple, beer). Once loaded up, we headed out of the neighborhood, jumped onto the San Gabriel River Freeway, and were on our way. The distance from our house to the beach was twenty-seven miles, which should have taken about thirty minutes to drive. Unfortunately, we were going on a gorgeous, warm, sunny, Southern California summer day; on a Saturday morning no less. As we sat in the parking lot called the freeway, I remember staring out the window and daydreaming. As I saw the five lanes of traffic at a complete stop, for as far as I could see, I began to imagine what would happen if I got out of the car and began to walk to the beach. I could walk across the top of all the cars in a single file line all the way there. I figured that I could walk faster than we were going in the car. As traffic began to move, I was rudely awakened from my daydream, and I began to think about the ocean and all of the excitement ahead of us. The thirty-minute trip turned into a nearly two-hour trek.

When we finally arrived at the beach, the four of us jumped out of the car and ran to the water so fast that we failed to hear the "Kids, help me unload the car" coming from Dad. We had no intention of hanging around the blanket with Mom and Dad or making a boring sand castle. (If we had created a sand castle, it would have only remained standing for a few minutes, and one or all of us would have been punished and a great time at the beach would have been ruined. No, the surf and sand were pretty much "Bay kid-proof," so that's where we spent most of the day.) We came to explore the ocean and the beach. As fast as we had jumped into the surf, we retreated much faster. The water was cold! Once we "warmed up" to the water temperature, we would go out into the ocean and let the waves crash over us. Occasionally, water would go down the wrong pipe, and we would have to take a small time-out from the ocean. A few warnings from Mom about jellyfish and how they would sting us if we touched them kept us a little wary, but even at a young age, we weren't awed by the vast ocean.

One fun thing to do at the beach was stand in the sand, where the tide comes in and out, and with our backs to the ocean, stare down at our feet. As the water retreated, we felt as if we were moving forward, gliding on top of the water. What a neat feeling! It was mesmerizing. As the water rushed back to the ocean, the sensation was that we were moving the opposite direction. While playing the "stand in the surf and splash around" game, we discovered something else that would occupy much of our remaining time on the beach. As the water rushed across our feet, in addition to shells and other small rocks and sea paraphernalia, we were startled to find a small animal; we soon found out that they were called sand crabs. I ran to Dad with prize in hand and excitedly said, "Daddy, look what we caught. It's a sand crab!" "That's nice" he replied. "Go put it back." Disbelieving what I'd just heard, I said, "But Daddy, can't we keep it?" "No." Wrong answer as far as I was concerned.

Even though Dad didn't see the value of the sand crab (they weren't good for much other than fish bait), we did.

We took the plastic buckets, the ones that were supposed to be used for the sand castle that never happened (these buckets looked an awful lot like the buckets we got at Easter, hmmm.), and decided to use them for collecting the crabs. We discovered a unique way of catching them. As we stood in the surf, we squatted down with the water about ankle deep. As the water retreated to the ocean, we would stick our hands down in the sand, palms facing up at an angle, and all of a sudden, we would feel a crab wash into our hands. We caught a million of them; well, not a million, but a bunch.

Even though the temperature wasn't particularly hot, the sun's rays were potent enough to burn the four of us blond-haired, blue-eyed, freckle-faced (a raccoon's face comes to mind) urchins. We would eventually brown (just like the girl on the Coppertone billboard that had the little black dog pulling down the bottoms of her swimming suit), but initially, we were a bright red color, like a lobster in a boiling pot of water. As the afternoon slowly eased into evening, the once bright white sun turned a glowing orange and methodically descended over the Pacific Ocean. The hour and the fact that four extremely tired and hungry kids can become a bit cranky led Dad to call it a day. "Kids, let's go. Pick up your stuff and get into the car." We all replied in unison… Come to think of it, this time we were all so tired we just obeyed for a change, without a word. As we loaded all the supplies into the car, Dad noticed that all of the buckets were full of sand and directed us, "Kids, dump out all of that sand and shake off your towels and shoes before you get in the car." Vicki, intelligently and slyly said, "But Daddy, we can dump all of the sand into the sand box next to the house. That way you won't have to buy anymore sand." Like I said, Vicki was the smart one.

Vicki had convinced Dad, and into the back of the car the buckets of sand went (unbeknownst to Dad, deep down in the wet sand were a bevy of creepy, crawly, stinky little sand crabs, soon to make residence alongside our house in the sandbox (mostly dirt with a little sand thrown in for effect). As we finished loading (not doing a very good job of removing the sand from our towels, shoes, hair, backs, legs, or anywhere else), we finally piled into the station wagon for the thirty-minute/two-hour drive back home. Once we got a little way down the road, we began shivering (our skin was extremely hot due to the sunburns), and the wet swimming clothes added to the cold. The wind through the window hitting our skin was painful, but if we rolled up the window, the car became stuffy, the air stifling. The salt from the ocean on our skin caused our sunburns to scream out in pain. Our normal shoving and hitting only brought tears, and Dad would have none of it. Much like the four of us, Dad too was hungry, cranky, and tired and it came out in his impatience. "You kids want me to stop this car and spank all of you?"

The threat shut us up rather quickly. It was enough of a threat in normal circumstances, but with the sunburns, we just weren't willing to push the issue.

As we arrived home, there was a smell beginning to emanate from the back of the car. We quickly grabbed the buckets of sand and ran to the backyard and dumped them in the sandbox. The next day, we began to dig through the sand, trying to find our new pets. As Dad shoveled sand out of the back floorboard of the car, we brought the dead sand crabs to him. Timmy, in tears, cried, "Daddy, ow sand cwabs ah dead." Kathy, as only she could, added, "Theah dead alwight." Dad found humor in the situation and said, "I thought I smelled something rank. I assumed it was you four kids."

For three of us, the sunburns were a minor agitation, but for Timmy, the burn turned into something much worse. On his shoulders, large water blisters formed, and the pain was excruciating. In order to protect us from further damage, Mom put white T-shirts on us so we could go out and play. Underneath Timmy's T-shirt were bumps, water blisters, which protruded two to three inches, obvious underneath his shirt. I, being the kind brother that I was, decided to terrorize Timmy. Chasing Timmy around the yard, I taunted him, "Timmy, I'm going to pop your blisters if you don't leave me alone." Running away from me, he replied, "I'uh tewh on you if you do."

The fear of a whipping almost, but not quite, prevented me from doing what I immediately regretted doing. I ran up behind

Timmy and smacked his shoulders, popping the water blisters. Timmy ran into the house bawling, his shirt now soaked from the popped blisters. As I was receiving my punishment from Dad's thick leather belt, it occurred to me that I was going to have a few blisters of my own.

One Easter, Dad decided that we would spend the holiday with his cousin Gene and Gene's wife Sue. In addition to being cousins, Dad and Gene were good friends from their youth. Gene and Sue lived in Indio, California, which was 120 miles straight east of our home. Straight east of Los Angeles leads directly into the desert. I loved the desert, never mind the heat. There were rattlesnakes, scorpions, lizards, horny toads, tarantulas, rocks, cactus, a plethora of things to fascinate and all potentially full of danger. We would have much fun.

The weather in the desert could vary as much as forty to fifty degrees in the March/April period, with highs ranging from the upper fifties to as high as the upper nineties. This was one of the hotter years. Dad and Gene had an idea that would cool things off a bit. "Kids, how would you all like to go on a trip to Salton Sea?" Dad asked. We had never heard of the place and Kathy asked, "Wheh is Salton Sea?" As if this explanation would suffice, Dad was precise, "It's about a thirty to forty-five minute drive southeast of here." "What is Sawhton Sea?" Timmy wanted to know. "It's sort of like a big lake…" But Vicki interrupted Dad with some knowledge she had just learned in school. "Teacher said that Salton Sea is one of the world's largest inland seas and lowest spot on earth at -227 feet below sea level. The saline level is not as dense as in the great Salt Lake in Utah, but much more than the Pacific Ocean." Dad cut Vicki off at this point and interjected, "Yes, thank you Vicki. You obviously know your geography, but we should have some fun here; playing in the sand and surf like we did at Huntington Beach." After hearing this, the four of us began jumping up and down with excitement,

"Yaaayyyy!" We had visions of lying at the beach, catching sand crabs, and diving into the cascading surf. Because of this new excitement, I grew impatient and asked Dad, "Are we there yet?" to which Dad responded, "We haven't even left the driveway."

It was decided to take Gene's car, an El Camino, on the trip. The El Camino was similar to a pickup truck in that it had a bench seat and what resembled a pickup bed behind the front cab. Along with the four of us, a cooler was loaded into the back of the vehicle filled with food and plenty of cold Schlitz. (In these simpler times, an entire family could be loaded into the back of a pickup truck, or in this case, El Camino, without fear of breaking any laws. No one ever fell out that I'm aware of.) Gene and Mom loaded up in the front seat, and off we went (Dad mysteriously decided to stay behind; he must have been tired from the previous night's activities).

As we headed down the road, the four of us were in pretty high spirits; visions of Huntington Beach in our minds' eye. Even though the air was extremely hot, the open air arrangements in the back of the car kept us relatively cool until we got there. Occasionally, one of the adults would turn around and yell at us to sit down (standing was much more fun than sitting, but in reality, it probably wasn't safe).

As we arrived at the beach and the car came to a stop, Gene began to unload the supplies and as he started to utter the words, "Kids, help me unload," we were already gone. We were soon to find out however that the beach at Salton Sea was not at all like the beach at Huntington Beach. Yes, there was sand and water, but the similarities ended there. As we ran to the water's edge, we noticed that there weren't any waves. "Where are the waves?" I wanted to know. The smart one replied, "This isn't the ocean. The waves are really tiny." "But, we can't dive into these waves," I said with much disappointment. Timmy too had some concerns. "Wheh's the suhf and how ah we going to catch sand cwabs?" Again, Kathy was in agreement, "Yeah."

As we ventured out into the water, we noticed that below the surface of the water, underneath our feet, was not the same as in the Pacific Ocean. Instead of soft sand beneath our bare feet, there were sharp rocks that hurt every time we stepped forward. It seems that the lake was full of volcanic residue including rocks of pumice and obsidian. There was a lot of tripping and falling as we tried to wade in the water, resulting in cuts and scrapes on our feet, legs, hands, and arms. It was not conducive for frolicking around in the surf. So in summary: no surf, no waves, no sand crabs, no wading without pain, lots of extremely hot sun. What in the world were Dad and Gene thinking? Dad stayed behind while Gene had the Schlitz and Mom to keep him company, and I doubt the four of us were paid much mind until the trip home.

It wasn't long before we were whining to go home. The thrill of going to the beach was gone, and now we were only thinking about what the Easter bunny would be bringing us the next morning. The adults relented, and we loaded up the car to head back to Gene and Sue's place. Unlike the gay ride to the beach, the ride back home was anything but. Whereas the wind was a soothing balm on the way out, it became an extreme irritant heading home. Not only did we have cuts and scrapes all over our legs and arms, but we also had really bad sunburns from the severe desert sun. As Mom glanced over her shoulder out the back window of the car, she saw four little urchins, shivering, crying, with tears (mixed with a little dirt) running down their cheeks: beach towels trying to serve as blankets. The cries were ubiquitous. "Waaahhh! It huhts! Pwease stop the cah." "Waaahhh! My sunbuhn huhts. Can I wide with you in the fwont?" "Waaaahhhh! The effect of the wind on these cuts, abrasions, and sunburns was brutal. Can we ride up front with you?" "Waaahhh! Are we there yet?"

Mom was truly concerned, and the look on her face was one of helplessness (there was room for one of us on the bench seat, but in order to remain fair, she decided that we would all suffer equally, sort of like the liberal mentality of taxing the rich to level the playing field). Unfortunately, there really wasn't a remedy to this situation. The thirty- to forty-five–minute ride home seemed like an eternity, and we cried and shivered all the way there. When we finally arrived at Gene's, I made a mental note to never visit the Salton Sea again.

Another family outing that is etched in my mind was our trip to Disneyland (this wasn't the trip where I got lost at age two). There were other neat parks around LA (Pacific Ocean Park and Knott's Berry Farm are two that we visited), but none compared to Disneyland. Located in Anaheim, Disneyland was about a thirty-minute drive from home, and it was such a quick drive that the normal buildup of adrenaline didn't have time to reach its peak before we were there. As we arrived at the park, in addition to the massive parking lot, we were in awe of the size and scope of what we were seeing. It was easy to spot the Sleeping Beauty Castle (the same castle that appeared on the Wonderful World of Disney at 6:00 every Sunday night).

In order to enter the park, you first had to stop at the ticket booth and buy your tickets. Dad dug into his wallet, surveyed the four of us, and determined that $30 worth of tickets was enough to entertain us for a while. Once the roll of tickets was purchased, we then went through the turnstiles and into the park. Our initial inclination was to immediately scatter and run to all points of the park, but two things held us back: Dad was with us and he had the tickets for the rides.

Disney was a genius when it came to entertaining people. The sights and sounds all seemed to have a ring of familiarity: from Mickey and Minnie to themed rides like the Teacups (from *Alice in Wonderland* and reminiscent of the Scrambler at the local fair) and the Dumbo ride (this was similar to the Octopus at the local fair, and in fact, Dumbo did fly in the movie). The great thing about the park was that it appealed to all ages. Walt Disney's movies were very popular at the time, and the characters and themes were evident throughout the park.

There was one ride in particular that we had heard about and just had to ride: The Matterhorn. While walking throughout the park, from almost any angle, you could see the snowcapped top of a mountain, jutting up above the parks other attractions. Each time any of us spotted it, we turned to Dad: "Daddy, theh's the Mattehhohn! Can we wide it now?" was Kathy's suggestion. Timmy caught on to the excitement and blurted out, "Yeah, theh it is! Can we wide it? Pwease?" Dad seemed to come up with any and all excuses and responded, "That's clear on the other side of the park. Wait until we get over there and we'll see." ("We'll see" was a phrase that all kids hated to hear. It was ambiguous and always left open the possibility of "no").

My favorite ride and one that I'll always remember was the Jungle Cruise. On this ride, a number of people load into a boat and begin a trip into the wilds of the jungle. The boat captain also serves as the tour guide, and along the way, he points out the many interesting things to see in the jungle. "Over on the left we see some beautiful butterflies. Did you know that these butterflies can have a wingspan anywhere from twelve inches all the way up to one foot?" Funny man.

In addition to the educational material, which I found fascinating, there was also room for jokes and humor, with a little drama thrown in. At one point on the trip down the river, a huge hippopotamus surfaced for air right next to the boat. The boat captain elevated the excitement level by pointing out how dangerous the hippo could be, and that if it were angry, it might charge the boat and we would all be in grave danger. The captain then pulled a pistol from a holster on his hip, pointed at the hippo, and fired a couple of rounds in its direction; the hippo then disappeared underneath the surface of the water. I wasn't sure if the hippo was dead or not, and for the remainder of the ride, I kept a wary eye on the water, just in case.

Along the bank, we saw snakes in trees, tigers, elephants, giraffes (none of these animals were real, but the simulation was pretty good, so it seemed real to me), and various other flora and fauna. At one point, as we rounded a bend in the river, the captain pointed out a palm tree on the bank that a couple of explorers were using as refuge. At the bottom of the tree, its horn almost reaching the trousers of the explorer nearest the ground, was a huge rhinoceros. As the rhino raised its snout in order to inflict damage on the helpless man, the man would shinny up the tree just out of reach. The folks in the boat exploded in laughter at the sight. It all seemed so real, but as we left the scene and moved down the river, I looked back and noticed that the rhino and man were continually repeating the same maneuvers, and I then realized that it was all a charade. Even so, I was having too much fun to worry about its authenticity.

After the Jungle Cruise, we continued to move around the park. There was one Disney character that I was interested in seeing, but to no avail. It was fine to see Donald Duck and Mickey, but I wanted to see Annette, one of the Mouseketeers (she had a nice sweater). We finally arrived at the Matterhorn, and the four of us became extremely agitated, almost to the point of wetting our pants with excitement. Our hopes were soon dashed as Dad surveyed the line that stretched halfway around the park and exclaimed, "The line's too long. I'm not waiting forty-five minutes to ride a five-minute ride." (We weren't asking him to wait, we would wait! He could go sit down in the shade somewhere. Get a cold drink. Talk with Mickey. We would wait!)

Patience was not one of Dad's strong suits, and this time was no exception. The one ride that we couldn't ride was the one ride that we had hoped for the most. I never experienced the Matterhorn, yet I was only a few feet away. What a tease. Maybe someday, I'll make it out to Disneyland again, and the line will be shorter. If I wish upon a star…

Another exciting place our family visited was the zoo, and we had two to choose from: the world famous San Diego Zoo and the Los Angeles Zoo. I only remember Dad going to the zoo with us once, and he slept on the park bench the whole time. (I think he must have "entertained" the night before and needed to catch up on some lost sleep.) With "Big X" indisposed and out of the picture, Blythe the Forger was left in charge. As I mentioned earlier, Blythe (Mom) was a quiet presence in the midst of the turmoil and liked to read and drink her tea, but herding us kids was not something at which she excelled. As much as she tried to keep us close, we would bolt ahead to the next exhibit, with her to catch up with us later.

From time to time, when a group of people are sitting around conversing, the following question is sometimes asked, "If you were an animal, which one would you want to be?" I always choose the rhinoceros. I had a picture book at home with all of the exotic animals from around the world, and I would open it to the rhinoceros page and read about the animal, all the while imagining what it would be like to be one.

What an awesome brute of an animal! One ton in weight! That's the size of an automobile. The rhino looks like a throwback to the prehistoric age with its armor-like skin, tree-trunk legs, and huge horn growing out of the top of its head. It is massive in size, extremely tough and strong, and doesn't take any flak from anyone or anything, exactly what I imagined for myself. It was the John Wayne of the animal kingdom. It was also as blind as a bat, just like me. The odd thing about my ferocious beast: it is a herbivore. That fact alone didn't deter me. It was still my favorite. When I finally saw one for the first time in the zoo, it was tough to drag me away. Staring into the rhino's cage I barely heard Mom's gentle nudging, "Ronnie, it's time to go. There are other exhibits to see." "But, Mommy, this is the rhino cage. That's a real rhino in there!" She tried again, "Son, you've been here for over an hour. What else is there to see? It's just standing there in the shade, occasionally pawing at the dirt and snorting." I answered with this odd fantasy, "I'm waiting for a zoo person to enter the cage so I can watch the rhino chase them down and gore them with the huge horn sticking out of the top of its forehead." I did have quite an imagination.

We saw elephants, and it was fun feeding them peanuts (it felt really weird when they sucked the peanut out of my hand and up into their trunk to later place in their mouth), and touching their skin was a unique experience (it was like touching rough leather with coarse hair growing out of it). I especially liked it when they sucked up the dirt around their feet and then blew it into the air, the whooshing sound emanating around the zoo.

The giraffe was beautiful as it gracefully moved from one end of the enclosure to the other (Fred Astaire was never this light on his feet), and as it got close to the edge of the cage, I realized how tall this creature was. No matter how many times I had seen it on TV or in books, the colors in real life were much more vivid. I wanted to reach out and touch it, but it never came close enough.

A couple of other favorites at the zoo were the monkey house and reptile house. The monkeys always gave us something interesting to see, and unlike most of the other animals, they were seldom idle, constantly moving to and fro (it's easy to see why rowdy children are often referred to as "little monkeys"). The baboons, with their red bottoms and canine-like teeth, were a little bit bizarre, whereas the gorillas, especially the huge silverback males, were fascinating. Although the gorilla often seemed docile, when something set them off, they could exhibit a sudden burst of power and strength, enough to make you thankful there were two panes of thick glass between you and them.

Once inside the reptile house, my inclination was to search out the large snakes: boa constrictors and pythons specifically. I liked the iguanas and other lizards, but the snakes held the most interest. There were copperheads, rattlesnakes, rare and exotic green snakes from Africa, most of them holding the potential of a poisonous bite. After a few minutes in front of any one snake, I got bored and moved on. The problem with snakes and other reptiles in cages is that they don't do anything. They just lie there, me staring at them and them staring back at me (with those weird elliptical eyes). No sudden strikes, no swallowing of rodents or even a pig (I saw a python swallow a baby pig on *Mutual of Omaha's Wild Kingdom*), no drama.

The zoo was a really fun place to go. I have to say though, that it was a bit muted, sort of buttoned down. I was hoping for a little more excitement. All of the animals, except maybe the monkeys, seemed a little tired. It was almost as if the zookeeper had slipped a little Ritalin in all of the animal's food (come to think of it, the zookeeper must have run out of Ritalin when he got to the monkey cage and instead spiked their meals with a few ounces of Red Bull). I daydreamed that it would be neat to have a button at each cage, that when pushed would energize the animals, and all of a sudden, they would run around attacking and eating their prey and an occasional human or two; wait a minute, that's already been done: *Jurassic Park*! Anyway, in addition to the above animals, I really enjoyed the hippos, zebras, camels, wildebeest, ostrich, alligators, crocodiles, lions, and tigers and bears, oh my! I'll go back again, if they'll have me.

A frequent and favorite outing for the four of us was a trip to the drive-in movie. Dad, as I mentioned before, was a kid at heart and enjoyed these outings as much as we did, and when it came time for the drive-in, he couldn't help doing something to tip us off and create a little excitement. After a great day of working around the house on Saturday, all of us playing our hearts out, Dad would sometimes take the garden hose and wash off the driveway. Then, about an hour from sundown, and this was the signal, Dad would back the station wagon into the driveway. Timmy began jumping up and down and shouted with glee, "Weah going to the dwive-in!" Kathy caught on to what was happening and excitedly asked, "Ah we going to the movies?" Dad directed us all, "You kids go get your pajamas on and grab your pillows."

While we excitedly put on our pj's, Dad would head to the kitchen to pop a batch of homemade popcorn. After burning a couple of batches and clearing the smoke out of the house, a good batch finally made it into the brown grocery bag. We then loaded up into the car, all four of us in the back (the backseat was folded down so that we could all lay out in the back of the car). Which movie we were going to see didn't matter, it was the entire experience that we enjoyed. In fact, I doubt that Mom and Dad really wanted us along most of the time: Dad asked Mom midweek, "Honey, did you call and get us a babysitter for Saturday night?" Mom seemed confused in her answer, "It was strange; I called seven different babysitters and they were all busy. Some of the excuses seemed a little weak to me, and one actually hung up on me. I can't figure it out."

As we approached the drive-in theater, the giant screen was visible from a mile away. The back of the screen faced the road with the name of the drive-in identified in large, bold letters. There was a marquee out front with the featured movies listed. The driveway circled around to the back of the theater, and at the back was a white building: the concession stand and restrooms. At the very front was the giant screen. Below the screen, there was a play area for kids: a swing set, merry-go-round, and slide. (While the theater was not in use during the day, on Saturdays, it was opened up for a swap meet. A person could find many bargains at a swap meet (think gigantic garage sale); that is where my first baseball glove was purchased for all of twenty-five cents.)

Once inside, the inevitable ritual of finding the right spot would then take place. The actual spaces set aside for each individual car were on mounds of asphalt that resembled giant speed bumps (in order to look up at the screen the front of the car had to be elevated). These bumps were in rows and ran from one side of the theater to the other. In between the bumps were aisles for driving. Between every set of two cars was a metal post that had two speakers, one for each car, hanging from it. The speakers were removable and were made of a heavy pot metal with a hook attached, designed to hang over the car window. On the front of the speaker was a volume dial. Where you parked, and ultimately how you parked, could greatly affect your movie viewing experience. It may appear that parking near the snack bar would be a good idea, but the traffic to the restrooms and refreshments was definitely a distraction when trying to concentrate on the movie. If you parked too far to the left or right of the screen, the movie was barely visible. The same for parking on the back rows with the added distraction of the teenagers making out in the cars surrounding you. No, Dad took this part of the adventure very seriously, and picking his spot was deliberate and intentional. He made sure that we showed up while the sun was still in the sky, much ahead of the late arriving moviegoers and while the parking choices were numerous.

There were a couple of incidents that happened during the drive-in experience that created a backlash from the patrons: a late arriver and a malfunctioning movie projector. The late arriver would drive around the theater with his lights on, looking for a place to park, and as he went through the ritual of parking his car, the people in his immediate area would get a little impatient and begin honking their horns. "Hey, buddy, turn your lights off!" was often heard in addition to the honking horns. Another incident occurred when the projector inside the concession stand malfunctioned and the movie was no longer up on the screen. The entire mass of people would lie on their car horns until the error was rectified. Much fun!

After Dad had decided on his spot, it then became a challenge of parking the car at just the correct angle and position. If he parked too far away from the post, the speaker wouldn't reach the car window. If he parked too far on one side of the bump, the kids in the back couldn't see the screen. He always had help.

I, being directly behind Dad said, “Daddy, I can’t see anything but the top of the people’s heads.” Kathy, in her normal spot in the center of the backseat whined, “The weawview miwew is in the way, I can’t see the movie.” “Mommy, can you move oveh so I can see,” Timmy chimed in. Vicki was more specific with her instructions, “Daddy, if you move the car five feet forward, we can all see better.”

Needless to say, Dad got a little frustrated, moving the car backward and forward until everyone was satisfied. Finally everyone was settled, popcorn and drinks, pillows and pj’s, the sun was down and the movie had begun.

Most of the movies that we saw weren’t for kids, and whenever there was a part in the movie that was a little risqué, Mom and Dad had a code word that signaled the four of us to scrunch down behind the seat and hide our eyes. The word was *Bluebird.* Why that particular word is a mystery, but whenever we heard it, we reacted accordingly.

Whenever we heard “bluebird,” down we went, but knowing that something was happening on the screen that I wasn’t supposed to see was unbearable, my curiosity eventually giving in to temptation. While “not looking,” I was finding every way possible to do just that: at the same time covering my eyes, opening my fingers just enough to get a good look, or peeking my head above the back of the seat, just out of Dad’s vision. There were ways. As the adult stuff wore on, we became bored, and the swing sets at the front of the theater became more and more interesting. After nagging Mom and Dad enough, they let us leave the car and run down to the playground (peering into all the cars as we went).

There were usually two movies playing on any given night, and due to the late start, we seldom stayed through the second one. In between the two movies was a cartoon followed by the intermission. The intermission was a great time for the advertisers to go to work luring everyone to the concession stand.

> Announcer (in a grand radio voice): "It's time for a tasty refreshing snack. Come visit the concession stand for some hot, buttered popcorn. We have cool refreshing Coca Cola. Come try our delicious candy and ice cream. How about a slice of some hot, delicious pizza pie?"

While the announcer was doing his utmost to sell some product, the product was on the screen selling itself. There were dancing hot dogs, boxes of popcorn, and cups of Coca Cola: each treat exhibiting legs and arms. There were people with huge smiles on their faces taking a bite of pizza or swigging down a soda. It was all a bit overdone, but effective, as the line coming out of the concession stand was long and winding. There was even an advertisement for attending church on Sunday! While all of this was going on, we were standing in line with Dad, going to the restroom, or playing at the playground. On the screen, in between the sales pitch, cartoon characters would appear, warning the patrons of the upcoming start of the next show. "Show starts in nine minutes" came the announcer's warning. And then a minute later, "Show starts in eight minutes." And so on.

Whenever the second show finally started, we would run back from the playground and see what the new movie was all about. Not too far into this movie, we usually fell asleep.

The theater must have had a problem with runaway speakers because this announcement usually came on during the show:

"Replace the speaker on the post when you leave the theater."

I suppose some people failed to remember to remove the speaker from their window and as they drove off, the speaker wire would snap and the cord would drag on the ground as they drove away. Thus this additional public service announcement:

"If torn from stand, please leave speaker in the box located at the exit."

Our camping trip in the Sequoia Mountains had ended abruptly, and I believe that Mom and Dad wanted to lay low for a while before attempting another campout. The time for a second adventure had arrived, and we went through the same ritual as the first trip:

> Extremely heavy and bulky canvas tent with holes in it: check
> Miscellaneous camping equipment: check
> Cooler full of Schlitz: check
> Applicable foodstuff: check
> Four kids: "Kids, get in the car!"

So off we went toward who knew exactly where. Dad didn't have a specific place in mind, only that it wouldn't be the Sequoia Mountains and the curious black bears. Once Dad came across the perfect spot for us to camp, he would know it.

In the movie *True Grit*, John Wayne's character, Rooster Cogburn, after a long day's ride and plenty of whiskey, falls off his horse. As he makes several attempts to regain his feet and mount his horse, he finally gives up and says, "We'll camp here for the night."

After driving through Ventura, California, we crossed a creek and after surveying the possibilities, Dad (our John Wayne) said, "We'll camp here for the night."

Dad had found a really nice spot for our camping trip (There was one concern though: being next to a creek with the threat of a flash flood if it happened to storm. But what were the odds of that happening?). Next to the creek was a small, mostly dirt-covered bluff that we immediately began to climb once we departed from the car. As Dad began to set up the tent and the campsite, we too were doing our part. Vicki fell into the creek (how do you fall into a creek?), which delayed the tent building.

Once the excitement of a wet sister had been calmed, we next saw Dad running around, swatting the air and shouting, "Ah, ah, ow, oh, ouch!" (We initially thought it was quite funny and entertaining to see Dad behaving in such a way until he gave us a look that caused us to immediately rethink our initial thoughts). Dad had apparently disturbed a yellow jacket's nest while trying to drive a tent stake into the ground, and the yellow jackets reacted in a way that most of us would if our homes were being invaded. (Thankfully, they weren't hornets; as yellow jackets are to hornets as my boxing abilities are to Muhammad Ali's of "float like a butterfly and sting like a bee" fame). Finally, the tent was up and the exploring, rock-throwing, bug-watching, animal-terrorizing, and other mischievous antics went on for the next few hours.

We finally tired of all the day's activities, and Mom called us to the campsite for supper. After supper, we all sat around the camp, soaking in the experience, listening to Dad tell one of his ghost stories. A family on an outing together, enjoying one another's company, well-behaved children (we were so tired by then that we couldn't raise a finger), a picture of bliss. Suddenly, out of the corner of his eye, Dad noticed a little commotion up the river about a hundred yards. There were two men, a little rough and scruffy looking, unloading what looked like camping supplies. (At that moment, I heard the faint sounds of what appeared to be music. As I listened more intently, I distinguished the sound of a strumming guitar. The sound of the guitar faded and was replaced by the sound of a banjo. First a guitar, then a banjo, back and forth, the sounds went. It was almost as if the two instruments were dueling.)

As we sat together, enjoying our experience, Dad was studying the men upstream. He was also studying the sky to the west, which was beginning to darken. Here we were, enjoying the beautiful stream, clear water, rugged terrain, campfire songs, and each other's company, and the fates were seemingly going to do to us what they did on our first camping trip; *campingtrippus interruptus* (sounds like a disease). As the sky darkened and night was coming upon us, it began to rain. The tent, as described previously, had issues, and once the rain began falling, the tent immediately began to leak. Dad decided that the leaking tent, impending flash flood, and the two hillbillies upstream were too much of a risk for us to stay the night. We packed up and drove home, banjo music ringing in our ears.

ABBY NORMAL

(STRANGE DAYS INDEED)

It may be a little strange, pardon the pun, for me to devote a separate chapter to strange behavior when the entire book is full of the same. However, when talking about me, the strange behaviors associated with other members of the family pale in comparison. I fully admit that my behavior was odd, and I do not shy away from talking about it. I suspect that all kids think their behavior somewhat abnormal, with this feeling culminating about the time of junior high school. Some of the behaviors I will tell about may seem bizarre to some, but after reading my explanations, the reader will come to the conclusion that, yes, this kid was crazier than a loon, nuttier than a fruitcake, one brick short of a load, well, you get the idea.

I don't quite know how the idea came about, but one day Mark P. and I got together and came up with an idea: Mark approached me first, so I have to assume what followed was his idea. Mark said, "Hey, the 'Z' family's not home. They left town this morning. Why don't we sneak over to their house and explore their backyard?" I was intrigued and agreeable when I answered, "Yeah! I've never seen their backyard. I wonder what's back there." Timmy, always the tag along, asked, "Can I come too? I'ah tewh Daddy if you don't wet me." "If you tell Daddy, I'll beat you up. Come on." He had convinced me to let him come after all.

Once past the gate and into their backyard, we noticed a swing set in the far left corner of the yard. We didn't have a swing set in our yard, so this was a good development. The remainder of the yard was nondescript, not much different than any other yard in the neighborhood. We wandered into the garage and surveyed the landscape there: tools, paint, and other materials lying around. Inside the garage was a window looking out into the front yard and out onto the street. We could see out, but passersby couldn't see inside. Then, out of the blue, one of us (to this day, no one knows or will say who it was) said, "Hey, let's take our clothes off and run around the yard!"

So we did. How exhilarating it was to be free of our clothes (I can understand why nudist colonies came into existence), totally nude, without a care in the world. The cool breeze gently caressing areas of the body that weren't normally exposed was a wonderful feeling. We hopped on the swing set and swung to and fro, hanging upside down on the pull-up bar. We chased each other around the yard, laughing and giggling all the way. Inside the garage, we stood in front of the window, daring the world to see us. The thrill of being caught added to the fun.

At one point, the excitement caused something else to happen. Something none of us had experienced before. A certain part of our anatomy became excited, just like the rest of us, and acted in a way that startled us, but intrigued us all the same. Oh, the joy of discovery. Somehow, we knew that if we were caught running around naked, terrible punishment would ensue, but if we were caught running around naked with a certain part of our anatomies at attention, we would be dead! We became paranoid and ran to the wall (man, was that murder, scaling a cinder block wall without any clothes), all three sides, climbing up to see if the neighbors had heard or seen us. We checked the gate, opened it a crack, and didn't see a soul. We ran back into the garage, staying away from the window, and slowly, we looked out into the front yard: nobody there either. By that time, the excitement had gone from a certain part of our anatomies, almost as quickly as it had arrived (funny how that works). After running around for a while longer, we decided that we had pushed our luck to the limit and put our clothes back on and went to our separate homes, no one the wiser. This tale remained a secret for years, you can understand why, and the looks I received when finally telling it were priceless. The urge to run around naked did not return for years until I learned of the joys of skinny-dipping, but those stories will remain untold for now.

My siblings and I often shared our ailments at the same time: chicken pox, measles, mumps, pink eye, etc., but whereas these were medical issues, we also had ailments of another kind, more of the psychological kind. To be specific: bed-wetting and thumb-sucking. Interestingly, these maladies affected us in pairs: Kathy and I were bed wetters (the scientific term for bed-wetting is enuresis), and Vicki and Timmy were thumb-suckers. Kathy was relatively young when she stopped wetting the bed. However, while she partook in bed-wetting, she was an absolute terror for her sleeping partner: Vicki (Kathy and Vicki slept in the same bed for many years, finally getting their own beds as teenagers). During the night, Kathy would wet the bed, somehow maneuver Vicki into that spot, and slide over into the dry spot: Kathy waking up dry, Vicki waking up cold and wet. For a little one, Kathy was extremely devious.

In my case, the bed-wetting lasted until I was eight years old (I had a tendency to excel at whatever I did, bed-wetting included). You may think this sounds funny, but for Mom and me, it was not a laughing matter. I would wake her up in the night crying because I was all wet. She had to change the sheets every time it happened, wash my pajamas (I hated that cold, wet feeling associated with urine soaked pj's), and she even came up with a plastic liner to put under my sheet (I was ruining my mattress!). At first, it seemed fairly normal, but as the years went by, Mom became quite frustrated. She was, at the beginning, very supportive and caring, but over time became angrier with me and couldn't understand why I was doing this. "Is it a physical thing or is my son mentally disturbed?" (This particular example would not necessarily answer that question.) She consulted doctors, stayed up all night (I suppose trying to catch me in the act), prevented me from drinking liquids after 7:00 p.m., made me go to the bathroom before bed, woke me in the night to make me go, anything and everything to try and correct the problem.

At one point, she was convinced it was psychological (she thought I was nuts). She tried to reason with me. "Why are you doing this! I can't take it anymore!" The plastic liner, although protecting the mattress, didn't keep the sheets dry or my pajamas for that matter, and Mom resorted to the only thing that had kept me dry as a baby: diapers. You should have seen my mom trying to put a cloth diaper on a relatively chunky eight-year-old child. (Now this was before going to bed. It's not like Mom would send me to school wearing a diaper underneath my jeans; don't be absurd!) She tried to stretch the diaper to fit around my hips and then insert the diaper pins, which often times stuck me, either accidentally, or out of Mom's frustration, on purpose. I would wear the diaper to bed underneath my pajamas (you don't think my brother and sisters were sympathetic and refrained from teasing me mercilessly, do you?): Vicki started in first, "Hey, Baby Huey; nice diaper."Timmy joined in, "Wook at the baby, weawing a diapuh. Ha, Ha." Even little Kathy, a bed-wetter herself, chimed in, "Yeah." I answered back with the only thing I could under the circumstances, "Yeah, well at least I don't suck my thumb. Ha!"

One day, I stopped. No reason or explanation, I just stopped wetting the bed. The smell lingered until the day I got a new mattress. (I can't blame Mom and Dad for not buying a new mattress. They had to be sure I was cured.) You may think that wetting the bed until I was eight years old was a little odd, but au contraire (that's French for "on the contrary," just so you know).

The statistics say that five to seven million kids suffer from bed-wetting and that many continue to a much later age. Here are the stats:

- 15 percent of children still wet the bed at age five
- 7 to 10 percent of children still wet the bed at age seven
- 3 percent of boys and 2 percent of girls still wet the bed at age ten
- 1 percent of boys and very few girls still wet the bed at age eighteen

All I can say is this: at least, I wasn't one of those really weird kids that wet their beds until age ten or eighteen.

The thumb-sucking duo portrayed different attitudes in their thumb-sucking. Vicki was a mad thumb-sucker, and she usually sucked hers in conjunction with a pout of some sort. When she got mad at Mom or Dad, she would retreat to her bedroom where you would find her sucking her thumb and pouting. She would insert the thumb into her mouth while the index and middle fingers tugged at the bottom of both eyes (the closest look I can come up with is a basset hound), which made her seem all the more pouty and angry. If you even tried to approach her, the daggers of anger would shoot from her eyes, whether you were an innocent bystander or the offending parent. Mom and Dad were very worried about this habit of hers and tried many remedies to get her to cease and desist in this behavior. Vicki hated peanut butter (at the time, they didn't know she was allergic to peanuts) so they put some on her thumb, hoping this would deter her. It didn't; she just wiped it off on something else and continued sucking. They tried a special elixir designed to stop thumb-sucking, and that didn't work either, she just sucked it off. I think she quit about the time they had given up.

Timmy's technique was much more interesting than Vicki's and a lot less violent. Timmy sucked his thumb in a way similar to a man retiring to his study to have a brandy and cigar, kind of as a relaxation technique. He would grab a blanket (we had a couple of blankets that were lined around the edge with a four-inch wide, silky/satiny blend) and crawl into bed with the blanket in one hand, thumb in mouth, silky edge under index and ring finger and over his middle finger. Then with the middle finger of the hand that had the thumb in his mouth, he would scratch the edge of the blanket. In addition, he brought the black-and-white family cat into bed to round out the idyllic scene, and every so often the cat would stick its head out from under the blanket. (No one remembers the cat's name, and I believe the cat was a visitor just passing through, or possibly the cat was being held by Timmy against its will and was looking for an avenue of escape.) The sound of his scratching reminded me of the sound a mouse makes when chewing on a cracker. For Timmy, it was a soothing sound, helping him get to sleep, but not for me. In the dark, I would hear the faint sound, coming from the top bunk (I slept on the bottom bunk, which gave Timmy an advantageous position when he wanted to throw something at me or spit down on me from above). "Mommy, there's a mouse in my room eating a cracker. Can you or Daddy kill it so I can get some sleep?" I offered to anyone who would listen.

Timmy eventually grew out of his thumb-sucking phase. The statistics for thumb-suckers are very similar to that of bed wetters:

- About 95 percent of babies suck their thumb
- About 10 percent will do so beyond the age of two to three
- About five percent will do so beyond the ages of four and five

The conclusion evident in all of this: the Bay kids weren't satisfied with being "average strange"; we strived to be in the top 10 percent of all kids when it came to bed-wetting and thumb-sucking. Like I said earlier, we excelled in all we did.

In another chapter, I mentioned that the Good Humor ice cream truck made regular runs through the neighborhood. I also mentioned that it was a rare occasion when we were behaved enough that Mom would give us money for an ice cream bar. Well, this particular day, the stars were aligned perfectly. I heard the Good Humor truck from a few blocks away. The tune that came out of the truck, alerting the kids that he was soon approaching, was a melody that not only stirred up excitement, but was one of those melodies that stuck with you long after you heard it. It was as if the Pied Piper of Hamelin was wandering through the neighborhood, luring kids to their eventual doom at the hands of the Good Humor man. I can still whistle the tune today. Anyway, I got excited as the truck got closer and closer to our street. I knew that I had been pretty good lately, that morning to be specific, and there was a slight possibility that Mom would come up with enough change to allow us to buy the coveted ice cream of our choice. The truck was now on our street and had stopped. Kids came running from near and far with dollar bills clinched between their grubby little fingers. I turned to Kathy and instructed her, "Kathy, run home and see if Mommy has any money, and if she does, if she'll let us have any for some ice cream. Hurry!" Kathy, obstinate as usual answered, "No, you go." Kathy was indeed an independent little cuss. I turned to Timmy next, "Timmy, run home to Mommy and get some money for ice cream. Hurry! I'll stay here and keep an eye on the truck." Timmy, eager for some ice cream, responded, "Okay. I'uh be back. Don't wet the twuck weave."

So the kids, one after another, picked out their favorite ice cream bar (on the inside of the door, there were pictures of all the favorite bars, so even the little kids could pick one without knowing the name), gave the driver their money, stuck the change in their other hands, and walked by those still in line, licking their ice cream with a triumphant grin on their faces. I was at this point getting a little nervous, Timmy still hadn't come back with the money, and the line was dwindling. I couldn't leave to go find Timmy. What if the truck drove away? I was getting very agitated and panicky. Finally, the last kid paid their money, and as they walked by me with ice cream in hand, stuck out their tongue. The driver looked at me and said: "Hey, kid, you want to buy some ice cream or not?" I blurted out in a panic, "I don't have any money, but don't leave; someone's coming with some money." "Sorry kid, I've got a big day in front of me and this stop's taken longer than I planned. Gotta go." I couldn't let him go and cried out, "Noooo! I want some ice cream. Wait!"

As the truck started driving away, with the wonderful, melodious tune beginning to warn the next street that the ice cream truck was on the way, I made a decision, one that in retrospect wasn't too bright. I ran after the truck, shouting for the driver to stop, but the truck kept going, slowly driving down the street. The truck was going so slow that I finally caught up with it and then I did it. I grabbed hold of the bumper with both hands, planning to do what, I'm not sure (I think I had just watched a Mighty Mouse cartoon and thought that I could grab the truck, pick it up, and shake it so that ice cream bars would fall all over the neighborhood and all the kids would love me), but I planted both feet on the ground and amazingly enough the truck didn't stop. It kept right on going, and I kept right on holding, and eventually, the truck dragged me down the street with me yelling, "Stop. Stop. I want some ice cream. Timmy's coming with some money!"

The driver must have finally realized there was something wrong at the rear of the truck, and he stopped and got out to see what was going on. As he stepped around to the back of the truck, he found me, still hanging on to the bumper, tears streaming down my face, knees ripped raw from the asphalt. I don't remember his exact words (something like, "Hey kid, get out of here"), but I immediately let go of the bumper and ran home crying all the way. When I came into the house and got to the kitchen where Mom was, I glanced over at the kitchen table, and there was Timmy, eating a bowl of ice cream. I was expecting some sympathy from Mom, what with the torn-up knees and other scrapes and bruises, but got nothing of the kind. "Ronnie, where have you been and why are your knees scraped up?" was all she could say to me. I replied indignantly, "The ice cream truck was driving away and I tried to stop it." Not surprised in the least, Mom replied, "Ronnie, go to the bathroom and grab the Merthiolate. I'll be right in."

I went to the bathroom (along with little sympathy), and when Mom got there, she applied her usual remedy for all cuts and scrapes: Merthiolate! Rather than apply a salve or ointment that made the sore feel better, Mom applied a substance that burned like fire! I believe Merthiolate was invented by the same man that invented the rack, crucifixion, and burning at the stake.

Merthiolate came in a glass bottle with a glass applicator, and once this bright reddish orange substance was applied to the wound (it would stain the skin and remain for days, long after the wound had healed), no matter how much the injury originally hurt, it would now hurt worse and the pain would be almost unbearable. The pain was so intense that the skin would shiver at the application.

Dad, especially, was fond of using Merthiolate (there were other less painful remedies such as tincture of iodine, but none of those would do. Apparently, if it didn't cause extreme pain, it wasn't effective) and usually had a smile on his face while doing so. Little did we know it at the time, but Merthiolate contained a poisonous substance called thimerosal, and in the late 1990s, the FDA banned Merthiolate in all over-the-counter products. I suppose we did our part for science. With us around, who needed guinea pigs?

I was a dreamer as a kid. I don't mean the John Lennon or Martin Luther King kind of dreams. No, I just dreamed things, some nightmares (to be explored later), and some reoccurring. One of my dreams involved me flying. Yes, I could fly in my dreams.

The scene was always the same. I would be in the neighborhood and all of the kids would be gathered around me, and I would begin to flap my arms (like a bird) and kick my feet (as if I was swimming), and I would slowly ascend, just out of reach of the kids, and hover about the height of the light pole. Once I had reached that height, I would begin to taunt the other kids, sticking out my tongue, letting them know that they couldn't get me. I was invincible up there. If I wanted to move, I would bend forward, flap my arms, and kick my feet and I would fly to a new location. This would go on for a while until my arms started to get tired, and then I would begin to descend toward the ground, the kids anxiously waiting for me to drop, just salivating at the chance to pay me back for my taunting. As I slowly descended, the other kids would grab at my feet as I got within reach. At this point, I would begin furiously flapping my arms and kicking my feet and would once again ascend out of their reach. This would go on for a while, repeating itself numerous times, and then as the kids were about to grab me, I would wake up. The feeling of flying was real and exhilarating. After waking up, I would close my eyes, trying to relive the dream and the feeling I had experienced. This was one of my reoccurring dreams.

Another dream that I often had was one that was as real as the flying dream, only this one was not fun at all. I was being chased by someone, a monster, a man, some nameless, faceless person. The first time I had this dream, earlier that evening the family had watched a variety show with Ray Charles as the special guest. While Ray was singing at the piano, wearing dark sunglasses, he would tilt his head back, rotating it back and forth, in a way that seemed as if he was in pain or a raving lunatic. It made an impression on me, and that night Ray came after me (nothing against Ray, I absolutely love his music). In my dream, I saw him, he saw me, and he started in my direction. I began to run, but my feet were really going slow. I couldn't seem to move. My legs were heavy and weak, and the faster I tried to run, the slower I seemed to go. As I looked behind me, there was Ray, chasing after me, his head tilted, moving back and forth. I turned back and tried to run harder. I couldn't seem to move, as if I was running in mud or quicksand. The funny thing, Ray never got any closer than when he started. I guess he was having trouble with his legs too. This went on for what seemed the entire night, and then I awoke. I was sweating and tired. That dream wore me out. Later, Ray was replaced by others, the same theme played out. I was being chased and I couldn't run. Psychologists say that this dream indicates a person is running from some kind of responsibility that needs sorted out. I was a kid! I didn't have any responsibilities. What do psychologists know anyway?

I had another reoccurring dream that wasn't fun or frightening, it was embarrassing. I grew up wearing tighty-whities (from JC Penney's), like a lot of other boys. No big deal as that goes, but when you dream that you are sitting in a classroom full of kids, wearing nothing but your tighty-whities, it's quite another story. Like the other two dreams, this seemed entirely real. I felt the eyes all around me, staring at me, pointing fingers, laughing at me. I couldn't move. I knew I had to get up and run home, but stayed glued to my chair. How did this happen? Where did my clothes go? I tried to figure this out, while at the same time I was aware of the stares. It was bad enough for my buddies to see me, but the cute girls were there too, staring and laughing with the rest. I tried to cover up, but other than a textbook, I didn't have anything to cover up with. Soon, I would wake up. My heart was racing, and my face felt flushed. It had all seemed so real.

Eating, for most people, is a benign activity that normally involves food. For me, it sometimes presented an opportunity for competition and didn't always involve food, at least the people kind. As a toddler, Mom would sit me out in the yard while she hung clothes on the line or did other yard work. I would play in the garden, and while doing so, I grabbed handfuls of dirt and decided that the dirt would be good to eat. It really wasn't all that bad, after all, worms eat it. After I was scolded and told not to eat dirt, I moved on to other nonfood items. The neighbor family had a dog named Trixie. Trixie had a big bag of dog food (the hard, dry kind) that looked scrumptious enough to eat (it had all the good ingredients: fish, carrots, potatoes, grains, liver, etc). I needed a partner in this crime and turned to little brother, "Timmy, doesn't that dog food look tasty?" Timmy, unusually compliant answered, "Yeah, wet's twy some."

So we did. It was hard and crunchy, but the flavor was similar to, well, dog food. Once the neighbor found out we were eating his dog's food, he ran us off (the dog didn't like us either).

In school, we were all given a small jar of paste that came with a plastic applicator. The paste had a pleasant minty smell that was very inviting. Once in the mouth, it didn't taste quite as good as it smelled, with a slight, grainy texture. It did seem to freshen the breath though. If paste tasted good, what about glue? Not the same effect. I ate chalk, crayons, lead pencils, and even erasers, but none of them tasted as good as paste.

For some reason, when it came to eating, I wanted to make a contest out of it. I couldn't chew just one piece of gum. I would challenge the neighbor kid, and he would put three pieces in his mouth. I would put four pieces in my mouth, he would add another, and I would put an entire package of gum in my mouth, barely able to chew, but I had won. (A few short years ago, we were all at a family reunion, and I noticed my nephew's pogo stick lying up against the house. I decided to try it out, me being fifty years old and all. Before long, I challenged all of the nephews and uncles to a pogo hopping contest. I hopped forty-nine times and won the contest. I say this to give you a brief glimpse into my psyche.) Before going to bed at night, I would take the entire wad of gum out of my mouth and put it on my headboard until the next morning, the gooey mass dripping saliva and sugar down the side of the headboard. The gum would be as good as new the next morning (ABC gum).

If I was lucky enough to have a package of Sugar Babies; instead of eating them one or two at a time, I would rip open the end of the bag and tilt my head back and pour out the entire bag, slowly chewing until the sugar had dissolved and I could swallow the remaining candy. I loved the Jolly Rancher Apple Stix. They were hard to eat because of the size and the fact that they were really sticky. I solved that problem. I put the entire Apple Stix in my mouth, the two ends poking out of both cheeks, and worked on the candy until it softened up. When it was softer, I was then able to remove it from my mouth, bend it in half, and reinsert it back into my mouth in a much more manageable condition.

A regular activity in our house was one of us kids standing in front of the refrigerator with the door open, asking Mom if there was anything to eat or drink. Her usual response was to tell us to look in the fridge. When it came to satisfying our thirst, we would sometimes drink water (out of the water hose was the best), but everything in the fridge was fair game. We drank Kool-Aid, lemonade, iced tea, milk (glug, glug, glug), brown vinegar (when playing cowboys, this was a great substitute for whiskey), olive juice, pickle juice (talk about puckering up); we really weren't particular. Once satisfied, we would run back outside to play and then repeat the above throughout the day. Our house needed a revolving door.

Long before ESPN had hot dog eating competitions, my siblings and I would have contests to see who could eat the most of Mom's tacos. Mom's tacos were the best, corn tortillas stuffed with ground beef and seasoning, then fried in a pan of Crisco oil until crispy. Once they were cool, you then filled them with tomatoes, cheese, lettuce, black olives, sour cream, and whatever else you could find. How many would we eat? Vicki issued the challenge, "I can eat more tacos than you." I defiantly shot back, "Cannot!" Vicki's retort was firm, "Can too. I'll betcha."

Mom and Dad were not involved in this competition and, in fact, were oblivious that the challenge had been issued. At the end of the competition, the score was as follows:

Vicki: nine tacos, Ronnie: seven tacos, Timmy: six tacos, and Kathy: three tacos

Vicki was the undisputed taco-eating champ. Her prize? A sore stomach. Today, when I eat, I eat food, normal portions, and I never challenge anyone to an eating contest.

Hairstyles for boys basically fell into three categories: burr head, flattop, or part on the side with a slicked-down look. Through the years, I experienced all three, but in stages. My head was big and round (think Charlie Brown), with ears sticking out a bit more than normal, and a serious cowlick on the front right-hand side of my head. The burr head look was the only cut that made sense when I was smaller, given the above parameters. Mom loved that haircut because she could do it at home and save the barber's fees. On haircut day, she would pull the high chair out onto the back patio, get the electric shears, strap me down, and begin shearing (yeah, like a sheep). A typical hair cutting encounter had Mom saying, "Ronnie, sit still! I'm going to nick you if you keep wiggling around." "Ow! That hurt. Am I bleeding?" Mom couldn't understand my reaction and while studying the clippers said, "That's funny; this thing must have a short in it." I disagreed, "I don't think it's funny!"

The electric shears did indeed have a short in them, but the haircut went on. With a number 1 clipper, the hair was cut down near the skin, all the way around the head. The haircut would last months and didn't get cut again until Mom said, "Ronnie, your hair looks like it needs a lawnmower."

As I got older, my next hairdo was the part on the side, slicked-down look. Because I had that serious cowlick, it took a lot of Vitalis (Vitalis contained alcohol, PPG-40 butyl ether, benzyl benzoate, fragrance, and a few other ingredients, but enough of it could lubricate an automobile for a year) to slick down my hair. With my glasses tilted a bit off center, ears sticking out, and hair firmly plastered to my head, I bore a striking resemblance to Ralphie from the movie *The Christmas Story* ("You'll shoot your eye out, kid").

When I was five, Mom and Dad decided that I needed to have my vision checked. When the doctor was through with the examination, he determined that I had what he called lazy eye, only mine was so lazy it was a bum (eye that is). I also had an astigmatism (a refractive error of the eye, or in laymen's terms, blurred vision), was farsighted, my lazy eye was 20/50, and my axis was off. In other words, I was as blind as a bat. My glasses, when I finally got them, had lenses that resembled the bottom of a pop bottle. The doctor suggested that in order to strengthen my lazy eye, I should wear a patch (no wonder I always liked being a pirate on Halloween) for a couple of hours each day, the intent being to cover the good eye and force the bad eye to get with the program. On the patch went, much to my dismay and dissatisfaction. I had to figure a way out of this, I couldn't see with my bad eye!

At night, when the family was gathered around the television, watching *The Red Skelton Show* or *The Wonderful World of Disney*, the four of us would lie on the floor, on our stomachs or sides (all of us in our pajamas), and watch the show. How was I supposed to watch TV with my good eye covered up? I had a plan. I would lie on my stomach facing the TV (back to Mom and Dad), my chin held up by both hands. In this position, I would then slide the patch up, ever so slightly, over my eyebrow allowing me to watch TV like everyone else. Leave it to my wonderful brother to ruin it for me. Timmy, always the tattletale squealed, "Mommy, Wonnie's not weawing his patch." (As if it was any of his business). I shot daggers at my squealing brother and said, "Timmy, shut up! I hate you." Our little back and forth just delayed the inevitable question from Mom, "Ronnie, are you wearing your patch?"

I became very adept at fooling Mom. After I lied and said yes, she would then tell me to turn around, and as I was making the move, my right hand would slide up, almost imperceptible to the human eye, and pull the patch back over my eye. It worked once. From then on, the patch wearing became so contentious (I would cry, hold my breath, kick my feet, and even feign death) that Mom finally gave up, and I didn't have to wear it anymore, except at Halloween. Aaargh!

I saved the most embarrassing story (the other stories weren't embarrassing?) for last. My siblings still tease me about this one. I might as well spit it out, *I choked myself.* No, really! Now, before you jump to conclusions, let me explain. One night, while lying on the floor watching TV, with my chin cupped in my hands, my wrists became tired, and in an effort to relieve them, I slid my hands down to the sides of my neck. Apparently, with the pressure applied to both sides of my neck, the blood flowing through the carotid artery to my brain was restricted, causing a light-headedness, euphoria, and a temporary brownout. The feeling was one of intoxication as if I had consumed one too many alcoholic drinks and was in the process of going from tipsy to drunk. Unfortunately, I liked the feeling and began repeating it often. Add to that my addictive personality and it was not a good combination. I would lie on the floor, back to parents, and repeat the maneuver until the euphoria came again. Mom and Dad finally discovered what I was doing and, as usual, didn't have any answers as to what to do. "Ronald, your son is choking himself again." Dad, trying to laugh it off said, "Which one? No, let me guess, Ronnie?" "Yes, Ronnie," Mom replied. Dad, again trying humor as a defense mechanism replied, "I've been tempted to choke that kid hundreds of times." Childhood behaviors have a tendency to stump parents, and my behaviors were a little more daunting than the usual. Mom saw me choking myself again and in a frustrated tone asked me, "Ronnie, what are you doing there on the floor?" I lied and said, "Nothing." Vicki, always the observant one said, "He's choking himself again." Mom was nonplussed and asked me, "Son, why would you want to choke yourself?" In a voice altered by the restricted flow of blood to the brain, I responded, "Because it feels good."

Mom and Dad were beside themselves. They chastised me, spanked me, pleaded with me, threatened me, nothing seemed to work. Whenever the chance presented itself, I was back to choking myself. I even tried to get by with it at the dinner table. My siblings made sure to point this out when they caught me in the act. "Mommy, Ronnie's choking himself," Vicki offered, trying to save me from myself. Timmy too wanted to help and said, "His face is tuhning puhpuwh." "He's huhting himself." Kathy added, almost in tears at the thought of her big brother dying.

This went on for months and not always at home. I would do it at school, on the way to school, wherever I could. It was really easy to disguise the act from people that weren't looking for it (although I couldn't disguise the red marks on my neck or the disorientation that came immediately after). While at my desk, I would hold my head in my hands, and from there, it was a slight change in position to get to the desired effect. Once, I nearly passed out at my desk (one of the desks that are chair and table all in one), and I must have "browned out" and fallen over in my desk. This startled everyone around me, including the teacher, so I had to act fast with a plausible excuse. I told the teacher that I was reaching for a pencil that I had dropped, and the desk tipped over. Little did I know it at the time, but what I was doing could have caused death or brain damage (I know what you're thinking). One day, I stopped. I don't know why, but I did.

I found out years later that not only do many others choke themselves, but there is actually a name for it. It is called the fainting game or the choking game, and in a 2006 behavioral survey in Ohio, it was determined that 11 percent of youths aged twelve to eighteen years reported having practiced it. Even today, my siblings still tease me, and I totally understand why.

The behavior is so absurd that it can only lead to a couple of responses: tears or laughter.

We were pioneers in drinking pickle juice (the BYU football team makes a practice of it), in the taco eating contest (hot dog and pie eating contests on ESPN), and I was a pioneer in the act of choking oneself (the choking game). If you would have known us as kids, you would never have figured us for being that talented.

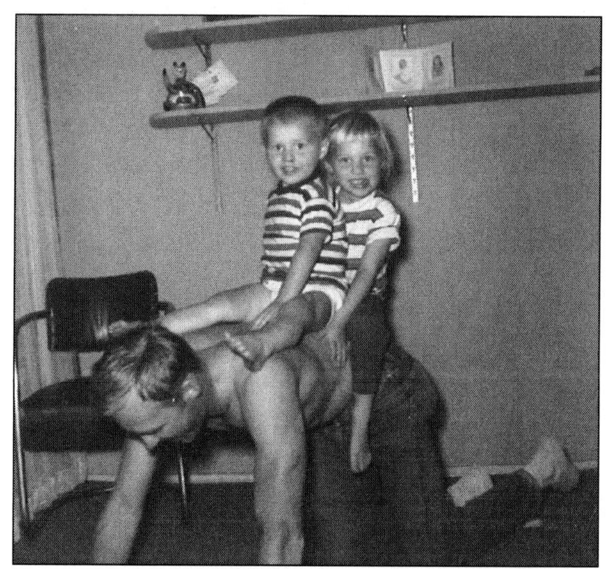

Dad the horse. An easy day with only two of us.

Dad seemed tireless when entertaining us kids.

You kids sit quietly while I rest. And don't move!

Ready to head off to school. Note the sack lunch and neat glasses.

Christmas morning. I was the happy cowboy
with six shooter on my hip.

Vicki and me climbing up the side of the hill
while on a camping trip.

In my baseball uniform. Still neat glasses.
Note the wall we loved to climb on.

The four of us with Dad inside a giant Sequoia.

SCHOOL DAYS AND ADD

To say that I was an active child is probably a bit of an understatement. Go to an older dictionary and look up the term "attention deficit disorder." Next to the definition, you will find my third grade class picture. My mom recently returned all of my report cards to me from kindergarten through the fourth grade (she must have found them in a box, and having read the teacher comments, she broke down crying and decided to get them out of her presence once and for all). The report cards that were sent home had an empty box next to the subject for the teacher to write in the grade, and there were four boxes for each quarter. In each quarter, there was also a space for the teacher to write her comments to the parent. In looking at all of the report cards, there was a reoccurring theme.

> Kindergarten—"Ronnie is progressing in his school work, but he has very much difficulty in getting along with others. He starts fights with other boys and girls."
>
> 1st grade—"Ronnie must understand that the classroom is for learning, not acting. He works well until his own work is finished."
>
> 2nd grade—"I'm hoping that Ronnie will improve in his study habits and citizenship, because he has outstanding abilities."
>
> 3rd grade—"Ronnie has become very careless with his work. Neatness is not part of his work and he hurries and does not do as good a job as he is capable of doing."

> 4th grade—"If Ronald will continue to improve his conduct, I hope he will have earned a "C" by the next grading period." The next grading period: "I believe Ronald could be an excellent student if he would take more thought in improving his conduct."

There is a definite pattern in these comments from five different teachers. They were obviously being as kind as they could, when what they really wanted to say was, "Mrs. Bay, your son is a hellion!" It seems that Citizenship-Conduct really had me stumped and a "D" grade was not uncommon. Thank goodness that particular curriculum was dropped off the report card after fourth grade.

It wasn't like I didn't get good grades; I generally received As and Bs. I think it was more the fact that the teachers had to spend an inordinate amount of time saying things like this: "Ronnie, please sit down." "Ronnie, please turn around." "Ronnie, leave Susie alone." "Ronnie, don't cut in line." While going through the report cards I noticed that I was in summer school in the first, second and fourth grades (Why third grade was skipped, I'm not sure. It had to be an oversight on someone's part). Since I got good grades, there had to be another reason. Hmmm. I also found out that there was a reason I started kindergarten at the age of four. Mom admitted that me being in school, in the care of someone else, would be better for all. I was as much of a handful alone as the other three siblings combined.

You get the picture. It was like I had ants in my pants and couldn't sit still. They didn't have drugs back then, well, at least the legal kind, and there weren't enough punishments to fix the problem. Maybe a frontal lobotomy might have done the trick. I have yet to visit a counselor.

From the first day of kindergarten, I knew that this school thing was going to be something I could really get into. Although I was only four years old, the memory is very clear to this day. My first recollection involved a boy named Guy, and what happened would haunt him for years. In the middle of class, the very first day of school, Guy wet his pants and started to cry. In front of all of his peers! The teacher left the room, presumably to call his mother; his mom showed up and off Guy went. That was pretty fun, and I couldn't wait for more.

The second event that sealed the school deal for me involved the cutest little girl I had ever seen (actually, I was pretty limited as to the number of girls I had seen, being only four years old, and limited in scope to the neighborhood and my sisters): Nicky. Round face, silver-dollar sized eyes, brunette hair (think Shirley Temple): I was smitten. Of course, all I could do was stare. I hadn't yet mastered the social skills necessary to actually hold a conversation with the opposite sex (I could only chase them around the playground or be chased by them) and in fact, wouldn't master those skills until approximately my senior year in high school. Nevertheless, school presented some mighty interesting possibilities for me, and I would take the bull by the horns and completely immerse myself in the experience.

In some of the earlier grades, we had a period that was called nap time (did they really think they could get me to take a nap with thirty other little distractions around me?). All the children were instructed to bring a towel from home, and at the appointed time, we would roll out our towel and all lie down and close our eyes, etc. For some reason, I couldn't sleep. In our class at the back of the room, there was a walk-in closet where all the kid's coats, sweaters, and lunches were stored. The teacher took me to the coat closet and told me that this was a special place to take a nap, and because I was such a special child, I would get to take my nap in the coat closet. Even though it probably seemed like a good idea to her at the time, it's only because she didn't think ahead far enough to realize what I might do in the coat closet by myself.

I eventually knew what every kid was having for lunch, and I tried on all of the sweaters and coats that the kids had brought to school. When I got bored with that, I began to bother the kids napping nearest the coat closet. Needless to say, when the report card came, next to napping, I received an incomplete.

The classrooms in LA were built independent of one another as opposed to all being in a single building like you would find in the Midwestern part of the country (with that wonderful LA weather, why enclose everyone?). One side of the classroom was all glass doors and windows, so the distractions were numerous: janitors walking by, other classes going to and fro, rain, and even the occasional kid being punished outside the classroom. There was a canopy that stood over the sidewalk in front of the class; I suppose it was there to keep people from getting wet while entering and leaving. Oftentimes, while all of the other kids were in class, presumably doing schoolwork, I would be out on the sidewalk, under the canopy, thinking; well, at least that's what the teacher told me I was supposed to be doing out there. The teacher, interrupting the class, berated me in front of everyone (not an unusual occurrence), "Ronnie, because you can't sit still and leave the other children alone, you will go outside on the sidewalk and think about what you should be doing while in the classroom." (I *had* thought about what I was doing in the classroom, and that's why I was in trouble.)

She instructed me to stand just outside the door, but I would get distracted and wander down the sidewalk, peering into another classroom. Sometimes, it was a bird, or when it rained a lot, the earthworms would come out of the ground and be crawling all over the sidewalk. Earthworms on the sidewalk were always good for a moment of my attention. When the worms would get waterlogged, they would come up on the sidewalk for a breath of air. Most would die on the sidewalk, and after the rain, they would dry out and shrivel up. They didn't smell too good when squished underneath my foot. If I wasn't squishing worms or watching the janitor, I was spinning around the poles holding up the canopy; first around and around to the left, then around and around to the right. The sound of my hand on the painted pole was a unique sound, similar to the sound of a hand spinning around on the jungle gym.

The teacher finally had me return to the classroom. I felt a little bit sorry for her knowing that she struggled with the answer to these two questions: Was I more of a distraction in the classroom, constantly bugging the other kids and talking, or was I a worse distraction playing with worms on the sidewalk and swinging around the pole? Based on future circumstances, it was evident to me that she wavered between two opinions.

I loved recess. I think I was born to play, the way some people are born to become bankers or lawyers. The best and longest recess was the one that came during the lunch hour. Mom would pack my lunch, usually a peanut butter and jelly sandwich or baloney, and then maybe some chips and a piece of fruit. She would also send a nickel with me to buy a carton of milk. When lunchtime arrived, the teacher would form all the kids in a single file line and then lead us to the lunchroom, which was located a good walk across the campus. It sounds pretty simple, but there was a lot that could happen in that line on the way to the lunchroom (it mostly always involved boys pushing and shoving). When one of those things did happen, the teacher had to stop the procession, go back down the line, correct the problem, and then start up again. I noticed that after a while, whenever we went to lunch, I was always second in line behind the teacher. I wondered why I got special privileges and the other kids didn't.

When we got to the lunchroom, all the kids would go buy their milk and sit down at different tables. Part of the lunch time ritual was comparing lunches with each other. Most of us had a sandwich of some kind, peanut butter and jelly and baloney being in the top two of sandwich choices. The main factor separating our lunches was the "dessert" portion. Was it cookies, or pudding, or a piece of fruit (what parent would consider a brown old banana as dessert)? Trading portions of your lunch was not uncommon. Once you were done with lunch, you could then proceed to the playground to play. On the way out of the lunchroom was a big box stacked high with balls: four square balls, dodge balls, bouncy balls, and my favorite, the kickball. While I was eating, I always had one eye on that box of balls by the exit doors; the kickball was never out of my sight. The setup was a first come, first serve sort of thing. The quicker you ate, the more time you had to play on the playground, and I was all about play. I initially tried to eat as fast as I could so I would be the first one to the box of balls, but realized that Phillip was a faster eater than I was, so I learned to throw my lunch in the trash (I kept the nickel to buy candy at Sam's Liquor Store on my way home) and head straight for the box of balls. I soon discovered that even if I was the first one on the playground, I still had to wait for the other kids in order to play the game.

On the playground, kickball was my favorite game. It was similar to baseball, but instead of hitting the ball with a bat, you kicked the ball. As the "batter," you could request of the pitcher how you wanted the ball presented to the plate. There were big baby bouncies, fast baby bouncies, slow rollers, etc. I always requested slow baby bouncies, and I became one of the best kickball players on the playground. Like baseball, you could "kick" a homerun, triple, double, or single. I soon began kicking the ball over the outfielder's heads. One difference between kickball and baseball was the way in which a player made an out. If the ball was caught in midair, it was an out, but the other way to get someone out was the best part of the game: you could throw the ball at them (only below the waist, but of course, there were times we threw a little high) and the added dimension of trying to dodge a thrown ball while going from first base to second base made the game that much more exciting (this part of the game was a cross between baseball and dodgeball). An overheard playground conversation like the following was routine. The playground monitor, seeing one kid chasing another, turned to a well behaved (was there any other kind?) little girl and asked, "Why is that little boy chasing the other boy across the field and who are they?" She answered knowledgeably, "The boy being chased is Ronnie and he's being chased by Phillip. They were engaged in a game of kickball and Ronnie threw the ball at Phillip's head, presumably to get him out. The rules specifically say that you aren't supposed to hit the opposing player with the ball anywhere but below the waist. Phillip, a stickler for the rules, got mad, and thus the chase." The monitor, having seen plenty of this kind of activity, was not moved and observed, "Well, it looks like they're headed this way. What's Ronnie saying?" Straining to hear, the little girl offered, "It sounds like aaaahhhhh!"

I loved that game!

My second favorite playground game was tetherball. Tetherball was a steel pole in the ground with a thin rope hanging from the top and a ball, resembling a volleyball, on the end of the string. Two players stood on either side of a line that ran through the middle of the pole. The line was drawn in the dirt and could not be crossed during the game. The goal was to hit the ball (you could not catch and throw it) so that it continued to wrap around the pole until it couldn't wrap anymore. At first, the ball would be on the outside edge of its arc, and in many cases, out of reach. As the rope wrapped around the pole, it became shorter and shorter, and the speed of the ball wrapping around the pole grew faster and faster. There were certain techniques that were the most effective: the main one being to try and keep the ball as high up the pole as you could and thus out of the reach of your opponent. As in kickball, I became one of the better tetherball players on the playground.

There were other playground games, such as foursquare, jump rope, hopscotch, and handball that all were fun in their own way. I especially liked the equipment on the playground, including the merry-go-round and teeter-totter, both of which are no longer found on playgrounds (we wouldn't want anyone to get hurt now would we?). The merry-go-round was fun alone or with others. If you were by yourself, you could grab one of the bars and begin running around as fast as you could, and when you hit warp speed, jump on and enjoy the ride. It was better if you were already on the apparatus and someone else pushed the merry-go-round. That way you could lie down and stare at the sky while spinning faster and faster; the centrifugal force always threatening to dislodge you and send you flying the closer to the perimeter you got. If you didn't want to fight the centrifugal force, you could go to the center of the ride, where it wasn't as difficult to hang on. The teeter-totter was also fun, especially when I had Kathy along with me. Being much smaller than I was, she soon realized the mistake of going on the teeter-totter with me. It wasn't my idea, but I was thrilled when she asked, "Wonnie, come and play on the teeteh totteh with me." Mischievously I answered, "If you insist."

As I sat on the opposite end of the teeter-totter, Kathy was lifted to the sky. She was so light that even if I tried to have my end go up and hers down, it wouldn't work. I just sat there, Kathy in the air, me on the ground. As she realized that I intended to leave her up there, she got a little frantic. "Let me down," she pleaded with me. "I can't. You're too light." Now she insisted, "Let me down, oh I'm telling."

At this point, I figured that I was in trouble either way, so I might as well enjoy it. After leaving her up there for a while longer, just to get her more agitated, I asked her again if she wanted me to let her down, just to make sure. Once she answered in the affirmative, I slid off the seat while still holding it to the ground and then I let her down. Hard! When we got home from school, after listening to Kathy's story, Mom somehow sided with her and I was punished once again.

Recess was over when the bell rang. Once the bell rang, all of the kids would come running from the outer reaches of the play area and form lines so that we could then be marched back into the school. If you were slow about responding to the bell, a playground monitor (teacher) would be equipped with a whistle and would blow it until you acquiesced. One very important rule that we all learned early on in school was the "no cut" rule. Kids have historically learned this rule well: try to cut in line at a movie theater or baseball game and see what reaction you get. Anyway, cutting was a cardinal sin on the playground. My goal at the end of recess was to run to the spot on the playground where my class would gather and be the first one in line back to class (I guess I was getting used to being first in line next to the teacher).

One time as we were forming a line back to class, my best friend Robert C. decided he wanted to cut in front of me. I would have nothing of it. We began to wrestle around, and I ended up putting him into a headlock and throwing him to the ground. The problem was, Robert didn't get up. The teacher called for help, and as the kids headed back to class, Robert was taken to the nurse's office and I was taken to the assistant principal's office. I knew I was in big trouble, and as I was being led from the assistant principal's office to the head principal's office, I walked by the nurse's office, and lying on a cot with his head bandaged was Robert. I began to cry. Turning to the nurse, I tearfully asked, "Is Robert going to be okay?" No response was given by the nurse. I didn't want Robert to be hurt, I only wanted to be first in line. As I walked by the office, I stuck my head in and told Robert that I was sorry. He didn't say anything and that got me even more worried. When I got to the principal's office, the principal sternly reprimanded me and asked me if I had known that Robert had a steel plate in his skull and that I may have seriously hurt him. This just got me to bawling even more. "I didn't mean to." The principal had me sit in a room for a while, presumably to think about what I had done, and finally, he returned with a legal pad. I knew what was next because I was becoming a master at writing "I will not fight on the playground" (1,000 times).

Even writing these sentences became a game after a while. When my hand became tired from all of the writing, I would change things up a bit. Instead of writing the same sentence over and over I would write each word over and over: I, I, I, I, I, I, I, I etc., and then will, will, will, will, will, will, etc., until the 1,000 sentences were complete. The page would look like this:

> I will not fight on the playground anymore.
> I will not fight on the playground anymore.
> I will not fight on the playground anymore.
> I will not fight on the playground anymore.

Even though I had been in trouble before (writing other "I will not fill in the blank" novels), this incident with Robert was a big one. After I had finished writing my 1,000 sentences, the principal loaded me up in his car (a Volkswagen bug) and proceeded to drive me home in the middle of the school day. Wasn't my mom surprised to see me coming home midday, in the principal's car, being marched to the front door by the principal? Mom answered the knock on the door and was a little hesitant when she saw who it was. "Well, hello, Mr. Brady. It's so nice to see you today. To what do I owe this honor?" Mom greeted him as politely as she could. Mr. Brady, through clenched teeth answered, "Hello, Mrs. Bay. Your son nearly killed another kid at school today. I thought I would bring him home to you. The school has run out of patience. You can send him back, someday. We'll let you know." As Mr. Brady quickly turned on his heel and headed back to his car, I muttered, "Uh-oh."

I won't go into detail as to my punishment at home, but suffice it to say, the punishment in this case surely fit the crime. What happened to Robert? He recovered rather quickly; we stayed friends, and we resumed our tussles on the playground while lining up from recess (I did learn my lesson in this instance and never again threw Robert to the ground).

There were punishments other than the ones I already mentioned. Once, Mrs. Pelton (second grade teacher) decided to bring me to the front of the class and have me sit on the floor next to her desk. I don't think she realized what I would do with this opportunity. I ended up sitting/lying on the floor (it's already been determined that I couldn't sit in one spot for more than a second) next to her desk. Your imagination will probably take you to the same place mine did as Mrs. Pelton, wearing a dress, stood next to her desk with me lying on the floor, glancing around to no place in particular. I think she figured it out, and I never received that punishment again.

Mrs. Anderson had a unique idea for punishment. While all of the other kids got to go out and play during recess, she held me back in the classroom where I had to copy word for word and symbol for symbol, an entire page of the *Webster's Dictionary.* I admit that this seemed to be a tedious and daunting punishment to endure, knowing how much I cherished recess and all. The one thing Mrs. Anderson didn't know was that I had a crush on her and spending the entire recess, just her and me in the classroom, wasn't punishment at all.

I was really a pretty good student, other than the 50 percent of the time I was standing outside the classroom, sleeping in the closet, sitting by the teacher's desk, or writing "I will not do something" 1,000 times. My favorite subject was spelling. The teacher did a pretty neat thing after all of the spelling tests were graded. She took the top scoring students and had a mini-spelling bee. I was often in the spelling bee as I usually had As on my tests. Before the spelling bee started, the teacher would go over the rules and here's what I heard her say, "Now, students, here are the rules for the spelling bee; wah, wah, wahwahwah." Once the rules were given out, the spelling bee would commence. "Ronnie, please spell onomatopoeia." I jumped right in, "O-n-o-m-a-t-o-p-o-e-i-a?" "I'm sorry Ronnie, you'll have to sit down." I was stunned. I heard her address the next contestant, "Leah, spell onomatopoeia." Leah, who must have listened to the instructions more closely than I did recited, "Onomatopoeia, o-n-o-m-a-t-o-p-o-e-i-a, Onomatopoeia." "Leah, you are correct. You now get to move on to the next word." I was indignant when addressing the teacher, "Hey! I got gypped. I spelled the word the same way that Leah did!" The teacher was blunt and put me on the spot in front of the rest of the class when she said, "Ronnie, if you had been paying attention when the instructions were being given, you would have heard that you must first pronounce the word, then spell it, and then pronounce it again."

It seems that during the instruction period I was either gazing out the window watching a squirrel or making google eyes at one of my friends in the back of the class. Otherwise, I liked spelling bees.

When the teacher would ask the class a question, students that thought they knew the answer would raise their hands, and the teacher would call on one of the students for the answer. I raised my hand quite often, but didn't get called on much. "Class, who knows which planet in the solar system is closest to the earth?" With hand raised and waving I said, "I know, I know!" The teacher overlooked me and instructed, "Go ahead Johnny and give us the answer." Johnny, not really wanting to be called on guessed, "Jupiter?" "I'm sorry, Jupiter is incorrect. Does anyone else know the answer?" This time my arm was waving furiously when I blurted out, "I know, I know!" Again, the teacher acted like I wasn't even there, sitting five feet in front of her desk, and asked another student, "Leah, do you know the answer?" Leah, one of the bright ones, incorrectly answered, "Uranus?" "I'm sorry, Leah, Uranus is incorrect. Does anyone else have the answer?"

By this time, my arm was getting so tired that I had to prop it up with my other arm. Each time a wrong answer was given, I excitedly waved my hand, said "wrong," and then "I know, I know!" but the teacher still didn't pick me. I didn't understand how she could overlook me. I was sitting on the front row (somehow, I ended up on the front row within a few minutes of the first day of class), right in front of her, yet she didn't call on me. Finally, the teacher called on Susan, the smartest girl in the class, and she gave the correct answer as Mars. There must have been some sort of conspiracy in the "raise your hand if you know the answer" tactic used by the teachers. Inevitably, the only time that I would get called on was when I didn't raise my hand because I didn't know the answer. "Class, does anyone know the formula for the theory of relativity?" Only one student raised her hand: Susan (the smartest kid in the class). "Ronnie, do you have the answer?" "I wasn't raising my hand! Why don't you ask Susan back there? She knows all the answers."

As I gazed at the worms on the sidewalk, I thought really hard about what I had done to deserve this most recent of punishments, here in the land of school days.

All in all, grade school was a blast, punishments aside. I met a lot of other kids and learned many things along the way: how to play kickball and tetherball, sleeping in the coat closet during nap time, standing on the sidewalk in front of the classroom watching worms die, how to read, how to spell, when to fight, and when to run, which brings up this next topic.

I suppose now is as good a time as any to discuss one of the other personality quirks that seemed to get me into trouble at school. You hear it said by many guys (usually when they've been confronted by someone bigger and tougher than they are), "Hey, I'm a lover not a fighter." Well, in my case it was the other way around (maybe I wasn't a lover because I was a fighter, I don't know). For some reason, I just got into fights. Each school year,

I would fight someone. I hated to be made fun of. That was it. I can hear the other kids now: "Who's going to make fun of that Ronnie kid this year?" I can't blame them though. If you've seen any of my class pictures from kindergarten through high school, you would see why I might be made fun of. I had an overly large head with a geometric shape somewhere between triangle and square. My ears were big and stuck out, and I was loaded with freckles. My hair was cut in the style known as burr head and then slicked down (all of the really neat hairstyles). On top of all that, I wore glasses from the first grade on. The glasses never looked quite right and had a tendency to pull my ears out further and sit cockeyed on my face (the Vitalis on my hair didn't help either, glasses constantly slipping off of my ears). "Hey, four eyes!" That's me of course and over the years that taunt was repeated often. I retorted, "So what, you're a Fatso." Bob elevated his taunt, "Four eyes, four eyes, pop bottle eyes. Ha ha." Proceeding to pound on Bob I shouted, "I'm going to kill you!"

I had a favorite fighting technique when I was younger, the headlock. The headlock served a couple of purposes. One, it allowed me to restrain my opponent while at the same time taking him down to the ground to minimize his abilities to fight and or flee. Secondly, it served to squeeze the life out of my opponent. The one problem with this technique was that when the opponent was having the life squeezed out of him, he would get so scared that he would gain super human strength and escape from the headlock. When that happened, I would run as fast as I could to the nearest authority figure. They would then be able to sort out the details while the mad man calmed down. As I got older, I relied less on the headlock and more on a newer technique called the double leg takedown. Once again, the main purpose of this move was to render the opponent helpless by taking him down to the ground, and while straddling him, beat him senseless with numerous blows to the face and head. Here is a list of my opponents over the years (some are missing because I forgot their names, but I didn't forget their face):

Third grade: Bob (the Fatso kid)—this was on the playground.

Fourth grade: Phillip—the headlock that came loose; I ran faster than Phillip that day on the playground.

Fourth grade is where this particular book ends, but since I'm on a roll, I may as well tell all of my fighting stories.

Fifth grade: ?????—not sure of his name, but I remember it was on the playground, specifically on the baseball/ kickball diamond. I was the new kid and once again, didn't like being made fun of.

Sixth grade: Rusty and Joe—this was an odd one as both Rusty and Joe were my friends. My other friend, Timmy, was being made fun of by the other two, so we decided we would have a fight or double fight in this case. We agreed to fight after we were dropped off at the bus stop at the end of the school day. I would fight Joe, and Timmy would fight Rusty. After the bus dropped us off and got out of sight, we began fighting. I was beating up Joe pretty good when I looked out of the corner of my eye and saw Rusty pounding on Timmy. I realized it was not protocol, but I left Joe and ran over to assist Timmy. I punched Rusty in the side of the face, and he immediately stopped pounding on Timmy. At this point, the fight came to a screeching halt, at about the time that the school bus came to a screeching halt, and the driver jumped out and rounded us up (the driver had circled back after dropping off the other kids; it seems that the fight was well publicized throughout the neighborhood). The punishment was me being kicked off the bus for the remainder of the school year. I never liked riding the bus anyway (too much fighting!).

Seventh grade: Mike—this one occurred in the field down from the school building.

> Eighth grade: Doug and Mike (not the same Mike as the year before. I found that once you fought a guy, you never had to do it again). The Doug fight was in the field down from the school building. The Mike fight was in the gymnasium up in the stands while we waited to go back to class from lunch. I really must have done some damage in this one because as the principal was shaking me, he kept saying that I may have broken Mike's jaw (he didn't seem too worried about my bruised-up fist). It just so happens that Mike was our immediate next-door neighbor. Funny thing: Mike's family moved away shortly after this incident.
>
> Ninth grade: Steve—this happened in the school hallway outside of shop class. The only fight I ever lost. It didn't last long. I took a swing at Steve, he ducked, he swung and connected, square on my nose. Tears ran out of my eyes and the fight was over.

There was a brief respite my sophomore through senior years. Maybe it was the wrestling that I decided to take up. Wrestling was an outlet for all of my aggression that was actually sanctioned. I did however get into a fight with my cousin David while at wrestling practice. It too was a one-punch affair. In this instance, I won.

> Senior summer: Ted—this fight occurred when I worked at the cheese factory. Ted couldn't help making fun of me because I was a college kid and was dating the plant manager's daughter and he was a factory worker with a family, and I guess he envied me in some way. Day after day, he would make fun of me. Hey, college, boy. You're a ———!" "———you!" I replied. Again Ted mocked, "——— you!" I shot back, "——— you!"
>
> It was arranged through intermediaries for us to meet in the back parking lot after our shifts were over. His second was Willie, and mine was Red. It was probably my favorite

fight of all time. I took pride in the fact that I whipped an older guy and did it in front of guys that I respected. I used the double leg takedown on old Ted, and it allowed me to be in an advantageous position throughout. Once I had him down, the fists and feet were landing blows at a furious rate. When I got home that evening, Mom and Dad, after observing my bent and broken glasses, torn shirt, and scrapes about the arms and neck, both asked, "What happened to you?" My response (with a smile on my face), "You should see the other guy."

I had one more fight after that, also at work, but I finally grew out of the fighting mode. I still think about it at times, but my superior self-control keeps me in check. Even though I have mentioned quite a few fights, I know I've left out many others due to memory lapse or possibly the insignificance of the opponent.

TO PLAY OR NOT TO PLAY?

(ONE POTATO, TWO POTATO)

If you would have asked the four of us kids the daunting philosophical question that has troubled mankind for millennia, "Why are you here?" I believe that we would have answered in unison, "To play!" Why have I come to that conclusion? Because it's what we did, what we thought about. It consumed our minds and occupied the majority of our time. "What are you kids doing today?" Mom asked us one day. "Playing." "Where are you kids going today?" "Outside to play," we answered her. "Where have you kids been?" she asked. "Playing" was again our answer. "What have you kids been doing all day?" In unison we all said, "Playing."

You see, playing was a word that covered a number of bases (even in my explanation, a game is referenced). Playing could mean an organized game, or it could mean sitting in your room all by yourself, pretending to be driving a truck through a mountain range (a mountain range created by inserting the hamper underneath the braided rug in our room, creating a mountain with numerous hills and valleys, or if a hamper was unavailable, having a sibling crawl under the rug to create a mountain range; man, was it dusty under that rug, and boy, did it tickle when a sibling drove a truck all over your body). The opportunities to play were endless. Not only did we have each other, but we had a neighborhood full of other kids to expand our horizons.

Inevitably, when it came time to play in the organized games (those involving more than two people), a ritual almost always took place that would determine either who was "it" or which side or team each individual was on. This ritual came about due to the numerous arguments that would ensue if the selection were more arbitrary. We would all stand around in a circle and insert both fists into the center of the circle, and someone (there often would be arguments as to who would be the person doing the counting) would begin tapping each fist in order, while repeating this phrase: "One potato, two potato, three potato, four, five potato, six potato, seven potato, more."

When the recitation got to the "more" part, you were either chosen as part of a team, or you were "it." This particular method of choosing morphed into something much bigger over time, maybe due to the fact that the first recitation was a bit boring, we had fertile imaginations, or that this method was more fun than the particular game we were choosing for. Anyway, the next recitation went like this: "One potato, two potato, three potato, four, five potato, six potato, seven potato, more. My mother told me to choose the very best one and out goes you."

And then, added to the end of this: "My mother told me to choose the very best one and out goes y-o-u."

Even with this method, we still had arguments, which led to more and more recitations, ever lengthening all the time. If you were chosen to be "it" in tag for example, you would argue the method of choosing and try again. Another way of choosing went like this:

Eeny, meeny, miny, moe,
Catch a tiger by the toe,
If he hollers, make him pay,
Fifty dollars every day.
My mother told me to choose the very best one,
and out goes y-o-u.

This rhyme has existed since before 1820 and is found in many languages including German forms (thought you might want to know). One particular "choosing" rhyme was a little different and didn't seem to have much to do with choosing: "I one it, you two it, I three it, you four it, I five it, you six it, I seven it, and you eight it."

The joke was the "you eight it" part, which was insinuated to mean you *ate* it. Ate what, didn't matter, but if "you ate it," it had to be bad and you were laughed at. If you forgot where to start on the rhyme and began:

> You one it, I two it, you three it, I four it,
> you five it, I six it, you seven it...
> Looks like trouble ahead, but a fast-thinking
> kid came up with this as a finish:
> You five it, I six it, you seven it, I jumped over it,
> and you eight it.

What fun! All the kids would run around in the yard, pointing their fingers at the one kid and laughing, "You ate it. You ate it. Hahaha." If you happened to be the one that "ate it," you would get mad, of course, and start chasing the other kids, with the goal of catching one of them and beating them to a pulp. When this activity was going on, the game we were choosing sides for became a distant memory and the ensuing pounding became the focus of the moment.

My favorite neighborhood game was hide-and-seek. When the call went throughout the neighborhood that a game of hide-and-seek was about to start, the kids came out of the woodwork. Here are the game specifics:

One person was "it" or the seeker. To start the game, the seeker went to the base, which in this case was the light pole in front of Russell's house. They then had to hide their eyes (you would fold one arm across your eyes while leaning on the light pole) and count to one hundred (sometimes, while counting, your eyes would accidentally slide off your folded arm and you might inadvertently notice where some of the other kids were going to hide). This allowed all of the remaining kids to go hide. One hiding rule that Russell and I usually broke was that you had to hide on our street and couldn't go around the block. Once the counting hit one hundred, the seeker would shout out, "Ready or not, here I come" as a warning to those that were still deciding on a good place to hide, that they better hurry up. Once the seeker had found someone, there was still work to be done. This hide-and-seek game involved a little athleticism as well as stealth. In order to catch the hidden person, it wasn't enough to say, "I see Ronnie." You had to run to the base and touch it while yelling out, "One, two, three on Ronnie." However, if you were fast enough and beat the seeker to the base while yelling out "free," you were safe and got to go hide in the next game. The first person caught in a particular game had to be "it" the next game. This was done so as not to penalize the ones who had eluded capture the longest. Once the seeker caught someone or gave up looking, they would shout out, "Olly, olly, oxen free" (some locales used "All-y all-y in come free" for the same purpose) to let all the rest of the players know that it was safe to come in.

In my inaugural game, I thought I had found the perfect hiding place, the sycamore tree in Neal's front yard. Not only was it the perfect tree to climb, but offered plenty of foliage to prevent the seeker from spotting me. I climbed up to the top of the tree and waited. As the seeker announced, "Ready or not, here I come," I felt pretty good about my position, but as they got closer and closer to my hiding place, I began to realize that I was in deep trouble if they saw me. By the time I came down from the top of the tree, the seeker would be back at the base and I would be "it" the next round. I had to hope they passed by without looking up. With my heart pounding, I held my breath and remained motionless, but hope faded as my eyes caught their eyes and I was done for. I vowed to never be caught first after that episode.

As the seeker, I finished counting to one hundred, and as I raised my eyes and began to look around, I noticed Kathy, standing in the middle of the street with a panicked look on her face. I quickly touched the base and said, "One, two, three on Kathy." That was easy. Unfortunately, Kathy's reaction was one that was quite familiar. "I wasn't weady" Kathy cried. Indignantly I replied, "I counted to one hundred. You had plenty of time to hide." With the tears flowing stronger and voice growing louder, Kathy wailed, "I'm telling!"

I quickly made a decision, partly because she was a little kid and I felt a bit sorry for her, but mainly because I didn't want to face Mom or Dad with a crying little sister accusing me of everything short of murder. I waived my rights, according to the rules of the game, and moved on to the next victim. I eventually caught one of the slow-footed neighbors and was out from under the seeker curse.

When the next game began, I decided that I needed a better place to hide, somewhere close to the base yet hidden. While the next seeker was counting to one hundred, I surveyed the scene and noticed a car in the driveway of Russell's house, no more than thirty feet from the base. I went to the opposite side of the car, hiding directly by the front tire so that even if they looked under the car they couldn't see me. The seeker shouted out, "Ready or not, here I come," and I waited. As they moved away from the base and out into the street, their back to me, I made my move. A few short steps and I was "free." Even though this was a great hiding place, it didn't take long for everyone else to notice, and when it was their turn to seek, they made sure they looked behind the car before going elsewhere to look.

The next game, I tried the car hiding place again, and as mentioned, the seeker also remembered the same location from the previous game, and after announcing that they were coming, headed straight for the car. As they approached the car, I was watching underneath to see which way they were going (the adrenaline rush I felt while hiding from someone, the anticipation of being found as they got closer and closer is something that everyone should experience. For a taste of that feeling, hide in a closet from someone in your house, and while you hear them call your name and hear their feet approach your hiding place, you will know what I'm talking about). As they moved around to the right side of the car, I moved, waddling like a duck, to the left side. Once they were directly across from me, and both of us about the same distance from the base (the timing on this needed to be perfect in order to work), I made my move and ran as fast as I could to the base. They also ran as fast as they could. Simultaneously, we arrived at the base, me shouting out "Free" and they shouting out "One, two, three on Ronnie." Although we touched the base at the exact same time, my phrase took a lot less time to say and I was technically "free" although the seeker didn't see it quite that way. The argument proceeded to escalate, and unfortunately, the game ended (arguments involving rules and other close calls have ruined many a good game). We would do it again another day.

Most of the hide-and-seek games were played around dusk and into the night. By playing after dark, the persons hiding had a definitive advantage. Couple that with Russell and I cheating by walking around the block, and the seeker could often become frustrated and not catch anyone. Eventually, at some point, we were all called in by our parents and the games ended.

Walking around the neighborhood at night was a particularly joyful time for me. I loved the shadows, the streetlights, and the soft glow of light from each house along the way. All of the senses seemed to be heightened in the dark. When running, I seemed to run faster at night than in the daytime. I also noticed that my shadow ran with me, although it ran much faster than I did. As I approached a streetlight and stood under it, my shadow stood with me. As I began to move away, my shadow moved with me, although it moved at a faster pace and grew elongated the farther I moved away from the light. If I ran, it ran with me. At one point, as I got far enough away from the light, my shadow disappeared. As I grew nearer the next streetlight, I looked behind me, and there was my shadow, elongated and shortening, chasing me, all the while I got closer to the light (my experiences with my shadow remind me of the Walt Disney version of Peter Pan and the sequence with Peter and his shadow dancing around the room). I felt freer walking through the neighborhood at night. I still enjoy the experience today.

Another popular game in the neighborhood was tag. Tag was a simple game; if you were fast, you did well, but if you were slow, you were perpetually "it" and spent quite a bit of time in frustration, trying to do something you were unable to do. Eventually, the slow kid would stand in the middle of the yard, tired out, other kids running by just out of reach, taunting him mercilessly. After a long while of watching the slow kid suffer, one of us would be gracious and offer to be tagged so that the suffering would stop and the game could start anew. Unfortunately, this scenario would repeat itself with the idea of the "survival of the fittest" playing out before our eyes, and the slowest kid getting tagged once again.

Dad, always the biggest kid in the neighborhood, introduced a newer version of tag to us that evened the playing field and limited the effects of the slow versus fast kids. This game was called king's base. In this game, each person had a home base. As a person left their base, they became objects to be captured. The last person off their base had the power to capture any of the others. If you were chasing someone who had left their base, you had to watch out for someone else leaving their base after you did, and thus nullifying your power. You also had to make sure that as you were chasing someone, attempting to capture them, you didn't chase them back to their own base and allow them to touch and then proceed to chase you. Sometimes, the game would stop with an argument taking place as to who was the last one off their base (if three or four of us were out running around and retouching our bases, it could become quite confusing). Vicki wasn't satisfied and stopped the game, "I captured you, Ronnie!" I didn't agree, "No, you didn't. I touched my base last. I captured you!" Timmy saw things totally differently and said, "I was wast off my base. I captuhed both of you." "Yeah," Kathy added to the dispute.

Once someone was captured, they were on your team, and they would help you capture the other players. The winner would be the one that captured all of the other players. I enjoyed the role of decoy, leaving my base, taunting the others, trying to entice them into chasing me so that they would be far off their base and could be caught by someone else on my team. What a blast!

Some games were seemingly great, but didn't last much longer than the first time played. One of those games was crack the whip. In this game, kids would line up hand in hand and the one at the head would begin to run, with the remaining kids following close behind. As the "whip" began to serpentine through yard after yard, the speed would increase. Due to centrifugal force, the person at the end of the whip ran the greatest risk of being dislodged from the rest of the group, dragged across the ground if still hanging on.

One particular time we played this game, the first and last, Kathy happened to be at the tail end of the whip. The speed escalated, and the next thing I remember, Kathy was flying through the air heading toward the Z house, luckily landing in the hedge in front of the garage wall. I approached the bushes and timidly asked her, "Kathy, are you okay? Are you hurt?" With leaves in her hair and scratches all over her face and slightly upset she cried, "I'm telling. Waaaahhh!" As I picked twigs out of her hair, I tried to console her and at the same time avoid future punishment with, "No. Don't tell. Don't tell. You'll be okay." Her unwavering, obstinate response was, "I'm telling."

I proceeded to the tree in the front yard to pull my switch and face the inevitable whipping. Meanwhile, the game of crack the whip came to an immediate and sudden halt.

Another game that didn't last very long was a game we called bulldog. In Britain, it is called British bulldog, and it was eventually banned there due to the rough nature of the game. One or two kids would stand in the middle of the playing area, a front yard would do, and the remaining kids would line up on one side of the yard. The kids lined up on one end of the yard would try to run to the other side of the yard without being caught by the "bulldog" in the center of the yard. Of course, the kid in the middle would try to tackle the kids running by. The object was to be the last one caught. I really liked the physical nature of this game, but that is what eventually ended it. I suffered a nice gash to my knee with other kids experiencing numerous abrasions as well. Moms throughout the neighborhood didn't like it, not only because of the injuries, but the torn-up clothes became rather costly to replace. It was fun while it lasted.

Hopscotch and jump rope were both games most often associated with girls, but I enjoyed and excelled at them both. Hopscotch required not only physical strength and agility, but hand-eye coordination as well. You could play it alone or with a number of competitors. As competitors were added, the game became more challenging. You had to toss your rock within a numbered square, and if the rock hit any of the outside edge of the square, you had to start again. Once the rocks were in place on a numbered square, you had to hop on one foot through ten squares, hopping over any squares that were occupied by a rock, and once to number ten, turn around and go back through the course, picking up your rock while on one foot and hopping out the other end, making sure not to touch any of the borders of the squares with your foot. Sometimes, you had to hop over three or four squares at a time on one foot. That's where the athleticism came in and the part of the game I liked best.

Jump rope also required athleticism and coordination, and if done properly was really good exercise. My buddies and I had a tendency to turn this game from jump rope to something that more closely resembled the high jump. The girls didn't put up with that for very long, and we were eventually ejected from the game.

When the weather became bad enough (the weather had to be really bad, as in another chapter, I told of the heavy rain soaked day that we played in the gutters all day) to keep us indoors, one game I particularly loved was what we called baseball with baseball cards. I mentioned in another chapter my passion of collecting baseball cards, and I realized that they could have multiple purposes. I had enough cards that I could put an entire unit of many teams on the field. So for the Cubs, I had Santo, Williams, Beckert, Hundley, Banks, Kessinger, Browne, and Phillips as well as Jenkins on the mound. If I was short a player on a particular team, I had plenty of cards to fill in the gaps. I laid out the players in the shape of a baseball diamond with certain elements in the room making up the outfield wall. The ball was the cap of a tube of toothpaste, and the bat was either a pencil or a green Tinkertoy piece. You would bend back the pencil and hit the toothpaste cap and send it into orbit. If the cap hit a player, it was an out. If you were on defense, you could assist your team in the field, and if you caught the cap in the air, it was also an out. Because the toothpaste cap could be launched twenty feet in the air, the game quickly became more of a home run derby than a true baseball game.

Late one fall, when I turned seven years of age, I was a member of the Cub Scouts and enjoyed my time doing the Cub Scout handshake and Webelos as well as Dens and Packs (one field trip, we went to a Hollywood movie set where they filmed the Tarzan movies). It was all fun, but when spring rolled around,

Dad approached me and said, "Ronnie, they're having baseball tryouts down at the park on Saturday. If you want, I can take you to the tryouts, but in order to play baseball, you have to give up Cub Scouts. You can't do both. You think about it and let me know your decision."

Dad should have known better than to ask. It took me no longer than the time it took for the words to go from Dad's mouth to my ears to decide. "Baseball!" Baseball became my favorite sport. I loved everything about it. I loved the feel and smell of the grass, the smell of the baseball glove (while in the field I would chew on the leather strings that held the glove together), the warm air, and sunshine, everything about it.

Dad bought my first glove at a swap meet, and although it was old and bulky (it really didn't look like a modern baseball glove, more like the ones used at the turn of the century. It was probably worth more than the twenty-five cents Dad paid for it since it was an antique), it served my purpose. With Dad's coaching, I became a pretty good ballplayer. My second year in the league I became an all-star. I was a good pitcher and an even better hitter.

At one point during the season, one of the other player's mothers caught me between innings and said that she would give me a dollar if I would hit a home run. I told her I would try. My next at bat, bam! I hit a home run (reminiscent of Babe Ruth's called shot in Chicago during the 1932 World Series, although on a much smaller stage). I collected my dollar at the concession stand in the way of food and candy. Not only did I have my baseball cards, but Dad and I listened to Koufax and Drysdale on the radio every weekend and I played baseball for many years to come.

In the neighborhood, we didn't have much room to play baseball, but with a tennis ball (we couldn't use a real baseball, too many car and house windows to damage) and bases made of old, wet newspapers, we set up a decent game in the street. Things were progressing pretty well until we all got tired of running into backyards looking for a foul ball or home run. We decided to improvise with a game that we could play in the street.

The new game was called "over the line" and worked well even without a typical diamond. We used a normal baseball bat, a tennis ball, and in the field, only hands were allowed, no gloves. If the ball was hit over a designated line without being caught, it was a hit, but if it was hit out of bounds (the gutters on both sides of the street), it was an out. A swing and a miss was also an out.

One day, we were playing over the line, and the bat rolled into the wet gutter, and even though we wiped off the handle of the bat with our shirts, it was still wet and slick. I was up at bat and swung at a pitch so hard (if I would have made contact, the ball would have ended up in the next neighborhood) that the slick bat flew out of my hands and toward the on deck/bench area and hit Matt P. in the head. I had that sinking feeling in the pit of my stomach, similar to when I killed the baby pigeon. Thankfully, he wasn't hurt too bad, but the game was put on hold until the furor died down, a couple of weeks later.

We played with many things as varied as boxes and toilet paper rolls. We also played with some really unconventional things, including vinegar and baking soda (someone in the neighborhood said it might be fun to play with these two ingredients). I told Timmy, "Go ask Mommy if we can have some vinegar. Don't tell her why." Timmy obediently asked Mom, "Mommy, can we have some vinegah?" Mom, always curious, asked him, "Why do you want vinegar?" "To pway with," was Timmy's vague and generic response.

And so it went. We got the vinegar, then the baking soda, and then the used pill bottle. Mom was pretty easy when it came to letting us play without much supervision or intervention.

You might ask, "How do you play with vinegar and baking soda?" With three ingredients: an empty pill bottle, two teaspoons of vinegar, and a portion of baking soda, you can create a rocket-like object. Here's how:

- Remove the lid from the empty pill bottle, then pack it tightly with baking soda.
- Add into the pill bottle about two teaspoons of vinegar.
- Carefully and quickly place the lid onto the bottle and snap it closed.
- Turn the pill bottle upside-down, place it on the ground, and stand back.

The four of us squatted like baseball catchers in a circle on the sidewalk, with the three ingredients in the center. (Kathy was a few feet outside the circle. Either she was apprehensive or smarter than the rest of us.) As I poured the vinegar in with the baking soda and clamped on the plastic lid, we all scattered and got as far away from ground zero as we could. The combination of the two ingredients created a pressure buildup as carbon dioxide gas was produced and the bottle shot into the air about twenty feet. We danced around in complete exhilaration and joy. We did it again and again. We had the imagination to take science and make a game out of it.

I always fancied myself a cowboy, a man of the west, rugged, tough, a type of John Wayne. When I was a kid growing up, westerns were pretty much in vogue. From the big screen to the small, from *The Hallelujah Trail* and *How the West Was Won* to *Bonanza* and *The Rifleman*. When we played games, almost always outdoors, it was often either "army" (it was the most fun to mimic the machine gun: "da, da, da, da, da, da," etc.) or "cowboys and Indians," my personal favorite.

When playing cowboys and Indians, our index fingers served as our guns. The sound most often used was a resounding "Pow!" The great thing about the index finger was that it never ran out of bullets. You could "pow, pow, pow" over and over and not even have to worry about counting to six and reloading. I don't remember pretending to shoot a bow and arrow; the index finger certainly wouldn't do, so the Indians must have had guns also. There were rules that went along with this game. Rules were important for a couple of reasons: games have rules, so whatever game we played had to have them too, and without rules, what would we argue about during the games? So we would be hiding behind a bush and the enemy would be sneaking around the corner and "pow, pow, pow." Kids running in all directions, index fingers pointed, conceivably at the target, and then the arguments would start. "Pow, pow, pow!" I pointed my finger and shouted. Timmy fired back, "Pow, pow, pow!" "I got you, you have to fall down," I said. "No you didn't," was Timmy's response. I argued back, "Yes I did. I got you on the arm." Timmy was indignant and shot back, "I got you fuhst. I shot you in the weg." I got technical on my little brother and admitted to being hit, "You only nicked me."

Now this type of dialogue could go on for quite some time and usually lasted longer than the actual battles.

The rules were pretty clear: if you got shot, you had to lie down on the ground and count to ten. Pretty simple? Here's where it got tricky: how did either one know if they were shot, what with the imaginary bullets and finger guns? Another great thing about this game was that no one ever died! You could be shot a thousand times and bounce back up to fight another day.

It must have been a kid frustrated with the idea of pointing his finger and shouting pow! pow! pow! over and over that decided to invent the cap gun. When the cap gun came into the neighborhood, it changed everything, at least for a while. The cap gun was a really genius idea. You opened up the side of the gun and inserted a roll of caps. Then you would thread the caps onto a spool (this took a bit of time, so the shooting and killing had to be put on hold until you reloaded), which would feed forward into the firing mechanism as you pulled the trigger. Conceptually, each time the trigger was pulled, the hammer would come down on the powder part of the cap and a distinct pop! sound could be heard. So instead of a group of kids running around in circles, pointing their fingers at each other, and yelling "pow, pow, pow," you would now have a group of kids running around in circles, pointing their realistic-looking cap guns at each other, pulling the trigger, and hearing a pop, pop, pop sound. Saved on the vocal chords.

There turned out to be a minor problem with the cap guns. As many times as you would pull the trigger and hear the pop sound, you would also pull the trigger and hear the dud sound. Not only that, the caps would get all jammed up inside the gun which required a lot of time to unravel and refeed into the gun. There ended up being a lot of time-outs in the middle of the battles. That got to be pretty frustrating. It was hard to convince the enemy that he'd been shot when there hadn't been any sound to go along with your trigger pull. I said to an enemy combatant, after obviously hitting him, "I shot you just now; you have to fall down and count to ten." "You did not. I didn't hear a single sound coming from your gun." He was right, but I had to respond, "I did too shoot you. Just because the cap was a dud doesn't mean you weren't shot."

We soon realized that we were better off with the fingers and pow, pow, pow. We put the caps from our guns to good use anyway. We found that if we took the caps out of the gun and strung the spool out on the sidewalk, we could take a hammer and whack each individual cap and get the pop sound that we were looking for. The success rate was much higher. Another use for the caps, other than those previously mentioned, was using your thumb to explode them. We found that if you had decent-length fingernails, you could set off the caps that way. Your thumb and finger would turn black and there was a little burning sensation, but the effect was worth the pain.

We had horses too. I know it sounds hard to believe, but if you can have fingers for guns, then horses aren't much of a stretch. One way to ride a horse was to get a broom, put it between your legs, grab the head of the broom, and start skipping around the yard. If you didn't have a broom or stick, you just held your hand out like you were holding the reins and started skipping around the yard. It sure seemed like riding a horse. Oftentimes, your free hand would be swatting the horse's rump to get it fired up into a gallop. It was fun times for all. Kathy, always being left behind, wondered aloud, "Why is my hohse sloweh than evewyone else's?"

One time the four of us, in order to authenticate the western experience, decided that we would cook out over an open fire (remember, we lived in the suburbs of LA). On this rare occasion, I brought up the idea and proposed to the rest of the group, "I think we should have a campfire, like the cowboys do." Vicki, the skeptic, argued, "We can't have a fire in the backyard, Daddy would kill us." "What about the Cave?" Timmy brilliantly asked. Vicki, mulling it over said, "Yeah, the Cave would work." "Great idea," I agreed. Kathy too saw the genius behind the idea and offered, "Okay."

The Cave wasn't what you might imagine it to be. Basically, it was the space between two houses on the other side of the block (we didn't know who lived there, but it was *our* place). It was probably three feet wide and twenty feet long with tall walls on both sides. For the western theme, it was probably more like a canyon, but we called it the Cave. There was dirt on the ground, including leaves that had blown in from season to season that crunched under our feet. We discovered something really neat about the Cave: when you reached out and touched both walls at the same time, there was a current that ran through your body. Neat! Of course, we didn't know where this current came from, but we would challenge each other to touch the walls and would giggle and laugh the whole time. This leads to a couple of obvious questions: were these two houses really secret government hideaways for radioactive materials? And the most obvious question: why, after the first kid noticed electrical currents or radioactive materials running from house to house through their body, did the other three kids then do the same thing? Obvious answer: we weren't too bright!

So we had the place picked out for our campfire, but what to cook? Cowboys had buffalo, steers, deer, and antelope, with a few beans sprinkled in for later effects. We had baloney! Barbecued baloney, what a connoisseur's delight! Timmy ran to get the matches, Vicki ran to get the baloney, and Kathy stayed by me and said, "Okay."

Now you might be wondering where Mom was in all of these adventures. I'm not sure where she was, home probably, and I'm sure she didn't know exactly where we were either. So we got the campfire going and the baloney cooking (the aroma emanating from the well-done baloney was reminiscent of some finer cuts of meat, such as hot dogs and Spam) and the leaves caught fire and smoke began to roll out of the Cave, and I'm sure some neighbor saw the smoke and called the fire department. We ran! Somehow, after the fire was tended to, the authorities ended up at our house. How in the world they traced all of this back to us, I'll never know (a little early in the forensic science discipline). I'm not sure of the punishment, but it may have been one of the "go get a switch off of the tree and bring it back to me" whippings. A switch doesn't look all that daunting as far as a parental weapon of choice, but when that thin branch comes whistling across your bare legs, it sure does sting.

Our cowboy activities weren't restricted to the outdoors. In all good western movies, your typical cowboy would frequently visit the local watering hole, step up to the bar, and ask for a shot of whiskey (red eye in some movies), and then proceed to knock it back in one fell swoop, wipe his mouth with his sleeve, and then either have another, look for a saloon girl, or in many instances look for a fight, which would then lead to a barroom brawl. We liked both of these, so we too enjoyed a little red eye and the occasional barroom brawl.

In the refrigerator, Mom always had a bottle of brown vinegar. We would get a couple of shot glasses out of the cabinet and pour in a full swallow of brown vinegar. Just like the cowboys in the movies, we would knock it back all at once and wipe our mouths with our sleeves. One difference was the look on our faces. When we swallowed the vinegar, our faces would pucker up and our voices would change; in some ways not really different than the movie cowboy, at least the tinhorn variety.

The barroom brawls took place in the girls' room (their bed was bigger and softer than the boys). We would pair up and one person would take a swing at the other, and at just the right time, the person being swung at would jerk their head back and flop out on the bed. Sometimes, we would have two or three fighting at the same time, like a real barroom brawl. Kids swinging, heads jerking back, bodies flopping on the bed. Much fun! This went along for a time until, "Kathy, I will swing at you and as my fist closes in on your face, you jerk your head back and flop on the bed. You've seen us do it, it's easy. Do you understand?" She seemed agreeable and bought in when she replied, "Okay."

I reached back to take a swing, and I'm guessing that even though Kathy said, "Okay," she didn't really understand how the whole thing was supposed to work. As my fist approached her face, the part about jerking your head back didn't happen and smack! "Waaah!" "Uh-oh!" "Kathy, Kathy, don't cry! I'm sorry. I'm sorry." "Waaahhh!" was all she said, but that was enough. She finally stopped crying and the tears were almost dry when Mom walked into the room and asked, "What's going on in here?" She started the crying back up again, "Waaaahhhh!" I was resigned to my fate and muttered, "I guess I'll go out and get another switch. Mommy, do you have a preference?"

Mom would often send us to our rooms to either take a nap and/or as punishment. To emphasize her point, she would lock us in the room. Our door was equipped with a hook-and-eye latch, which wasn't really much of a deterrent to us getting out (remember, it wasn't a stretch for us to sneak out the window), but made Mom feel in control. She assumed that we were either napping or suffering in our punishment. Not hardly. I wasn't interested in taking a nap and from inside the locked door asked, "Mommy, do we have any kite string, and can we have it in here?" Mom suspiciously answered, "Yes, we do, but what do you want it for?" "To play with," was my pat answer. "Well, you can have it, but you're not in your room to play." Mom was a master at stating the obvious.

That's what she thought. We had just been out in the yard, examining a spiderweb and its occupant when we were called into the house. Why not create a spiderweb of our own in the bedroom? Thus the kite string and a large spool to boot (our kite flying didn't last long in the neighborhood: too many trees and power lines. A lot of string, not much in the way of kites).

So we began weaving our web, from doorknob to bedpost to bookshelf to light fixture. Back and forth across the room, the web was taking shape. It became so thick that the only way to navigate across the room was on our hands and knees. Mom finally unlatched the door and began to enter as I yelled, "Don't open the door! The bookshelf is tearing out of the wall and the lamp is sliding across the roll top desk." When Mom realized what we'd done to the room she giggled and asked, "What have you kids done?"

Nothing fazed Mom, definitely not our creative ways of playing. Well, there was one incident that fazed Mom, and it involved me, movie blood, my bicycle, and some of the neighborhood kids.

One of the neighbor kids across the street gathered all of us around and showed us something that none of us had ever seen:

movie blood! This fake blood came in tubes, and after quite a bit of discussion, we still hadn't decided what we could do with this blood. Then somebody came up with a plan. Mark suggested to the group, "Why don't we pretend that one of us is hurt, put blood all over us, and go get somebody's mom?" Ronnie across the street wasn't volunteering, "My mom's at work." Even though Mark had come up with the suggestion, he too had an excuse, "My mom went to the store." Mark P. had an even weaker excuse, "My mom is drying her hair." It was up to me and I said, "Hey, my mom's home. She's not doing anything. I'll do it."

As mentioned before and quite obvious to most, my decision-making skills were questionable at best, and this instance was no exception. The execution of the plan went like this. I lay down on the grass, halfway in the street and straddling the gutter, with my bike lying on top of me. The other boys took the fake blood and applied it to my face and my shirt, layering it on pretty thick. Then, after arguing about who would go tell Mom that her son had been hit by a car, one of the boys ran to the house and spun the tale. It's a blur to this day as to Mom's reaction. Here is how I anticipated it to be (my anticipatory skills were quite limited in that I had trouble thinking past the next five seconds): Mom, running breathlessly to my prone body, tears on her cheeks and fear in her eyes, "Oh, Ronnie!" Are you hurt? My poor, dear, sweet, beloved son. Somebody call an ambulance!" All the while Mom's tears would be dripping down onto my lifeless body, her soft tender hands stroking my hair while holding my head in her lap.

Here's how it really happened:

Mom came quickly running out the front door and as she approached me she realized the hoax that was being perpetrated, and as flames shot forth from her eyes said, "Ronnie, you go to your room immediately! Don't bother pulling a switch from the tree, I'll take care of that. Now get!"

What had happened? How did she catch on so quickly? Maybe it was the fact that I kept looking up toward the house while I was supposed to be unconscious. Or maybe it was the fact that all the other boys were standing around my "lifeless" body, grinning and giggling. Whatever the reason, only in my imagination did I ever try to pull that "woe is me" act again (anytime I was upset with Mom or Dad, I imagined myself deathly ill or injured and how heartbroken they would be at the thought of losing me. I would show them). Just like a possum, I even played dead.

SKATEBOARDS, BICYCLES, AND OTHER MODES OF TRANSPORTATION

The modern-day skater dudes might think that they've invented a new sport with the X Games and all that goes along with them. However, back when I was a kid in the early and mid-1960s, skateboards were a staple of the neighborhood, and it wouldn't be abnormal to see two or three going up and down the sidewalk at the same time. I do have to admit, the new, modern skateboards are as superior in comparison to ours as the auto is to the horse and buggy. The tricks that are done today couldn't have been done back then, due mainly to the fact that the equipment is totally different, even though the basic design is the same.

The skateboard design is basically a board on two sets of wheels. That's about as far as the comparison goes. Our board looked like a typical 1" × 4" piece of pine wood and was generally about 24" in length. Underneath the board were two sets of wheels made of steel and ball bearings that were mounted to the wood with basic wood screws. When these wonders of modern technology went down the sidewalk, at each crack, there was a tremendous bump that shocked the system and often resulted in a tongue that was nearly bitten in two at each thump, thump. I believe that riding skateboards may have contributed to my knee problems today. We did tricks on ours too, such as popping wheelies and spinning around. Not a lot of jumping though. No ramps to do a 900 (a 2.5 revolution aerial spin performed on a skateboard ramp), although I do believe on a few occasions we did 2.5 revolution aerial spins, just not planned. No ollies, kickflips, or varials either. In fact, our skateboard wasn't used for tricks at all, more as transportation from point A to point B. It made the mundane task of going to a friend's house a little more interesting.

To liven things up a bit, we came up with the brilliant idea of mounting the skateboard with a plain cardboard box, and in some cases, an actual wooden crate. By doing this, we turned a simple skateboard into a car of sorts, a convertible sports car to be exact. One key ingredient needed to make this work was someone to push you around in your new sports car since the skateboard didn't have pedals or a motor (because the boxes weren't secured to the skateboard, you had to be very delicate in your pushing technique). So who would push me up and down the sidewalk? I approached little sister and gingerly asked her, "Hey Kathy, how would you like to have some fun pushing me up and down the sidewalk in my new car?" I asked gingerly because I anticipated her "No" answer. I begged her, "Pleeeease? I'll push you next." Surprisingly she agreed, "Okay." No bribe this time. My candy and baseball card collection were safe.

In order to make the sidewalk realistic and more like a road, we came up with some pretty neat ideas. Sidewalk chalk wasn't invented yet, but plain old chalk worked just as well (the neighborhood parents didn't like it very much because the chalk didn't wash off the sidewalks and driveways and probably this frustration led one of them to invent sidewalk chalk). On the sidewalks we would draw arrows, directing us to go straight, go left, go right, do a U-turn, stop, and various other traffic signs and signals. These directions would go on the length of the block, up and down each driveway, and once we got to the end of the block the arrows and signs would repeat themselves all the way back to where we had started. The amount of chalk on the sidewalks and driveways was amazing. From an outsider's point of view, all of the arrows and drawings didn't make much sense, but to us, it was according to design (if an aerial shot was taken, there would be some talk of aliens leaving behind cryptic messages on the sidewalks). We even took detours and went "off roading," which made it a little more bumpy and much harder to push (through the grass and dirt and bushes, a bit of a woodsy feel). It was all quite fun until you went from riding to pushing. I believe that pushing that skateboard and sister up and down the sidewalk for hours on end is partially responsible for my back problems today. When you were the one being pushed, the pushee, you had total authority over the pusher. "Tuhn left, back up, slow down, tuhn wight, now stop." Kathy seemed to enjoy her newfound authority. I didn't as I moaned, "Oh, my back!"

After a time, the box on the skateboard game became tiring and we had to spice things up a bit. The skateboard soon morphed into the scooter. Same design as the skateboard with another 1" × 4" board nailed to the front with an additional brace to keep it in place, and across the top, a smaller board nailed on for handle bars. The scooter was more exciting than the skateboard and allowed for passengers. The bumps were the same, however, and I can understand why the skateboards of that day didn't lead to X- Games, the steel wheels were murder on the body (besides, if we were to fly through the air with our units, once returning to earth the thing would blow apart, wheels falling off and rolling down the sidewalk, boards splitting, etc.).

We also had roller skates, similar in design to roller blades, but only in design. They too had steel wheels, but with a twist. The skates of that era were not designed like a shoe or boot on wheels, where you would slip your foot into the boot and lace them up and skate down the road. Our skates were made of steel and had little grips on each side on the front and back of the skate with a flat surface. You would step on the flat steel platform, and then with your key, you would tighten these side grips (like a vice) until your shoe was snugly gripped. Sometimes, you would see a skate lying in someone's front yard with a tennis shoe still tightly gripped on the skate, due to the key being lost and the kid having to exit quickly.

They were a far distant cousin to the roller blade. If the roller blade is capable of going twenty miles per hour, the old skate would allow you to crank it up to six or seven miles per hour, which was slower than running and probably led to the old steel skate being phased out. It was pretty embarrassing to be skating along one hundred yards behind your friends, who were without skates, and if someone called you a name while you were skating, you couldn't catch up to them to pound them into submission, and it took too long to get them off your shoes.

After skates and skateboards came cars; not adult cars, little kid cars. One Christmas, I got a police car. The outside of the car was painted black and white and looked just like a real police car. Inside was a seat and steering wheel with pedals to move the car forward and backward. This car was much fun and was a definite step-up to the box on the skateboard that we had been using. There were a couple of issues with the car: lack of speed (other kids would taunt you and run away and you were stuck inside the car going slower than an old man with a cane: one time a snail passed me). The other issue: the older we got, the longer our legs, and it soon became impossible to pedal the car, with knees up to your chin and wrapped around the steering wheel. The car was soon parked alongside the house, abandoned, and eventually eaten by rust (kind of like real cars down in the Ozark Mountains). We had a tricycle too, but it too was outgrown and had similar drawbacks to the police car. While we had skateboards, scooters, and tricycles, the neighbor kids had bicycles.

Dad, being the good dad that he was, realized that we were coming up short in the neighborhood in the transportation department. He couldn't just give us bikes, so he came up with a plan. Gathering us around him Dad said, "Kids, how would you like to earn some money so that you can each buy your own bicycle?" Excitedly, we replied in unison, "Yay! What do we have to do?" "Well, I will pay each of you thirty-five cents per week to do some chores around the house. Boys, you can take out the trash and help mow the lawn. Girls, you can help do the dishes and fold the laundry. All of you can make your beds every day." Now those expectations seemed reasonable. Timmy, thinking ahead to the end prize, asked, "How wong wiwh it take untiwh we can buy ouh bikes?" "It shouldn't take long at all (either he hadn't done the math or he was just being kind, but at thirty-five cents per week it would take us two years to earn enough money to pay for the bicycles). I'll keep track of how much you've earned and let you know when you have enough money saved."

Every day, every week, we would ask Dad if we had enough money. One day, it couldn't have been more than a few months since the allowance started, Dad took us all to the store and bought four brand-new bicycles (he must have tired of all the asking and nagging). Timmy and I got identical, bright red, shiny new bicycles. Vicki got a big blue, shiny girl's bike (girl's bikes didn't have a bar running from the seat to the handlebars, whereas the boys bikes did, which didn't make much sense to me since that bar could really do some damage to the boys if their feet slipped off the pedals). Kathy's bike was a bit smaller than all of ours and had training wheels. Timmy and I were not tall enough to touch the ground while sitting on our bikes, so it was crucial that we learned to ride immediately.

Dad had a unique way of teaching us how to ride our new bikes. He would pick us up, set us on the bike, and with one hand on the handlebar and the other on the seat, proceed to push us at a high rate of speed down the sidewalk. He would then let go (now here's where it got tricky). I had an advantage over my brother in that I had borrowed (stolen in some circles, borrowed in others) the next-door neighbor girl's bike out of her garage and learned how to ride her bike prior to graduating up to the next level. It's much easier to learn on a smaller girl's bike than on the ones that we got new. After letting go, Dad shouted words of encouragement to us. Once we were flying down the sidewalk at a high rate of speed, Dad shouted behind us, "Don't crash the bike, son. Steer it straight. Keep pedaling. Watch where you're going." All helpful advice. Meanwhile my return answer, barely audible due to the distance and wind in my face, was "Aaaahhhh!"

There was one thing Dad forgot to teach me prior to propelling me down the sidewalk at a high rate of speed: how to stop the bike. In lieu of braking the bicycle as designed, I found out that running into a tree worked almost as well. Timmy didn't fare any better than I did, even after he had the opportunity to watch my disaster first-hand. He didn't hit a tree; his fate was the family station wagon. I only had to hit the tree once to come up with a different plan. From that day forward until the day that I could touch the ground, the preferred method of stopping the bicycle was to dismount in full flight, basically jumping off the bike while it was still moving. The neighbors, seeing a bicycle rolling across the yard unmanned had to be a little curious. "Hey honey, come out here and see this bicycle. It's going down the street without a rider." The neighbor man called to his wife. Rather than coming to look, being aware of the unmanned bicycle phenomenon, she replied, "Dear, if it belongs to one of the Bay kids, I'm not surprised. I've seen their bikes go from the street, into the garage, and come to rest alongside the garage wall, all while the kids are already in the backyard playing baseball."

Once we learned to ride and stop our bikes, it wasn't long until we were doing tricks on them. We learned to ride, standing on the seat, lying down on the seat, riding side saddle (like the Indians we'd seen in the movies), jumping back and forth over the seat while holding the handle bars, and jumping off ramps we'd made. It became quite a spectacle, which led to the big event: the neighborhood parade.

The boys lined up at the end of the street with their bicycles, while the little kids, Kathy and friends, sat one by one on the curb, feet in the gutter, waiting patiently for the parade to begin. The boys then came down the street, one at a time, doing the aforementioned tricks, while the little ones clapped and cheered. It was all quite fun and the cheering and clapping created an atmosphere that felt like a real parade indeed. The cheers inspired a little showing off which in turn led to more cheers. Only when one of the tricks ended in skinned knees, elbows, and a few tears did the parade come to an end, and the little ones shuffled off to their houses, the excitement still fresh in their minds.

We weren't satisfied with our bicycles after a while. They didn't make any noise, and noise is a prerequisite in any child's play life. One of the older neighbor kids showed us how to rev up the noise on our bikes. All that was required were some clothespins and playing cards. Mom had the clothespins, Dad had the cards, not that we asked them, just that they had them. Vicki instructed Timmy what to do, "Timmy, go get some clothespins off the clothes-line in the backyard." Timmy, needing a little more information, asked "How come?" "Just go, or I'll beat you up!" "Okay, I'uh go, but if you beat me up, I'm tewhing." Vicki wasn't moved. "Go get the deck of cards out of the drawer in the kitchen," I directed Kathy. She was unusually acquiescent and replied, "Okay."

Once we had the deck of cards and the clothespins, we wrapped the card around the bars on the sides of the wheels, the yoke, and attached them to the bars with the clothespins. This left the card sticking about halfway through the spokes. When the cards were in place and the bicycle wheels turned, the sound of the spoke hitting the card was glorious, and when you duplicated that sound with numerous cards, it was truly awe-inspiring. It didn't really sound like a motorcycle, but it was a great sound any way (it sounded a little like playing cards in the spokes of a bike). Like all good things, the joy didn't last all that long. After a while, the clothespins would turn sideways due to the continued beating and the cards would no longer be in the spokes and the sound would stop. You then had to stop the bicycle, adjust the clothespins and cards, and then start all over again. The other drawback to this great fun was the reaction from Mom and Dad when they realized that certain things were missing from the house. Dad, looking through the kitchen drawers, asked Mom, "Honey, have you seen the deck of cards? The Pike's are coming over tonight for a game of canasta." Mom, in the meantime, was looking for something else and answered him, "I haven't seen the cards, but I'll help you look as soon as I find my clothespins. I thought for sure that I had plenty of them on the line out back, but I just went out there and they're gone." They both came to the realization at the same time and shouted, "Kids! Do any of you know where the deck of cards or the clothespins might have disappeared to?" I responded first, "I don't know," with additional, "I don't know's" being heard in succession. Kathy played dumb and said, "What pins?" while Timmy the squealer blamed his sister, "Vicki made me."

One of the neighbors thought they would "one up" us on the cards/clothespins, when they mounted a "Vrooom" on the side of their bike. Vrooom wasn't the sound as much as it was the name of the plastic, battery-operated sound machine that was supposed to imitate the sound of a motorcycle. It didn't, and it didn't last long. Not only was it an issue with batteries, but the other kids were merciless in their teasing and the Vrooom was soon found in the "ash heap of history."

My best friend Russell and I would often ride our bikes around the neighborhood, sometimes venturing far outside of our block and into the next neighborhood (bicycles expanded our neighborhood exploration by several blocks). This was pretty exciting and mysterious: to go into a strange neighborhood with strange streets and strange dogs (dogs had a way of making me pedal my bike so fast that my feet couldn't stay on the pedals). Timmy, two years younger than me and three younger than Russell, often wanted to tag along.

Russell and I, being a little ornery (mean), would play a game that we aptly named "ditch 'em." The game was really quite simple and didn't have any rules. The three of us would be riding along, talking, just casually taking in the scenery, when all of a sudden, Russell or I one would yell, "Ditch 'em!" At that point, we would proceed to pedal our bikes side by side, as fast as we possibly could, with the intent of leaving poor Timmy in the dust. We knew we had accomplished our goal when we would look behind us and Timmy, with tears in his eyes and turning his bike around, would say, "I'm tewwing Daddy when I get home." This didn't seem to have much of an effect on Russell (why should he worry?), and I sure knew what that meant for me, but the exhilaration of the moment and the fact that I had to save face with Russell led me to say in return, "Go ahead and tell Daddy, you big baby. Haha." Needless to say, I didn't have the last laugh when I got home.

Bicycle riding was relatively safe (unlike today when you need a helmet, knee pads, elbow pads, rearview mirror, survival kit, fire extinguisher, jaws of life, etc.), but there were some hazards that we did encounter. I mentioned earlier that we saved our allowance for two years (well, that was what we were told it would require), which totaled around $30 for our bikes. Needless to say, they weren't Schwinn's, but a lower echelon bike bought at the dime store, which probably led to some of the hazards we had to deal with. I am not mechanically oriented at all, but I did learn a few mechanics with my bike. We had an ongoing issue with the chain coming off the bike while we were pedaling down the road (the worst timing of all happened when a dog was chasing you and the chain came off; it's amazing how fast a kid could run while pushing a bicycle!). All of a sudden, right in the middle of a pedal thrust, the sprocket would spin around, causing you to bang your ankle on the chain guard, and when the chain came off, there was another little problem: no brakes! Because we'd learned to jump off our bikes while still traveling at a high rate of speed, neither of these issues were a bother.

Getting the chain back on, however, took some practice. Not only that, the chain was really greasy. To fix the chain, you had to flip the bicycle over on its back, resting on the handlebars and seat, with the two wheels sticking up in the air. You then had to put the chain on the back wheel sprocket, start the chain on the front wheel sprocket, and then slowly rotate the pedals forward. It really was easy. The bigger question was why did the chain keep coming off? We obviously weren't mechanical enough to figure out that if you loosened the two nuts on both sides of the back wheel and pushed it back as far as it could go and then tightened the nuts back, the chain would be tighter and come off at a far lesser rate than before. We thought the answer was in removing the master link (someone told us about the master link) to shorten the chain. Shortening the chain didn't work out too well.

Another hazard of riding bikes was getting your pants caught in the chain. Bell bottoms weren't the best for riding apparel, and when this happened, unlike at other times, you couldn't jump off the bike and the resulting "stop" was a bit uncomfortable. In addition to long billowy pants, we found out that you should never ride your bike barefooted (not real good on the toes).

Flat tires were also a problem to deal with and required a certain skill set to fix. Inside of the tire was the inner tube. Whenever we ran over nails, glass, sharp rocks, or other debris, the possibility of a flat tire was very real. Dad would buy an inner tube repair kit so that we could fix our bikes whenever he wasn't around. A screwdriver was used to pop the tire off the rim of the bike and then the inner tube was pulled out of the stem hole and the inside of the tire. The repair kit came in a cardboard tube that had a metal lid. The lid had a rough surface that was used to prepare the tube for the application of the patch. In the kit were rubber patches and some adhesive. To find out where the hole in the tube was located, you could do one of two things. You could blow it up with the bicycle pump and feel around the tube for a tiny air leak, or if that didn't work, you could dunk the blown-up tube into a tub of water, and when the bubbles appeared, you found your hole.

Once you located the hole, the lid of the kit was scraped on the surface of the tube around the hole (this prepared the surface for the adhesive and patch to stick better). Once the adhesive was spread around the hole, the patch was applied, and while it was drying, we would lay a heavy object (a brick or two usually worked) on top of the patch to help it stick. After waiting a while, the patch would be dry, and you had to test the tube to make sure it didn't leak. In order to get the tube back in the tire, all of the air had to be let out via the stem, the tube inserted back in the tire, and the tire forcefully squeezed back around the rim. The tire was then pumped back up, and presto, as good as new.

There were two major incidents that happened in my life involving bikes. One involved Vicki and the other a neighbor kid. One day, Vicki and I decided that we would race our bikes around the block. As we came to the first corner, we were neck and neck. I, unfortunately, had the outside lane. As I was watching Vicki and looking for an edge going around the corner, I looked up and wham, I ran into a car coming down the street. As I flew over the handlebars and the hood of the car, I landed in the neighbor's yard. The driver of the car came to a sudden stop and got out to see if I was okay. Meanwhile, the entire neighborhood came running to the corner (well, maybe it was only a handful of people). Somebody ran to get my mom. All in all, there wasn't much damage (a slight groin injury) to me, my bike (the handlebars were bent sideways, but that was easy to fix), or the lady's car. Instead of consoling me, Mom was extremely angry (I may have interrupted the afternoon showing of *Let's Make a Deal* with Monty Hall or more likely, fear was causing Mom to act out of character). She berated me the entire way home; me and the bike limping along together.

The second major incident was a much bigger deal than my encounter with the car. The neighbor kid across the street was David. David and I were not friends; in fact, we were close to mortal enemies. That day, for some reason, we decided to ride bikes together. As we got a few blocks away from home, we noticed a street cleaner going up one side of the street, then making a U-turn, and coming back down the other.

The street cleaner was a large vehicle, similar to a dump truck in size, that not only had four sets of large wheels on the back of the truck, but a large brush underneath that rotated around and around and swept up the dirt from the gutters in front of everyone's house. David came up with the bright idea to ride alongside the street cleaner, just out of the view of the driver, and hang on to the rear bumper and get a free ride. I was too scared to do it myself, but I rode along with him and watched him for a short time. I decided to turn around and go home when the street cleaner started to do a U-turn and come back up the street. David didn't let go, and as the cleaner made the turn, he was pulled under the truck and was run over by the back wheels. I raced my bike back to where he was, and as he tried to get up and walk, he fell down. I remember some blood and teeth missing and a few other frightful things (I had nightmares for weeks).

People came around from all over, the ambulance showed up, the policemen asked me questions, and it was a really traumatic experience to go through, especially for a small boy like myself. David recovered and returned to school, but was on crutches and did not return to normal for quite some time. Unfortunately, he was not a nice kid and told others that I had pushed him into the street cleaner. David will be featured in other stories in this book.

All in all, my first bike was really special. As I got older, I would have many other bicycles, a stingray with banana seat and a ten-speed racer, but my first bike was the one that I will always remember most fondly.

DOCTORS, NEEDLES, AND DEAD MEN

I like doctors. I like them when I have my recurrent kidney stones and I'm rolling all over the floor, yanking on my hair, writhing in uncontrollable pain, and they stick in the intravenous drip full of happy juices: morphine, codeine, I'm not particular. I like doctors when I have pneumonia and they prescribe an antibiotic that knocks out the inflammatory infection in my lungs. Yes, I like doctors…today. Once, I hated doctors. Maybe hated is a little strong. I was terrified of doctors is a better way to put it. Doctors were no more or less scary than the mummy, Frankenstein, or the Wolfman. The funny thing is, as a kid, I was always going to the doctor. The truth is, it wasn't the doctor I was afraid of; it was the pain or fear of pain associated with the doctor. Although doctors are supposed to alleviate pain, in my case, they caused pain more often than not. It was all of those darn shots and vaccinations. Tetanus, polio, and smallpox are some to name a few. Every time some malady visited me, it required a shot.

I remember going to the doctor on one occasion due to an injury that happened while playing with the lawn mower. Although most people wouldn't consider the lawn mower something to play with, the Bay kids considered almost anything worthy of entertainment. Dad's lawn mower was the old-fashioned, hand-reel lawn mower. It had a two-pronged handle that ran down to the two large wheels on either side. Between the two wheels were six or seven horizontal steel blades that when the mower was pushed, would rotate in a circular motion and cut the grass. Dad wasn't trying to be environmentally friendly, he just found the cheapest mower on the market, and it happened to be man-powered, not engine-powered.

So here the four of us are in the backyard, Dad at work, Mom somewhere in the house, and we get the lawn mower out of the garage and gather round. As I was examining the blade construction, I stuck my finger down into the blade cylinder, and for some reason, one of my siblings decided to give the mower a push. I was impressed with the construction and mused, "Wow, these blades are really sharp. I bet you could lose a finger in here if this mower was moving." Timmy, holding the handle, must not have heard me clearly and as he pushed the mower forward said, "Okay, I'll move the mowa." My response was one of agony and pain, "Aaaahhhh! Ow, ow, ow!"

After running around in circles, with my finger swinging wildly through the air, I stopped long enough to examine the wound and realized that stitches were a strong possibility. I also figured that a tetanus shot was also on the agenda. We were told that anytime you got a cut, you had to get a tetanus shot. What I didn't know was that tetanus had another name: lockjaw. Lockjaw! That name sent fear throughout the neighborhood kids. The legend went like this: step on a rusty nail and you would get lockjaw (it was always stepping on a rusty nail that caused it, nothing else, and what are the odds of stepping on a rusty nail?). Anyway, the legend said that if you got lockjaw, your mouth would become sealed shut, and you couldn't eat and then you would die. We were all scared that we were going to get lockjaw. This turned out to be a catch-22 situation: if you got lockjaw, you would die. If you got a tetanus shot, you wouldn't die, but the shot would hurt so bad that you wished you had. In the final analysis, I didn't get to make that choice, Mom did. Missing out on the beginning of this ordeal, Mom saw me running around the yard and asked, "Ronnie, what's the matter with you? Why are you wailing and crying and running around the yard?" Holding my finger in the other hand with blood squirting with every heartbeat, I responded breathlessly, "I cut my finger in the lawn mower!" Mom asked an odd question, "Why did you do that? (What kind of question was that and what kind of answer would suffice?) Now I have to take you to the doctor to get a tetanus shot."

See there; right out with the tetanus shot. She didn't even consider the lockjaw option. Off we went to the doctor's office. The entire trip there, all I could think of was the tetanus shot and how big the needle would be (the needle had to be a foot long if it was an inch). As the doctor came into the room (after I had sat on the table, the one with paper spread over it, for what seemed like an eternity; sweating, shaking my leg, unable to sit still), he kept the needle down by his side in an attempt to keep me from seeing it. All the while I was craning my neck, trying to see exactly how big that needle was. As he brought the needle up, I saw it and I began to say in a loud voice, "No, I don't want a shot. Please don't give me that shot!" "Now son, turn your head. This will only hurt for a few seconds." He admitted it! It was going to hurt. A few seconds? A man could fall from a hundred-story building in a few seconds. A foot-long needle sticking in my arm for a few seconds was an eternity. I began to get louder and more agitated, kicking and flailing about. "No, no, please don't! Mommy, don't let him hurt me!" The doctor called for reinforcements, "Nurse, come in here. I need help holding this patient down. And bring the other nurse with you."

All three of them couldn't hold me still. Somehow, they got the needle in my arm. After the needle incident, the stitches seemed like a breeze. I did overhear a conversation between the doctor and my mom when the ordeal was finished. "Mrs. Bay, please do not bring your son back here in the future. We will refuse to treat him." Mom was apologetic and said, "Doctor, he's really not a bad boy. He just gets a little scared of some things. Where can I take him then?" Without missing a beat the doctor replied, "The psychiatric hospital down the road has strait jackets in ample supply. Try there."

I wasn't the only one of us four to get their finger nearly chopped off in Dad's lawn mower. It happened to two of the others. Always helpful, I told the little ones, "Hey guys, you ought to stick your finger in the lawnmower blade while one of us pushes the lawnmower. You get to go to the doctor's office and get a sucker."

Timmy and Kathy, after seeing their older brother's example, decided that they too wanted to visit the doctor (he was a nice man). How they didn't learn from my example, after all they were intimately involved in the first experiment, is a question that may never get answered. Because she had smaller hands and fingers than Timmy or me, part of Kathy's finger was cut off. Mom, thinking I was involved in some way, told me, "Ronnie, run out in the yard and see if you can find the rest of Kathy's finger. We need to take it with us to the hospital." I wasn't going to take all the blame and grabbed Timmy. "You pushed the lawnmower. Help me find it."

The finger was sewn back on, and we all lived to play another day. It would be years before another lawnmower incident would occur.

It may seem strange, but the doctor's office wasn't the only place you had to watch out for needles. Sometimes, it wasn't safe in school.

You would be sitting in the classroom, minding your own business, glancing at a classmate's paper, when the school nurse would come into the classroom and whisper something to the teacher. A few minutes later, the teacher would say, "Children, thirty minutes prior to the lunch hour the entire school will be getting a smallpox vaccine. We will line up on my instruction and march down to the cafeteria, single file. Ronnie, you will walk next to me."

A smallpox vaccine? I wondered what that might be when the whispers started. Some said it was like a rabies shot (rumor had it that if you were bitten by a dog, squirrel, bat, skunk, wolf, bear, elk, rabbit, possum, or other wild animal, you would get rabies, and the only cure for rabies was to have a humongous needle inserted into your stomach twelve times). Once again, fear began to creep in, and I started to get really antsy and I couldn't stand still. We got into a single-file line, me next to the teacher, and began the journey to the cafeteria. As we approached, we noticed another line, even longer than ours, that wound its way toward the cafeteria. Great, I would have to think about that huge needle being stuck in my stomach twelve times, with each passing moment the needle increasing in size. I was close to wetting my pants when the line finally reached the cafeteria. I was told to roll up my sleeve, only I didn't see a needle. The next thing I knew a device was placed on my shoulder, I felt a sharp pain, and then it was over. That wasn't so bad. Later, the place where the device had been formed a round sore that eventually turned into a scab. I now have a round scar on my shoulder for memories sake.

When I was five years old, I had my tonsils removed. As a young child, I suffered a lot with asthma and other respiratory ailments, so the doctors thought if they removed my tonsils, it would solve these other illnesses. They were wrong. At the same time I had my tonsils removed, so did Mom. They must have had a two-for-one special on tonsillectomies. I remember being wheeled into the prep area and the nurse placing a breathing device over my nose and mouth. They were very gentle with me; they must have heard from the needle doctor that I could be a volatile patient. They asked me to count to ten backward. "Ten, nine...."

The next thing I remember was waking up in a large room lined with gurneys along one wall. As I was coming out of the anesthesia, after throwing up, I looked to my left and noticed an old man on a gurney (old being a relative term, he may have been forty). He wasn't moving. I started crying. The nurse noticed me crying and tenderly said, "Ronnie, what's wrong? Why are you crying? Do your tonsils hurt?" (How could they hurt when they had just been removed?) "That man's dead," I cried some more. The nurse, knowing the truth chuckled, "No, he's not dead. He's only sleeping. He'll be okay."

I didn't believe her. I was sure the man was dead. I cried myself back to sleep. When I awoke, I looked to my left and the man was gone. I'm convinced that while I was sleeping, the nurses rolled the dead man out of the room and buried him out behind the parking lot. And yes, I did feel a lot of pain, but the ice cream made up for that. Mom, being much older than I, had a much tougher recovery than I did.

Growing up with three siblings created an interesting phenomenon; when one of us came down with an ailment, we all did. At some point, we all had the mumps, measles, chicken pox, and pink eye. In fact, there is a family picture of the four of us, all with pink eye. We look pretty goofy in the photo, but not because of the pink eye necessarily. Contrary to the way we should have behaved (a loaded statement if I ever heard one), when we came down with these diseases, we treated it like a vacation, something to be celebrated.

One morning, as we all were waking up, we noticed that our eyes were glued shut with mucus. This caused us all to become really excited. We felt and bumped our way into Mom's room. With Mom asleep, Vicki was the first to whisper, "Hey Mommy, wake up. We can't see." "Hmm? What time is it? You kids go back to bed." Mom hadn't looked at us yet and so wasn't aware of the situation. I pushed the issue, "But Mommy, we can't see." "Yeah Mommy, ow eyes ah gwued shut!" Timmy was a little more descriptive than Vicki had been. Kathy, in her own world said, "Wheah is evweybody?"

We thought it was fun. We went to the mirror by Mom's bed and tried to pry open our eyes. After creating little slits so that we could barely see, we walked around with arms outstretched and chased each other around the house, acting like monsters.

We had the beginnings of pink eye, but we thought we had won the lottery. Measles? No problem. We compared our red splotches with each other, and again, thought it was really neat to have measles. Ditto chicken pox. It must have been the fact that we were all home from school and it seemed more like a Saturday than a school day. The neighbor kids came over to the house and knocked on the front door. After a knock on the door, Mom addressed some of the neighbor kids who had come over to play, "Hi children. The kids can't come out to play. They have the mumps." One of the neighbor kids asked, "What are the mumps?" "Well children, mumps or epidemic parotitis is a viral disease of the human species, caused by the mumps virus. It causes painful swelling in the salivary glands and may be accompanied by a fever, loss of appetite, and fatigue. So you see, the kids can't come out to play." "Oh" they said as they walked away.

The neighbor kids proceeded to go from the front porch to my bedroom window, I suppose to get a better view of this mysterious mumps thing. They banged on the window, and I opened the curtains, raised the window, and basked in the attention I was getting as I showed off my swollen salivary glands. Too bad I didn't have diseases all the time; they were great attention getters.

Not everything about the doctor visits was scary. I did enjoy the time in the waiting room, waiting for the doctor to beckon us back to his domain. All of the office areas were equipped with a special magazine for kids called *Highlights*. This magazine was especially designed for children and featured hidden pictures, puzzles, fiction and nonfiction stories, jokes and riddles, science experiments, and other interesting reading. There were two sections of the magazine that I looked forward to on every doctor's visit. The first was an ongoing story about a family named the Timbertoes. The family includes Pa, Ma, Tommy, and Mabel Timbertoes. One particular story was concerning the Timbertoes' beginnings. Pa and Ma Timbertoes were made of wood, and when they got lonely, they made Tommy and Mabel to be their children. They also made a dog, a cat, and a goat. And they lived happily ever after.

The other section that I loved even more than the Timbertoes family was the Hidden Pictures section. Within a larger picture, the artist drew in common items that blended in to the rest of the picture. The idea was to locate within the picture a hammer, baseball bat, hat, saw, thimble, teacup, etc. It was a really fun exercise and diverted my attention so that I wouldn't have to think about the foot-long needle and the shot that was coming my way.

As mentioned earlier, I grew up with asthma. For the most part, I functioned as normal (normal being a relative term here) as any other child. My mother was very concerned about my asthma, and because I had experienced a few severe bouts with it, she watched me like a hawk. I was an extremely active boy, always on the go and wanting to play, so Mom would, from time to time, stop me in the middle of a run in and out of the house to listen to my chest. She would tell me to breathe in and out as she listened for the slightest wheeze. If she heard anything, she would cancel any further play activities and make me come into the house and rest. Well, I obviously didn't like that and learned how to circumvent her little test. When she would listen to my chest and tell me to breathe in and out, I would breathe as slowly as I possibly could so that the wheeze could not be detected. It seemed to fool her most of the time, although I think she figured it out early enough, but didn't want to break my heart since I had worked so hard to deceive her.

Asthma then was treated much differently than it is now and not nearly as effectively. Pills and inhalers were not available at the time, so a warm air vaporizer was the solution.

Later, the nebulizer, a step up from the vaporizer, became available. The nebulizer was a glass tube, shaped like an L, which had two holes, one for breathing and the other for airflow. A medicine in liquid form, such as salbutamol, would be placed into the unit, and a slight squeeze on a rubber bulb attached to the end of the unit would shoot the medicine into the mouth, while at the same time, the patient would inhale the substance into the lungs. Although much better than the vaporizer, it wasn't as good as what would come next, Primatene Mist. This inhaler, with a couple of puffs, would bring instant relief to my asthma attacks. Unfortunately, for the millions of asthma sufferers throughout the country, the government very recently banned Primatene Mist under the assumption that the fluorocarbons they emitted did damage to the atmosphere, and if one million inhalers were used at the same time, the earth would spin off its axis and hurl endlessly into space. Or if one million inhalers were used at the same time, the earth's temperature would instantaneously rise by two degrees, leading Al Gore to crank down the air conditioner in his 20,000 square foot home by three degrees as an offset, the hydrofluorocarbons from the air conditioner exceeding all one million inhalers. So now, presumably, millions of asthma sufferers will still suffer and the planet will breathe as originally intended. Don't get me started!

When I did have a severe attack, I was put to bed, and Mom would turn on the vaporizer with a little Vicks VapoRub (made of camphor, eucalyptus oil, and menthol, it was a soothing mixture to make me feel better) on my chest and under my nose. At first, I didn't like this remedy, but grew to love the smell (it was like chicken soup when you didn't feel well). The vaporizer emitted a warm mist that we imagined was a thick fog. Our bunk bed became the ship, and we had to steer through the fog on our way to the pirate hideaway (on the bottom bunk with the above bunk's blanket pulled down the side, it felt like being below deck on the ship with limited sunlight). Even at my sickest, I still had to play.

It was very difficult to breathe, and it felt like a belt was tightened around my chest. Each breath was laborious. There were a couple of environmental things that exacerbated the problem: Dad smoked in the house and car, and I loved to run around in the cool night air (playing took precedence over all other considerations), which are not good for asthma. I eventually conquered the disease, either because Dad quit smoking and I no longer ran around in the cool night air or I outgrew it.

One day, I was in the backyard next door, playing with the neighbor kid, when another incident occurred similar to the "finger in the lawnmower." The kid's father had a hammock; not the kind strung between two trees, but the kind that was strung over a metal stand shaped like a gondola. As I entered the neighbor's backyard I heard David say, "Hey Ronnie, I'm going to put all of my weight on one end of this hammock and push it down to the ground. The other end will then be lifted eight feet in the air. You stand on the other end and I will slowly raise my end back up and you catch the other end as it comes back to earth." I was incredulous and responded, "So, you will slowly lift your end off the ground and I will eventually catch the other end as it returns to the ground? Did I get that right?" "Yeah," he replied. For some reason I responded, "Okay," not grasping what was about to take place.

After the end of the metal stand came crashing down on my head and after letting out a murderous wail, I began making my way next door to the only person in the world that might show me some sympathy, Mom. Meanwhile, in the midst of my misery, the siblings seemed to enjoy the entertainment. Vicki was the first to make fun of me. "Ronnie, I realize that you can't see right now, with all of the blood running down in your eyes, but you should see yourself. You're probably going to need a tetanus shot." In a taunting, rhythmic voice Timmy said, "Yuh gonna get wockjaw, yuh gonna get wockjaw. Ha, ha, ha, ha, ha, ha!" Kathy was the only one really worried about my health and asked, "Is Wonnie going to die?" Mom didn't turn out to be as sympathetic as I had hoped and sternly said, "Ronald Dean Bay, Jr., what have you done?!"

Back to the doctor's office, more Timbertoe family, and another tetanus shot. I realize the tetanus shots are only required once every ten years or so, but I think in my case, they were only making sure I didn't get lockjaw, or the doctor was paying me back for all the trouble I had caused him in the past.

I had my stomach pumped, either once or twice, I'm not quite sure. It could have been for the time I swallowed a quart of used motor oil, or it could have been the time I ate an entire box of ex-lax (ex-lax is a stimulant laxative that is guaranteed to work gently and effectively overnight or your money back and should not be taken for any purpose other than the relief of occasional constipation unless directed otherwise by a doctor) thinking it was chocolate candy. Grandma had a linen closet where she used to hide candy. I saw the box and read "chocolate flavored" and didn't bother to read any further, not that I would have understood laxatives or constipation anyway. I ate the entire box not wanting my siblings to have any. Needless to say, I did not suffer any constipation symptoms.

The motor oil incident is a little harder to explain. In the garage was a shelf that was approximately five and a half feet off the floor. On the shelf was a quart-sized coffee can. I didn't know what was in the coffee can, but was curious and I had to know. As I stretched as far as I could, my fingertips just gripped the top edge of the can and I pulled it toward the edge of the shelf to tip it back and see what was inside. As I tipped it, a black flood poured out into my face, and because of the shock, my mouth was wide open. I sputtered and choked and spit oil out of my mouth as much as I could, but the remainder made its way down the gullet and into my stomach. Motor oil has a unique flavor that I don't recommend you try. I had eaten dirt, dog food, and paste before, but never had the complications that the used oil brought on.

One night, after all of us kids had been put to bed, I noticed a light coming into our darkened room. It was Mom with a flashlight. Of course, this was a little unusual, but what came next was even more so. As Timmy and I slowly awoke to the strange glow of a flashlight, we heard Mom tell us, "Boys, I want you to take off your pajama bottoms and underwear and lie face down on your beds (like I said, a little unusual)." I was curious and asked, "Mommy, what are you doing, and why do we have to lie face down on our beds with our bottoms off?" Timmy was curious and just as concerned as I was and asked, "Why do you have that fwashwight and why ahn't you tuhning on the wight in ow woom?" "I have to check for worms," Mom replied.

Pinworms to be exact. It seems that pinworm is an intestinal infection caused by tiny parasitic worms. Pinworm infections affect millions of people each year, particularly school kids (thank goodness we weren't the only ones). People who have pinworms aren't dirty, kids can get pinworms no matter how often they take a bath (again, thank goodness we weren't any dirtier than other kids). The symptoms of pinworms are itching in the anal and vaginal areas. Mom must have recently read an article in the *Reader's Digest* titled: "Itching and Scratching in School Children May Be an Indication of Pinworms"

So Mom proceeded to check our, well let us say, private areas (all of us were subjected to this indignation) in the dark with a flashlight (when I look for worms in the night with a flashlight, it usually indicates I'm going fishing the next day). After a thorough examination, Mom didn't find any pinworms and came to the ultimate conclusion that her children were naturally itchy and scratchy (probably more a result of playing in the grass or ivy than pinworms).

I haven't gone into the normal childhood ailments such as the stomach flu (when some of us threw up, it was a major ordeal with much noise and activity, whereas others would quietly go to the restroom and wretch our guts out in private), the common cold, earaches (man, those things hurt and Mom had a remedy of sorts: she heated up some type of mineral oil and squirted a few drops in the ear and inserted a piece of cotton to keep it from running out. This didn't cure it, but like many other things Mom did, it made it feel better), cuts, bruises, and other afflictions associated with childhood. Mom was the best at being our doctor at home when the other doctor wasn't available or we were too scared to go.

You might think that I was the only one of us that had traumatic injuries, but you would be wrong. I'm not talking about the normal injuries that all kids get, stubbed toes (when you ran around barefoot like we did, stubbed toes were as common as the morning sunrise), scrapes, bruises, minor cuts, and abrasions, etc. The injuries worth writing about are a little more unusual and, in some cases, pretty bizarre. Take for example, my brother Timmy.

Timmy was a hard-headed kid in more ways than one. I mean, he must have had a hard head because he kept falling on his and was none the worse for wear. Dad built a roof over the brick patio that was made of two-by-fours and bamboo, which was woven across the two-by-fours and formed the roof. It was a nice patio. On the outside edge was a trellis that ran from the roof to the flower bed. Timmy and I decided to climb up onto the roof of the house and see if the bamboo roof of the patio was strong enough to walk across. Like Peter on the water, he made it a short distance until the bamboo began to give way and crash. Timmy fell headlong onto the brick patio (in this instance I was smart enough to let him go first). He ran into the house to find Mom, the doctor, and she applied ice to the egg-sized bump on his forehead.

Another time, and I don't know how this happened, but I was lying in bed, sound asleep, when I heard a loud thump and then a loud wail. Apparently, Timmy had fallen off the top of the bunk bed and hit his head on the corner of the roll top desk. He still has the scar on his head.

Speaking of scars, I have one right along the hairline that came about when my little brother shoved my head into the kitchen table. I didn't respond at the time, preferring to wait until just the right moment.

One afternoon in the backyard, Timmy was doing his normal pestering when I decided that I'd had enough. With the "shoving my head into the kitchen table" incident still fresh in my mind I yelled at him, "Timmy, I'm going to kill you, or at least beat you up!" Taunting me he replied, "You can't catch me. Ha, ha, ha, ha, ha!"

Timmy was right, I couldn't catch him, but as he was taunting me and running away, he failed to realize that he was headed straight for the wooden trellis on the side of the patio. Of course, I wasn't going to warn him. Bam! "Waaah!" Timmy lost his two front teeth that day. Lucky they were his baby teeth. You will notice the missing front teeth in many family pictures from that period.

Kathy wasn't immune to these major injuries. In addition to the ponytail cutting incident from David next door, David also decided to throw a large pointed rock in Kathy's direction; I assume trying to hit her with it. He was a good aim because the rock hit Kathy right in the lip, putting a hole beneath the lip that you could look through and see her teeth and gums. Kathy was apparently on David's list because she was also the one that he dragged onto the freeway, presumably to go get candy and ice cream at his Grandma's house. A likely story. If I hadn't come along to save her, no telling what the outcome would have been.

SCAREDY-CATS

(NOTHING TO FEAR BUT...)

The year was 1933 and America was in the depths of the Great Depression. As our newly elected president was contemplating what to say in his inaugural address, here is what he and the nation faced: There was a 25 percent unemployment rate leading some people to starve and many others to lose farms and homes. This was the time of the hobo riding trains across the country (giving Jimmy Rodgers and Woody Guthrie something to sing about). People from the Midwest migrated westward in the hopes of striking it rich in the land of plenty: California. Times were tough and fear was rampant and real.

Franklin Delano Roosevelt rightly sensed that Americans needed some confidence, some words of encouragement, a shot in the arm. In the midst of his address, he uttered this now famous line:

> *So first of all, let me assert my firm belief that the only thing we have to fear is fear itself.*

My comment on that comment was uttered by an even more famous president, Abraham Lincoln:

> *You can fool some of the people all of the time, and all of the people some of the time, but you cannot fool all of the people all of the time."*

With all due respect to Frankie, I have to side with Abe on this one. He may have fooled the others, but he doesn't fool me. Nothing to fear but fear? You have to be kidding me. I was afraid of everything (this list is exhaustive, but not all inclusive): needles, spankings, scary movies, doctors, dogs, lockjaw, fear itself, girls, neighborhood bullies, cows, loud noises, Dad, dying, etc. I had nightmares. I avoided going into certain places (anywhere dark to be exact). I was even known to scare myself; it didn't take much to frighten me. Of course, like me but not as severe, were my three siblings who were afraid of a few things themselves.

In school, I wasn't much of an artist, but Brad (the kid that Mom warned me to stay away from and whose own mother warned him to stay away from me) and I discovered that we could make some pretty scary drawings using crayons and lead pencil. During "quiet time" in class, we were allowed to read, draw, or daydream as long as we were quiet and not bothering the other kids (I usually missed that last part).

We came up with a design that resembled the face of a wolf combined with that of a man: a wolfman! For the eyes, we drew big round circles with a deep, dark black center. We really ground the crayon into the paper to magnify each color and its effect. From the black pupil, we had scraggly red lines for bloodshot eyes that resembled the spokes of a bicycle wheel. Again, the crayon was pressed extremely hard into the paper to create a red that almost glowed. On top of the head were ears like that of a dog. In the mouth were numerous teeth, all sharp and resembling a canine. The inside of the mouth was in black crayon and on top of the black crayon were the teeth, done in #2 pencil. When drawing over the black crayon with the lead pencil, the color was a bright glossy silver that became even more glossy the more the pencil was rubbed in (we rubbed it in to the point of almost tearing the paper). The remainder of the face was filled in with a few other colors in the brown or black family. When the portrait was completed, we were pretty pleased with ourselves and showed it to all the other kids, some of whom recoiled in horror at the sight. This was all well and good while we were in school, during daylight hours, and the portrait was set aside to take home later. That afternoon, I brought my artwork home to show Mom. "Ronnie, what is that you have there?" "It's a drawing that Brad, the kid you said I couldn't play with, and I worked on together. He has one too. Do you like it?" Mom didn't take to it like I thought she would and muttered, "It's uh, very nice. Take it to your room now and don't show it to your brother or Kathy."

I took it to my room and created some space on the bulletin board for my masterpiece. Once it was tacked up, I went about doing other things, occasionally glancing up at the hideous creature I had created. When Timmy came home, I immediately showed him my picture and he ran out of the room; I guess he was as excited about it as I was. It finally came time to go to bed, and the new picture on the wall would soon make for a sleepless night. As the night progressed and the room became darker, there was an eerie glow emanating from the wall on the other side of the room. The silver teeth! What had I done? I had created a monster literally. The picture was haunting me, and I couldn't go to sleep. I also couldn't take my eyes or mind off the picture on the wall. I finally rolled over with my back facing the wall and eventually drifted off to sleep.

I suddenly awakened as the monster with the bloodshot eyes and silver teeth was within a few feet of grabbing me. I began to cry and ask for Mom (for some reason I never asked for Dad), and the volume escalated until Mom finally awoke and came to my bedside to see what was going on. "Ronnie, what's wrong? Why are you crying?" Mom said as she sat on the edge of my bed. I cried, "My picture scared me. I had a bad dream. Boo, hoo, hoo." Mom tried to assure me, "It's just a picture. It can't hurt you. Now go back to sleep."

A few minutes later, I was crying again. Mom returned to my room and tried to console me once more. This time I insisted that I sleep in Mom and Dad's bed. Reluctantly, Mom gave in (she must have figured that letting me come into her bed was better than being awakened throughout the remainder of the night). All seemed to be going well until later that night, I wet the bed. I never slept in Mom and Dad's bed again, nightmare or no nightmare.

Even after all of the drama from that night, the next day, Timmy and I decided to draw more of these scary pictures. It was a contest to see which one of us could create the scariest monster. It was arguable who had won when the creative juices finally dried up. Timmy, as I had, created a monster that made him have nightmares (because he was a thumb-sucker and not a bed wetter, he was allowed to sleep in Mom and Dad's bed after his nightmare). He named his monster Oil Stirhurt. Somewhere, deep in Timmy's subconscious, there is a reason for that name.

Some people would refer to the four of us as "a handful" (in the same way a trek up Mount Everest would be referred to as a "good stretch of the legs"), yet Mom seemed to maintain her sanity for the most part. There were times, however, that she needed to get away from us (not to be confused with us getting away from her), a time to engage in adult conversation with regular human beings. There was one hurdle to overcome: finding someone willing to babysit us if only for a couple of hours. After numerous phone calls to potential sitters, it seemed strange that they all had "sudden emergencies" to attend to during the two hours in question. Not to be deterred, Mom came up with another plan. She decided to drop us off at the movie theater, and while we were safely in the care of the public, she would go to the beauty parlor and get her hair done. The timing couldn't have worked out better for her. The particular movie didn't matter much to Mom, and as she drove away, the three of us turned to Vicki who had all the money. "Vicki, what movie ah we going to see?" Kathy asked.

"It's a comedy called *The Nutty Professor* and stars Jerry Lewis and Stella Stevens." "Jewwy who?" Timmy wanted to know.

This movie seemed innocent enough; after all, Jerry Lewis was a comedian, so what could possibly be amiss? In *The Nutty Professor*, Lewis plays a nerdy professor who discovers a potion that when consumed, turns him into a suave, handsome, ladies man, and this allows him to pursue the girl he has a crush on, played by Stella Stevens. The movie was initially pretty boring for us kids until one particular scene.

As the professor drinks his magic potion, the music begins to turn eerie, which perks up the attention of four little kids sitting side by side in the dark theater (other than us, there weren't many people watching the matinee). Our eyes became as large as saucers when the camera panned to the professor's hand, which began to grow thick brown hair and resembled something more like that of a werewolf. This was all I needed to see, and within seconds, I was out in the lobby (I could still hear the scary music and other sounds emanating from the professor and my imagination went into overdrive). If I had stayed in the theater, I would have seen the complete transformation of the professor as he knocked over test tubes and beakers, falling to the ground and finally emerging as Buddy Love. The entire scene lasted around a minute, but I wasn't taking any chances. Out in the lobby, the young man at the concession stand asked me, "Hey kid, what are you doing out here? Are you going to buy some popcorn? Candy?" Startled out of my daydreaming I replied, "What? No, I don't have any money. Can I stay out here for a while?" "No. You have to go back in the theater. You can't stay out here."

By this time, it was all four of us out in the lobby. We huddled together and weren't going back into the theater until an usher came out and coaxed us back in. The movie was now back in the boring mode, so we stayed put for a while. When the scene switched to the laboratory and the music changed to scary, we didn't wait around for the transformation, instead moving en masse to the lobby once again. This time, we were threatened. The usher was firm when he said, "You kids get back in there, or I'll go get your mother." I flippantly replied, "Good luck if you can find her. She went to get her hair done, and we don't know where she is."

We stayed one step ahead of the usher by moving between the lobby and the bathrooms and even hiding behind the cameraman's perch. When the movie finally ended, Mom was out front to pick us up.

What most people considered a comedy, we considered a scary movie (out of only twenty-seven kids in the entire world that would be frightened while watching a comedy, four of them happened to live in the same house). *The Nutty Professor* wasn't the only movie that had that effect on us. Abbott and Costello played in a movie titled *Abbott and Costello Meet Frankenstein*. In addition to Bud and Lou, the movie starred two of the most recognizable horror movie villains of all time: Lon Chaney Jr. (the Wolfman) and Bela Lugosi (Count Dracula). With these two in the movie, it was sure to be scary. It didn't disappoint. The Frankenstein monster was included, and the trifecta was complete.

Bud and Lou were their usually funny selves, but when the monsters were on screen, I couldn't watch (this time we were in the relative safety and comfort of our own home rather than a movie theater). It was bad enough when Frankenstein was chasing Lou around (Frankenstein always walked really slowly with arms outstretched; I often wondered how he could catch anyone) or when Dracula was staring into Lou's eyes, hypnotizing him with his piercing, menacing, penetrating gaze. I was definitely on edge during these parts of the movie (it didn't help that Dad thought it was extremely enjoyable and funny to slowly creep up behind us and scare the living snot out of us whenever the movie was in the most suspenseful part), lying on the floor in such a manner that I was ready to run at a moment's notice. That moment came when the Wolfman appeared.

Lon Chaney Jr. played Bud and Lou's friend Larry Talbot. Unfortunately, he also played the Wolfman. He kept warning them to lock him in a room whenever the moon became full as he knew the transformation that would inevitably take place and didn't want to hurt either of them. In one scene, Talbot has Lou on the phone, when the music all of a sudden becomes intense and scary. Talbot begins to growl and falls down in a chair, presumably passed out. The camera focuses in on his face, and the transformation takes place as his face slowly grows thick fur, while canine teeth are seen forming in his mouth. At one point, his hand appears over the back of the chair and looks like the paw of a canine, claws, fur and all. Even though the interaction between the two of them was funny, I sure didn't see it that way. This scene had barely begun, when I was on the move. I quickly jumped up and said, "I need to go to the bathroom. I'll be back."

I could hear the music and growling sounds through the bathroom door, and I waited in there with my hands over my ears until the tone of the movie changed. Once the coast was clear, I rejoined the family in the living room. Sometimes, I could get through a scene with my fingers covering my eyes (I couldn't cover my ears and eyes at the same time, although I tried), but there were several times during that movie that I had to go to the bathroom. I must have had an overactive bladder.

In addition to comedies, there were other movies that left an impression on me and have stayed in the recesses of my subconscious to this day. Here are some of the movies and the parts that made me "duck and cover":

> *Captain Sinbad*—1963
> Starring Guy Williams, this is typical Sinbad the sailor fare.
>
> The story is very simple: Sinbad must rescue his fiancée Princess Jana from the evil wizard El Karim. Our hero gets attacked by birdmen dropping rocks on his ship before he can reach the shore, and when he does arrive on land, he is arrested and imprisoned. During his imprisonment, he has

to do battle with an invisible monster. In a resourceful bit of ingenuity, the area surrounding the monster's foot goes bright green as it takes steps toward Sinbad. Of course, he eventually escapes to find the princess and kill El Karim in the ivory tower. The way to kill El Karim is to destroy his heart, which is removed from his body and placed in a glass container (aluminum foil colored red). There's a lot of fun to be had with an array of strange creatures. Along the way, Sinbad encounters man-eating plants, giant alligators, a hydra (a multi-headed dragon), and a large fist with spikes. Sinbad saves Jana and kills El Karim by throwing his heart out of the ivory tower.

What's not to like? It was scary enough with the flying birdmen, invisible monster, man-eating plants, giant alligators, hydra, and giant fist with spikes, but the thing that really got the hairs standing up on the back of my neck was the beating heart inside the glass container. The director seemed to take much pleasure in repeatedly showing the glass container with the heart beating, pa pum, pa pum, pa pum! I couldn't watch. As in most of these movies, due to closing my eyes, I missed half of the scary parts, but that didn't stop my imagination from wreaking more havoc than the actual scene.

The Wizard of Oz—1939
Starring Judy Garland as Dorothy with Frank Morgan, Bert Lahr, Ray Bolger, Jack Haley, and Margaret Hamilton as the Wicked Witch of the West.

The story is about a girl named Dorothy who feels mistreated at home and longs to run away to find adventure. Meanwhile, she gets caught in a tornado, and when she is knocked unconscious in the storm, she drifts off into a dream world where she encounters a myriad of creatures and people (talking trees, munchkins, lions, tigers, and bears among many others) that assist or block her efforts to get back home.

You might be wondering what in the world would be scary in this movie. Need I remind you? The Wicked Witch was pretty scary (green with a long crooked nose), especially when she hurls the fireball at the Scarecrow. Or how about the talking trees that throw apples at Dorothy and her friends? Even the Wizard is scary on the giant screen, at least until Toto discovers the "man behind the curtain." However, the scariest creatures in this movie, the ones that actually made me run into another room, were the flying monkeys.

On a dark, cloudy, windy day, Dorothy and her friends were in the deep and dark woods when all of a sudden, out of the sky came a legion of flying monkeys sent by the Wicked Witch to terrorize the innocents and take Dorothy to the Witch's castle. They looked like monkeys with giant wings on their backs and flew around causing havoc at the Wicked Witch's behest. Worst of all; they had bad attitudes.

I feel it's safe to assume at this point that the aforementioned movies, *The Nutty Professor, Abbott and Costello Meet Frankenstein, Captain Sinbad,* and *The Wizard of Oz* didn't deliver the same level of fright to the average movie viewer as they did to me (I find it difficult to believe that flying monkeys and nutty professors wouldn't scare most sensible people, but I'm willing to move on at this point). The following three movies are sure to instill a level of fear in even the most hardened horror movie aficionado, and being a "fear" expert, I would know.

> *The Beast with Five Fingers*- 1946
> Starring Peter Lorre among others.
>
> Locals in an Italian village believe evil has taken over the estate of a recently deceased pianist where several murders have taken place. The alleged killer: the pianist's severed hand. The severed hand runs amok throughout the movie, wreaking much mayhem, and apparently murdering much of the cast. The movie culminates with Peter Lorre throwing the hand in the fire to burn it up, and the hand subsequently crawling out and choking Lorre to death.

Even though the plot was extremely interwoven and complicated, seeing a disembodied hand running around, playing the piano, and choking people was just too much for my senses to handle. After watching this movie, I would have trouble going to sleep at night, imagining the crawling hand under my bed. In order to remain safe, all of my limbs had to stay under the covers, which would remain wrapped tightly around me. The only part of my body that would be visible outside the covers was my head, from the eyes up. My siblings too would lie in bed, safely tucked under the covers, making sure that no part of their bodies got anywhere near the crawling hand, hiding just out of reach, underneath the bed. Vicki was so buttoned down and tucked in after watching this movie that I thought Mom had given her a special "tuck in" that the rest of us missed out on. She must have pulled the sheets underneath her from inside the covers, in effect, tucking herself into bed. This was a talent that she alone had mastered.

> *Donovan's Brain*- 1953
> Starring Lew Ayres, Gene Evans, and Nancy Davis.
>
> The plot is yet another version of Curt Siodmak's novel about an honest scientist who keeps the brain of a ruthless dead millionaire (Donovan) alive in a tank. Donovan manages to impose his powerful will on the scientist and uses him to murder his enemies.

The plot really didn't interest me. All I cared about was the numerous times in the movie when the camera focused in on the glass tank where Donovan's brain was being stored. How was I able to tell that the brain was alive? The brain was "breathing" (contracting and expanding) inside the glass case! This truly unnerved me, and the result was the same as the crawling hand movie: under the covers, wrapped up like a caterpillar in a cocoon, unable to go to sleep with a brain lurking underneath my bed.

Of all the scary movies I saw as a kid (*The Exorcist* wouldn't come along until my teenage years), *Hush, Hush, Sweet Charlotte* wins the prize as the one that terrorized me the most.

> *Hush, Hush, Sweet Charlotte*- 1964
> Starring Bette Davis, Olivia de Havilland, and Joseph Cotton.
>
> An aging, reclusive southern belle (Davis), plagued by a horrifying family secret, descends into madness after the arrival of a lost relative (de Havilland).

I'm not sure what frightens me (notice I used the word *frightens*; it still does to this day) most in this movie: the decapitated head rolling down the stairs or the severed limbs (all done with a cleaver) or maybe the additional murders that ensue. Each of these was definitely frightening, but there was one other feature that made all of the others even scarier: mysterious harpsichord music that haunted Davis each night after dark. Whenever that harpsichord started up, I started running.

All in all, it was an excellent movie, although I've never mustered the courage to watch it again (when I hear the title song, I still get goose bumps). Timmy was so shaken by this movie, he tried the "I'm scared can I sleep in your bed tonight" with Mom, but it didn't work any better for him than it had for me, and he didn't even wet the bed! If you were to poll the four of us and have us rank movie genres, from favorite to least favorite, I'm quite sure that "horror movies" would be nowhere on the list.

In the overall theme of "Scaredy-Cats," the chief protagonist in this drama was none other than Dad. Not only did he enjoy showing us scary movies and secretly smiling as we ran out of the room, purportedly to go to the bathroom, he sometimes *became* the movie. Dad really enjoyed scaring us because he was:

a. A sadist
b. A fun-loving guy
c. Secretly Doctor Jekyll's alter ego
d. All of the above

In reality, I think he enjoyed our reaction of not only frenzied terror, but the stranger reaction when we were frightened of running toward the one who had scared us! How odd that our natural impulse was to run toward Dad in the end and not away from him (we did run away at first, but eventually turned and came back). Somehow, deep inside us, we knew that Dad was still our ultimate protector (definitely some theology in there somewhere).

He had many characters he liked to play, but the one I remember most was his version of the mummy from *Abbott and Costello Meet the Mummy* (funny thing about those two comedians: they seemed to meet a lot of monsters). Like Frankenstein, the mummy spent an entire movie chasing the good guys around. And like Frankenstein, the mummy moved very slow and deliberate; so slow, it seems strange that anyone was ever caught (those caught must have been cut from the track team in junior high school).

To be a classic mummy, there were specific behaviors that had to be imitated. First: you had to perfect your limp, the dragging of your right leg as you slowly walked toward your prey. Second: your right arm had to be positioned across the chest with your wrist bent as if the linen wrappings were still intact and had the arm pinned against the body. Third: your gaze had to be as if you were staring miles in front of you (like a zombie) not really seeing where you were going, being driven by an evil that was beyond your control. Finally: you had to let your tongue hang out of your mouth and groan from time to time; this added some additional flavor to the character by making him seem totally out of his mind. Dad had this character perfected. On one occasion, Kathy, highly agitated, came running our way and shouted, "Wonnie, Timmy, and Vicki; wun foh youh lives! Daddy's tuhned into the mummy again. He's coming this way!" As we ran for our lives the three of us cried out, "Aaaaahhhhhh!"

One minute he's Dad, the next minute he's the mummy. We never knew when the change would occur, but it definitely didn't bring out the best in us; it became every kid for him or herself.

Once the alarm went out, we scattered, each to his or her own hiding place. Some chose closets that at first glance seemed pretty safe, whereas I chose behind the door in my room. I could see the hallway through the space between the door and wall, but didn't want to look, preferring to close my eyes and wait (an ostrich with its head in the sand comes to mind). Hiding behind the door in my bedroom, I could hear the thump, ssshhh, thump, ssshhh of the mummy, slowly walking down the hall, dragging one leg behind him, right toward my room. My heart was beating extremely fast and the sweat began to form on my brow. As the sound of the mummy drew closer, I was faced with a difficult choice: stay put and possibly be discovered, or run like the wind, which would only expose me and put me at greater risk. As the mummy finally stood right outside my door, a low groan heard as he slowly breathed and waited, I did neither. Instead, I jumped out from behind my door, temporarily startling the mummy, and ran and jumped into the mummy's arms, which ended up being the safest place. The other three cowards soon followed suit, and this episode came to an end, if only for the time being.

Did I mention that loud noises scared me? This frightened behavior was not to be confused with a normal person being startled. I doubt I would have made a good soldier in battle. "Where's Bay?" the corporal shouted out over the mortar fire. A private turns to the corporal and yells, "He didn't like the loud noises, so he's hiding in the Humvee. The windows are rolled up and the radio's on, playing classic rock."

I could have known ahead of time when the noise was coming, and it wouldn't make a difference. I was still scared and acted accordingly. Like Al Gore and the Internet, duck and cover was my invention.

Unlike me, Dad loved loud noises. He would sit out on our front porch, waiting for an approaching thunderstorm. Off in the distance, the lightning would be flashing and the delayed rumble would slowly reach the porch. He often invited one of the four of us to join him on the porch to enjoy the festivities. I have to admit, it was a beautiful sight until the storm got close enough that the rumble became more of a crash, boom, or bang. Even though I could time the loud bang based on the lightning flash, it didn't help. I couldn't take it. Once Dad realized that I was no longer sitting next to him he turned and yelled, "Ronnie, get back out here." By this time I was safe inside and answered him, "I'm scared. I don't want to watch the storm." Dad was not concerned and said, "Okay. Send out the next one."

Even in my bed, with the window shut tight, some of the thunderclaps were so loud that they woke me up, and I couldn't go back to sleep. I saw the flash from each bolt of lightning and knew the result would be the inevitable boom! As the storm came closer, the interval between flash of light and thunderclap became shorter and shorter. Knowing this didn't help. I lay there with hands cupped over my ears, my body tense with the wait.

Dad also loved to take us to the fireworks display each Fourth of July celebration. The family would load up in the station wagon, and Dad would drive us out to the city park. Once we arrived, the four of us would climb up on top of the car while Mom and Dad sat on the hood. There were families all around us: some on their cars and some in their cars, with many on blankets around the park. All awaited the upcoming show. As the anticipation was reaching a boiling point, off in the distance, a red light ascended from the horizon. Suddenly at its apogee, the red light became a brilliant flash of light accompanied by a loud bang. This demonstration signaled the beginning of the display and had me on red alert. Early in the show, the different bursts of light had a mild "pop" immediately following. This I could handle. The colors and patterns were exquisite. However, as the show progressed, the sound that escorted the light became louder and eventually the "pop" became a loud boom! Kathy, trying to get me into trouble, noticed me gone and told Mom, "Mommy, Wonnie is in the cah with the windows wolled up." "Why did he go in the car?" Mom queried. Timmy, not minding his own business, offered, "He's scahed of woud noises." Peering at me through the car window, Mom instructed me, "Ronnie, come out here so you can see the fireworks. They're beautiful." Trying to position myself to see the display, while remaining inside the car, I said, "I can see just fine in here."

Fireworks and thunderstorms were similar in many ways:

1. They were both beautiful light shows.
2. Loud booms followed flashes of light.
3. They happened in the dark.
4. They scared the tar out of me.

Timmy had a couple of things that terrorized him, one for which I was mainly responsible. Whenever a police, ambulance, or fire truck siren was heard in the neighborhood, Timmy became extremely scared to the point of crying hysterically. The noise of the sirens bothered me too, but not to the extreme that it did Timmy. There was a reason: me. You see, for every siren we heard, I told Timmy that the police were coming to get him. He believed me.

Timmy was also afraid each time we drove down Telegraph Road. It wasn't the road that scared him, but what was located along each side of the road. There were oil wells up and down the road, and they were actively pumping oil. Timmy thought they were monsters, and each time we drove by them, he would hide down in the floorboard of the car until we were a good distance beyond. I didn't see the scary aspect myself, but scary is often in the eye of the beholder. I thought they smelled bad though.

The list of things that scared me as a kid is long and extensive, but too lengthy to catalogue in its entirety. There were bugs, spiders, dogs, cows, Dad, needles, the belt, the dark, bullies, losing, girls, monsters, ghosts, loud noises, heights, close places, my sister, movies, whatever was under my bed at night...

STICKS AND STONES

(WHAT YOU SAY IS WHAT YOU ARE)

Children are known to say some pretty bizarre things and not necessarily the things they've heard and repeated from their parents. In fact, in many ways, children often have their own language. Some of the language is meant to inflict damage on the recipient, whereas other times, it is meant for an entirely different purpose. Art Linkletter coined the phrase, "Kids say the darnedest things." He surely had to be listening to us and writing down every word when the thought came to him. We not only had phrases, we had musical jingles as well, and like many of the phrases, the songs often made little sense. With some of the phrases, there was a subsequent comeback that immediately followed. I will list some of the phrases below and add meaning and context in order to give some perspective.

"Liar, liar, pants on fire, nose as long as a telephone wire." This well-known and beloved epithet was directed at a sibling, friend, or foe whenever their previous comments were judged to be full of baloney. If a friend told me that their dad was in the CIA or had climbed Mt. Everest, when I knew perfectly well they were a janitor at the school and had never left the country, this phrase was the perfect comeback. The "nose as long as a telephone wire" was an obvious reference to the Pinocchio story, recently done by Disney. If Pinocchio told a lie, his nose would grow, and with each lie, it would grow ever longer. Where the "pants on fire" came from, your guess is as good as mine.

"Made you look." There were many tricks used to get the other kid to look, at what didn't matter. The fact that your trick had "made them look" was the point. You might sneak up behind them, lightly tap them on the right shoulder, while easing slightly toward their left, and when they looked back to their right, thinking someone was there, you'd utter the phrase "made you look." You may say something like "There's a monster behind you," and when they turned to look, "Made you look." Or you could be telling the truth (not likely, but possible), and they might assume you weren't and call your bluff, with the impending result being disastrous. "Timmy, Daddy's standing behind you with the belt in his hand." "Ha! I'm not fawhing foh that ohd twick. Besides, I'm not afwaid of Daddy."

Well, at least Timmy could say, "You didn't make me look" after he and Dad had danced. The inexplicable thing was not how many times we fell for it, but how many times we tried to fool each other.

"Wanna bet!" or "I'll betcha!" Since we had limited debating skills, we often resorted to this when faced with an argument that we couldn't seem to win. There were a couple of problems with this approach: one, we didn't have anything to bet with (maybe that's why the stakes were seldom mentioned with the phrase). Two, how would it be proven one way or another who was right? When we were absolutely sure of being right, we might say something like, "I'll betcha a million dollars."

"Shut up. Make me. You're already made, but too dumb to know it." If, no when, a sibling told you to shut up, often times it was hard to think of a decent comeback. You could say, "No, you shut up," but that sounded pretty weak, so "Make me" had a snappy ring to it and rolled off the tongue rather naturally. This pattern would oftentimes be repeated over and over ("Shut up, make me, shut up, make me"), but finally, in order to break the stalemate, "You're already made, but too dumb to know it" pretty much ended the back and forth. There really isn't a comeback to this particular phrase. Genius! There was one other that was pretty neat also. Someone would say, "Shut up," and the comeback would be "Make me," and then the ultimate comeback to stop the other person in their tracks, "I don't make trash, I burn it." Wow!

"I know you are, but what am I?" Although Pee Wee made this famous, it was already in use for years before he came along. Another version of this was "What you say is what you are." Either would work when the right moment came. For example, Timmy might say to me, "Wonnie, you'ah a butt head."

Now I could have responded with a number of things: "No, you're a butt head, shut up, I'm telling, I hate you, I'm going to beat you up, you're absolutely correct," the possibilities were endless. However, the easiest response, especially if you weren't in the mood for the usual back-and-forth, was one of the two mentioned above. When he said, "Wonnie, you'ah a butt head," my response in a matter of fact tone would be, "What you say is what you are."

What could Timmy possibly come back with? It was almost like a game of chess, and his king had just been cornered and he had no way out: checkmate! If for some reason, your mind froze up and you couldn't think of "what you say is what you are," there was one more that worked perfectly, a secret weapon in comebacks: "I'm rubber, you're glue. Whatever you say bounces off me and sticks to you."

Not a kid in the land could insult us without paying a severe price in a volley of comebacks that seem to be much more insightful than kids our age could have come up with. In this case, the saying, "A great defense is the best offense," became a reality. Like Superman fighting Mighty Mouse, who would win?

"He touched me." This particular phrase could mean a variety of things and may not even be true. Sometimes, just the inference of a touch would elicit this response (these episodes weren't limited to, but inevitably happened in the family station wagon). In fact, that was part of the game. The offender would stick their finger in the other kid's face, just close enough, within a sixteenth of an inch from their nose, but never actually touch them. At that point, if the other kid's finger was within a sixteenth of an inch from the nose, you couldn't slap their arm out of the way because then you would be the one touching them. It wasn't even limited to touching, but could be a number of offenses: he/she looked at me, made a face at me, crossed their eyes at me, stuck their tongue out at me, etc. "Mommy, Ronnie touched me." "Did not," I replied. "Did too," Vicki shot back. A little louder this time, "Did not." Louder yet, Vicki shouted, "Did too." Louder by far than either one of us, Mom ended it, "Would you two kids shut up?"

Mom's next move would be to separate us in the backseat of the car. We now had our own space, our own side so to speak. This seemed like a good idea to Mom, but actually led to the next argument. Knowing that there was an invisible line that separated us, the temptation was to find out just where that line was. Kathy and Timmy were typical when she said, "Timmy, you'ah on my side." "No, I'm not. This is my side. You'ah side is ovah theah."

Carving up territories worked in beds, cars, chairs, couches, wherever we happened to be at the time. It was like we were each sovereign nations with borders and the neighboring country was invading. The only thing left to do was launch a counterattack.

"None of your beeswax." There you were, playing with your truck, and your sibling walks up and says, "What are you doing?" It would have been just as easy to respond, "Playing with my truck," but for some reason, "None of your beeswax" was what came out. It was as if every question was a challenge that deserved a sharp retort. "Where are you going?" "None of your beeswax." "How old are you?" "None of your beeswax." Was this a case of just being obstinate or were there other motives at play? If your answer was "playing trucks," then that might lead to another question such as, "Can I play?" If you had wanted to play trucks with someone else, you would have invited them. So the "none of your beeswax" retort was more of a defense mechanism designed to keep the other kid at bay. Sometimes, the phrase was used to keep information from the other party. If Timmy, for example, walked up eating a bowl of ice cream, Kathy might ask, "Hey, wheah did you get that ice cweam?" Being the snot that he was Timmy would respond, "None of youah beeswax."

This little exchange inevitably led to the next oft-uttered phrase.

"That's not fair!" As in "beauty is in the eye of the beholder," so too is what constitutes fair or not. If you have something that I don't have, then it's not fair. If I have something that you don't have, fair really doesn't matter. If Timmy received a spanking and I didn't, I of course thought it plenty fair. Timmy, on the other hand, and by his very nature, figured that fair would be all four of us getting a spanking, even though three of us didn't commit the offense that he was being spanked for. The reality: Mom and Dad were the sole arbiters of what was fair, and we were left with the woeful cry, "That's not fair!"

"I'm telling." "I'm telling." "Shut up." "Shut up." This technique was designed to drive the other person nuts and often came close. No matter what they said to you, all you had to do was to repeat it word for word. If pushed too far, violence often ensued.

"Booger nose, snot grass." A derogatory slur, this one has to be an original. It makes sense that little kids would recognize in their sibling or playmate a tendency to have boogers and snot running down their nose. Some little kids even ate the boogers and licked the snot from underneath their noses. Because the above activities, if viewed by another person, were a little embarrassing, the terms became ones of derision. Booger nose is obvious as to meaning, whereas snot grass leaves a little to the imagination. Snot is often green and so is grass, so… "Booger nose" I said to Timmy. His response of "Snot gwass" was similar but not quite the same. I combined the two and retorted, "Booger nose, snot grass."

"You think you're hot snot, but you're cold boogers!" Note the similarities with the previous entry.

"I'm telling!" This phrase could be used as a threat or in some cases as blackmail. Say for example, and this is completely hypothetical of course, that I "accidentally" punched Kathy. She would normally begin to cry, and I would normally try to calm her down, bribe her, stuff a shirt in her mouth, hide her in the closet, or try some other way to keep her quiet. Then she would utter two simple words that I dreaded to hear, "I'm telling." I knew then, no matter how much she had stopped crying, no matter how much time had elapsed, that the minute Mom was anywhere in sight, I was a dead man. Another use of this phrase was more as a bribe or blackmail. Say for example, and this too is purely hypothetical, Timmy had taken one of Dad's tools, a hatchet in this case, from the garage and was throwing it at a tree. "Hey Timmy, what are you doing?" "Thwowing Daddy's hatchet at the twee" was his response. "Can I try?" I asked. "No" was his blunt answer. My next comment was all I had left, "I'm telling."

In most cases, you didn't have to say specifically who you were going to tell, but it made a much stronger impact to say "I'm telling Daddy" than it did to say "I'm telling Mommy" (it could have been the belt versus the switch that made the difference). In this particular case, the inference was enough. Most of the time, you never ended up telling because (a) the other kid gave in or (b) there was the chance that not only the tellee would be in trouble, but the teller as well.

"I'm going to beat you up." This phrase was usually uttered as a last resort, when your patience had been totally exhausted. You never said it to anyone that you knew could beat you up. It was most often an idle threat and very rarely ended up in fistcuffs. The only person that followed through on the threat was Vicki, who frequently ended up on top of Timmy, pounding him into submission. Knowing Timmy, Vicki was justified.

"My dad can beat up your dad." Once again, mostly a lot of wind (it's not like there were dads in the street duking it out every day). In Dad's case, we said it with all of the confidence in the world. I saw Dad call out a neighbor kid's dad from the street (the other dad stayed in his house: smart move). In our minds, Dad was the real-life version of all the characters played by John Wayne. Other similar phrases: "My dad is smarter, bigger, stronger, better, meaner, richer than your dad."

"Wait up!" When with a group of kids, there were times that the group would decide to move, en masse, to some other location. If you weren't paying attention, they would start off in another direction. If you noticed them leaving and they were fairly close, you would shout, "Wait up!" Sometimes they would, and other times, you had to run to catch up. If you didn't notice them for a while, and they were a ways down the street, you would then shout, "Hey, guys! Wait for me!" If you were left on purpose and didn't notice it until later, you went home.

"I get the window." To be repeated later as teenagers as "Shotgun!" This was really a lot more significant than it seems on the surface. There were four of us and only two windows in the backseat of the station wagon. One of us would be in the far back, rolling around with the twists and turns, and the remaining three would be in the backseat. If you didn't get either one of the windows, it was pretty miserable sitting in the middle. For one thing, if Dad was reaching back to smack someone, for any number of reasons, the middle person was the only one he could reach. If you sat in the middle, you couldn't make faces at Dad when you got into trouble because he could see you in the rearview mirror. Besides, sitting next to the window had an air of freedom about it. The scenery always changed and kept your mind off other more unpleasant things, like the sibling sitting next to you.

"Is not, is too, is not, is too." No explanation necessary.

"I hate you." This phrase was rarely used and usually followed by tears and a dramatic running away, usually back to the house. We didn't really understand what it meant, but knew it was a pretty big deal to use it. Your emotions had to be pushed to the limit before engaging in its use. It was a final act of desperation, when all other words and actions had failed. Once I said this to Mom. I never said it again.

"Cross my heart, hope to die, stick a needle in my eye." Often when in a dialogue with another little minion, whether related or not, there sometimes came a point of incredulity from the other side. In order to prove your sincerity, this phrase would suffice. If you were crazy enough to suggest dying and sticking needles in your own eye, then you must be telling the truth.

"Missed me, missed me, now you gotta kiss me." This phrase was used in many of the games we played, like tag, and dodge ball, but generally when someone was throwing something at someone else (rocks for example) or spitting or any number of things. The part about kissing was a really low blow; after all, kissing girls would lead to cooties and kissing a boy, well, that wasn't even a consideration.

(Of all the indignities that we would inflict on one another, spitting had to be the worst. The smell of the other person's spit was more than gross, and even if wiped off, the smell would linger. Often in the movies, the bad guy spits in the hero's face, and from that point on, the hero lets loose a flurry of energy that completely dominates the bad guy. Don't ever spit in the good guy's face!)

"Dick and Jane, sitting in a tree, K-I–S-S-I-N-G." You never really believed that a particular boy and girl were sweet on each other, but it was fun to throw this at them in a derisive fashion. Usually, it was one or the other of them playing with someone else, and being jealous of their time, this phrase came out and inevitably led to being chased around the yard and threatened with a pounding. Even if you did like the person of the opposite sex, when you heard this phrase thrown your way, you could never admit it.

"I'm not going to be your friend anymore." As in some of the other phrases, this was used primarily as a bribe, but could even be used if you were tired of playing with someone and a disagreement had ensued. Usage of this phrase generally caused two people to go their separate ways. It was never meant to be permanent, and the two would usually be seen playing with one another the next day. As Vicki sat playing with her dolls, Kathy approached and asked, "Can I pway with youh Bahbie doll?" "No. You have your own dolls to play with." Indignant, Kathy responded, "I'm not going to be your fwiend anymoh." Vicki wasn't concerned and said, "I don't care."

Here are some phrases reserved for Mom and Dad only.

"Wait 'til your father gets home." We all knew what that meant, but what was the alternative to waiting? It obviously was a threat, a threat that we knew was not idle, designed to stop us in our current activity and to warn us of the impending danger coming our way. It also was an admittance on Mom's part that when it came to doling out punishment, she was no match for the master, Dad.

"Straighten up and fly right." This phrase was the sole property of Mom and usually preceded the "wait 'til your father gets home" utterance. At this point, Mom had yet to lose her patience and the phrase usually followed "You kids better." Another warning which we often ignored.

"You kids want something to cry about?" or "I'm going to give you something to cry about." This was Dad's and usually followed a recent whipping or punishment of some sort. He would only use this if our crying volume escalated to a point that he couldn't take anymore. I assume the first was rhetorical; after all, what would a proper response be?

"Do you kids want a spanking?" Again, rhetorical. An obvious theme has developed here, and all of the parental phrases revolve around one activity: our misbehavior.

The songs that we sang didn't necessarily fit with our age. One of our favorites (we liked it because adults would always react with mock horror every time they heard us) went like this (sung to the tune of "The Old Gray Mare"):

> Great big gobs of greasy, grimy, gopher guts.
> Chopped-up monkey meat, mutilated birdies' feet.
> All topped off with French fried eyeballs, swimming in a pool of blood.
> I forgot my spoon, but I brought my straw.

This song, unbeknownst to us at the time, was a children's song originally released in 1959 and had many interchangeable lyrics. You can see by the format that the possibilities of other lines, animals, and parts are pretty much endless. This was the chorus and was the only part of the song that we knew, although there were many additional lines.

A song with a similar macabre theme went as follows:

> The worms crawl in
> The worms crawl out
> The bugs play pinochle on your snout (the actual line here had worms again and not bugs; we improvised)

This, like the previous song, was all that we knew, and we repeated it over and over again. The actual song is titled "The Hearse Song," and in case you wanted to make it your family favorite, the remaining verses contain coffins, death, worms eating eyes and noses, jelly between your toes, green worms crawling in your stomach and out your eyes, pus like whipping cream, etc. Pretty neat song, don't you think? It's sure to make your mother squirm every time you sing it. It also works well at Halloween and scares the little ones.

Sung to the tune of "Jingle Bells," here's our own version of that song:

> Jingle bells, Santa smells, happy Halloween.
> Oh, what fun it is to ride in a yellow submarine.

Like most other songs, we didn't know any other lyrics and just kept repeating these over and over. There is a variation on the same theme that goes:

> Jingle bells, Batman smells, Robin laid an egg.

There was a second line, but we didn't know it, preferring instead the Santa smells version.

Some of our songs were meant entirely for the car, on those long boring trips to somewhere. Here are a couple of favorites:

Sung to the tune of "Johnny Comes Marching Home":

> The ants go marching one by one hurrah, hurrah.
> The ants go marching one by one hurrah, hurrah.
> The ants go marching one by one, the little one stops to suck his thumb
> And they all go marching down, underground, to get out of the rain boom, boom boom.
> The ants go marching two by two, hurrah, hurrah.
> The ants go marching two by two hurrah, hurrah.
> The ants go marching two by two, the little one stops to tie his shoe,
> And they all go marching down, underground, to get out of the rain boom, boom, boom.

This song absolutely drove Mom and Dad nuts on those long boring car trips. For their sakes, we usually tired out when we couldn't think of anything to rhyme with twelve.

Another song that we sang in the car that was even more monotonous and that brought the parents to the boiling point was:

> 99 bottles of beer on the wall
> 99 bottles of beer
> Take one down, pass it around
> 98 bottles of beer on the wall.

This particular song, unlike the "ants" song, hit a little closer to home, since Dad frequently imbibed large quantities of Schlitz (the beer that made Milwaukee famous). Even though his preferred vessel was the can, the theme was close enough. After getting through the nineties, Dad had pretty much had enough. "You kids want me to stop this car?"

I'm sorry, but that really wasn't a very good question since the answer was so obvious. We knew that if he stopped the car, all of his attention would be focused on us and he would have the mobility to move around and get to each of us, whereas if he continued to drive, most of us were pretty safe, except the unfortunate kid sitting in the middle seat. Needless to say, we shut up. That song was getting boring anyway.

H-BEES AND GOLDEN GARDEN SPIDERS

(RENFIELD WOULD BE AMUSED)

In the famous novel by Bram Stoker, *Dracula*, there was a character named Renfield that exhibited an abnormal attraction to bugs and spiders to the point of eating them. He was considered clinically insane. We too exhibited a fascination with bugs, spiders, rodents, reptiles, and other creatures, although we didn't eat them, and as far as I know, we weren't considered clinically insane (in order to be clinically insane, one needs to be interviewed and observed by a psychologist or psychiatrist for a diagnosis, and to date that hasn't happened yet).

One day, while traveling through the neighborhood, in between houses, up and down the street, a sparkle of light, a gleam in the sun, caught my eye. I had to stop running and take the time to investigate. As I got closer to the area where the gleam had appeared, I noticed between two bushes on the side of a house, a beautiful, perfectly formed spiderweb, approximately two feet in diameter. It was glorious. Mankind in all his wisdom could not make something as perfect and beautiful as this web. And yet, in the midst of the beauty, there was also an accompanying feeling of dread and fear. I stood and stared at it for a while and then ran to get Timmy. I figured that he would want to see this thing too.

As we came back to the spot that held the spiderweb, we noticed that not only was there a web, there also was a huge, beautiful spider. This spider hung head down in the center of the web. It had bright yellow and black markings on the abdomen and legs with a white head. It was approximately one inch in length, not counting the long legs. We later found out that the spider was known as the golden garden spider and is harmless to humans, but we didn't know it at the time and our fear was very real. We watched the spider, from a safe distance, and it stayed in the web, motionless. At one point, the spider began to move from the center of the web back to the outside edge. We jumped back in excitement and slowly approached once again. "I wonder what spider's eat?" I muttered in hushed tones. Timmy wasn't sure, but guessed "I don't know. Maybe bugs?" "Let's go ask Vicki, she's smart."

Vicki informed us that the spider would probably eat flies, moths, and other bugs. It seems that Timmy was right. So we decided to feed the spider. Our first offering to the altar of the golden garden spider would be a fly, and we proceeded to search the neighborhood for a likely fly spot. Like hunting any animal, when you are trying to find them, they're never around, but when you're not looking for them, they're everywhere. We finally found some flies buzzing around a trash can. I smacked one down, stunning it, closed my hand around it, and then Timmy and I ran back to the spiderweb with lunch. The spider was nowhere to be seen, but we had the fly and decided to throw it into the web. "Timmy, stand back! I'm going to pitch the fly into the web." "Shouldn't you stand a wittew cwoseh?" Timmy suggested. With an air of confidence, I stated "First, if I get too close, the spider could jump off the web and land on me and then bite me and I could die. Second, I'm a pitcher and I know how to throw a strike. Move back."

I wound up and threw the fly with all my might, but as we gazed into the spiderweb, there wasn't a fly to be seen. Timmy said he saw the creature fly away. I didn't see it fly away because as soon as I let it go, I turned the other way and ran. Well, back to the trash can for another fly. This time, the fly wouldn't fly away because we pulled off its wings. (Which is crueler, pulling off the wings or throwing the fly into the spider's web to be devoured? It's all a part of nature.) The second time was much more successful. As the fly hit the web, it began to struggle, but to no avail. Finally, the fly stopped struggling, and the web became still once again, save a slight breeze causing a minimal swaying. Up until now, we thought the experience had been really neat. Here's what happened next. The spider showed up on the web from wherever it was hiding and proceeded down the web to where the fly was trapped. Here are the specifics of the process we saw unfold before our eyes:

The spider does not see very well, but by detecting vibrations of the trapped insect in the web, knows when lunch or dinner has arrived. It injects its prey with venom and quickly wraps it with silk. When it eats its prey, it injects digestive enzymes to break down the soft tissues into a liquid, which the spider sucks into its mouth. The exoskeleton of the prey is dropped to the ground.

This was great! Far better than television (with only three channels on a black-and-white TV, it wasn't hard to beat). Well, we'd done a fly, why not a moth? We proceeded to find and catch a moth, a big one, and took it back to the web, where we watched the same process once again.

From that day on, I had a new respect and admiration for the golden garden spider. (It seems that the golden garden spider and Renfield are fellow travelers when it comes to cuisine preferences.) I pretty much left the spiders alone out of a newfound respect, although I did try to destroy a web once by spraying water from the garden hose, but the web withstood the onslaught, and I gave up and went on to other mischief.

I have described Vicki as the fastest kid in the neighborhood. Not only was she faster than all the other kids, but she was also faster than a lizard. The type of lizard most often seen in southern California is the southern alligator lizard. Although the name seems a bit frightening, they are really quite small and harmless. They are seen during the daylight, along houses and garages and in bushes. Even though they are often seen, catching them is another issue completely. Once spotted, they will move very quickly to an area of cover, underneath a rock, debris, a crack in the wall, etc.

This particular day, we were walking through the high school and spotted a lizard on the side of the wall, basking in the sun. He also spotted us, and the chase was on. The wall was lined with bushes with just enough room between the bush and wall for us to squeeze behind. Vicki came up with a plan. "Ronnie, you go down to the end of the wall and wait there, in case he runs that way. Kathy and Timmy, you go down the line of bushes and separate, in case he decides to make a run for it across the sidewalk. I will go behind the bushes on the other end, opposite Ronnie." "Okay," we all replied.

As Vicki entered in behind the bushes and began herding the lizard down the wall, the remainder of us stayed in position until we heard further instructions. Soon, Vicki instructed me to begin moving in her direction. The lizard was to be the victim of the pincer movement, a classic military movement used by Hannibal at the Battle of Cannae in 216 BC. As Vicki and I both closed in, with Kathy and Timmy blocking any avenue of escape, the lizard had only one option: jump to the bushes. As I mentioned earlier, Vicki was fast, and as the lizard leapt toward the bushes, Vicki quickly reached to the point where the lizard was intending to land and grabbed it, tightly grasping it in her fist. The four of us triumphantly headed home, victorious over the once happy and carefree lizard.

Once home, the intention of the owner, Vicki, was to keep the lizard as a pet, but where? After looking around the house and garage, a large cardboard box was found that looked like a pretty good living arrangement for the lizard. We wanted to keep it in the house, but Mom had other ideas. "Mommy, I caught a lizard. Can I keep it in the house?" "What? You're not bringing any stinky little reptiles into our house." Mom's response was firm.

The box in the backyard would have to do. Vicki, always the smart one, told us that the lizard, like the spider, feasted on various insects, but unlike the spider, its diet also included small rodents. Added to the box, with the idea of duplicating the lizard's natural habitat, were rocks, dirt, and various branches and twigs. If the aforementioned insects and rodents didn't show up for supper, we would take care of that later. The lizard in the box was left outside, on the sidewalk near the garage, while we went off to other pursuits. All but one of us.

There was an urban legend going around at the time that if a lizard lost its tail, it would continue on like nothing ever happened and the tail would grow back. Apparently, Timmy had heard this legend, and being the inquisitive lad that he was, he decided to test the theory (Vicki was not asked her opinion on this theory, nor was she asked if her lizard could be the object of a scientific experiment). In the garage was a short-handled axe, which was Dad's and off-limits to us. In this case, Timmy could think of no other instrument that would serve his purpose, so he went into the garage, removed Dad's axe, and headed to the big box housing the lizard.

Later, Vicki went to the box to visit her pet, and as she peered into the box, the lizard was not visible. She was a little panicked, and she assumed, quite logically, that one of the three of us might know where the lizard had gone. "Ronnie, did you see my lizard?" she asked. "No, I've been playing trucks next door in David's side yard." "Kathy, have you seen my lizard?" "No. I've been in my woom." By now Vicki was a little desperate and called out to the usual suspect in these situations, "Timmy!" Feigning ignorance Timmy replied, "What lizuhd?" Vicki went back to Mom, "Mommy, my lizard's gone and nobody knows where it went." Not that Mom was that concerned, she offered, "Maybe it climbed out of the box and ran away. They are good climbers, you know."

Seeing Vicki in a state of panic, looking all over for the lizard, we all decided to look one more time in the box. After removing all of the foliage, Vicki noticed a tail sticking out from under a rock in the corner of the box. Lifting the rock, she was shocked to see the bottom half of the lizard, cut in half midsection. Lifting another rock, the top half of the lizard was found. All of us turned to Timmy. Vicki confronted him again, "Timmy, what happened to my lizard?" In tears Timmy cried, "I twied to cut off its taiuwh to see if it would gwow back, but when I swung the axe, it moved and I missed."

Although the lizard had made a great pet, albeit for a very brief moment, Vicki decided that her lizard catching days were over. Other pets would come, one even meeting a similar fate as the lizard's, but that story will come later.

Did you ever notice the similarities between the snail and the slug? Well, we did. As far as we could tell, the only real difference was that the snail had a house on its back. Other than that, they both were ugly, slimy, and left trails of mucus on the sidewalk (slugs and snails will never get lost as they always leave a trail behind them, like bread crumbs) and were extremely slow (we didn't need Vicki to help us catch either of these creatures). Once located, either one of them could be observed, untouched, for an extended period as they slowly moved down the sidewalk. For some reason, as we observed (observation is usually the first step taken in a scientific investigation) this mollusk moving along the sidewalk, the thought entered our minds: is there any salt around here? Now what put that thought in our minds, I cannot say. Some would say Satan, but my guess is it was one of the older kids in the neighborhood. Into the house we went. Timmy asked first, "Mommy, do we have any sahwt?" "Of course we do. What do you want it for?" Not wanting Timmy to spill the beans, er, tell the truth, I interjected, "We are doing a scientific experiment, and salt is needed in order to complete it." Mom seemed impressed and replied, "That sounds very nice. I love it when you kids learn new things. How much do you need?"

Outside we went with the salt shaker in hand. The slug had gone another couple of inches down the sidewalk (this particular slug was in pretty good shape and moved rather quickly as slugs go). We all got down on our hands and knees, surrounding the slug, and I poured the salt from the shaker onto the slug. It recoiled in agony and began to shrivel up. As I moved closer to the slug to observe the effects of the salt, I could have sworn I heard this coming from the slug (having recently watched *The Wizard of Oz*, what I heard sounded very familiar), "Aaaahhhh! You cursed brats! Look what you've done! I'm melting, melting. Ohhh, what a world, what a world. Who would have thought that some little kids like you could destroy my beautiful wickedness? Ooohhhh! Nooo! I'm going....ohhhh...ohhhh..." So much for the slug. If it worked on the slug, why not a snail? But where could we find a snail? I asked Timmy, "Have you seen any snails?" He replied, "I saw one in the ivy oveh by the cohnuh house the otheh day. Maybe it's stiw theh." With salt still in hand I said, "Let's go."

After digging through the ivy for a half hour, we finally spotted a snail, crawling, sliming through the dirt right off the edge of the sidewalk. We refrained from touching the snail, not because it was dangerous, but because we were afraid it might be. A stick we held in hand continually blocked its path, eventually steering it onto the sidewalk where we could conduct our experiments in the open.

Snails, as well as slugs, have a couple of antenna like tentacles extending from their heads, and on the end of each tentacle is the eye. Part of the experiments we conducted included the tentacles and eyes of the snail. As we put anything close to the tentacles, and at the time we didn't have any idea that the eyes were located on the ends of them, the tentacle would begin to retract to the point of receding all the way into the body. Really neat! Each tentacle operated independently of the other, which was also pretty neat. We waited awhile and the tentacles would again extend out to an inch or so away from the body, and the snail would proceed down the sidewalk. Now back to the original experiment.

If the salt worked on the slug, it should also work on the snail. Unfortunately for us and our experiment, the snail proved to be a much craftier mollusk than the hapless slug. Maybe it was the additional house on its back, but whatever the reason, when we tried applying the salt to the snail, it just retreated into its shell, out of harm's way. Similar to a turtle, once it went back in its shell, it became a waiting game. How much patience did we have? Not much. A couple of times playing out this scenario and we got bored with the snail and moved on. I'm sure that if the slugs would work hard and save enough, they too could afford a mobile home, just like the snails. After all, there's no place like home.

At this stage of our young lives, we, as a family, decided to try the pet thing. Dad, being the big kid that he was, wanted us to experience growing up with a dog. One day, out of nowhere, there was this little puppy in the house. The four of us were extremely excited and could barely contain ourselves, each wanting to smother, er, hold the puppy and shower it with love in the form of hugs and kisses. Shortly after the puppy arrived and the excitement had died down a bit, we were all back to our normal routine, when the front door was left open and the puppy, as puppies do, ran out the front door. Within a moment or two, the sound of a car screeching to a halt in the street in front of the house was heard, and then the sound of a wailing puppy running back into the house. We didn't quite know what was wrong, but the puppy would not let anyone touch it, biting each hand that reached in its direction. Dad and a neighbor man finally caught the puppy and took it away, never to be seen again. At the time, we didn't know the fate of the puppy, and obviously, Dad didn't want to tell us. We hadn't even named it yet and it was gone.

Months went by, and Dad, ever determined, decided that just because the first dog didn't work out didn't mean we couldn't try again. We all loaded up into the station wagon and headed down to the pound. Of all the dogs we visited, the family favorite was the white German shepherd. We all agreed that this was the one until Dad found out how much it would cost to feed this large animal. The dog that we finally came home with was a black curly-haired dog, resembling a poodle, but basically a mutt. She was fairly large and very active. We named her Paulette (why, I couldn't tell you, but that was her new name and her subsequent behavior was probably her rebelling against us for naming her that). It was decided that Paulette would not be a house dog, but live in the backyard. Dad built a doghouse, and it seemed that things were headed in the right direction for a day.

Paulette had issues. The first night as a part of our family, the dog barked incessantly all night long. Not only was this difficult for us, but the neighbors didn't much care for it either. One neighbor decided to call our house and bark into the phone, repeatedly. We never found out which neighbor it was, but couldn't really blame them. Paulette also liked to dig, not with any purpose in mind, she just liked to dig. She dug with a passion.

Once, we went on a family excursion and left the dog locked up in the backyard by herself (big mistake). When we arrived home and finally went out to the yard to check on her, the yard looked like Dresden after the allies had dropped 3,900 tons of high-explosive bombs and incendiary devices on the city in February of 1945. There were huge, deep holes all over the backyard. Only later did we realize that Paulette had been planning her escape via tunnels, but she couldn't dig deep enough to get under the wall (if she had only been able to enlist the help of Danny, the Tunnel King, she might have made it). Dad was not too happy to say the least. The veins on his neck were just beginning to bulge.

Paulette was an equal opportunity offender. Mom wasn't immune to the shenanigans she pulled on the family. Back in those days, our clothes dryer was the outside air. Mom had the clotheslines, clothespins, and laundry baskets with plenty of southern California sunshine to work with: primitive but effective. At any given time, the clothesline would be full of clothes, drying in the warm sun. Paulette wasn't impressed. Vicki, looking out the kitchen window, said to Mom, "You better look out in the yard to see what Paulette's done." Kathy saw it too and said, "Mommy, clothes ah all ovuh the yahd."

In the meantime, I was out back warning Paulette to hide, as Mom was on the way and wouldn't be particularly enamored of what she had done. Clothes were strung from one end of the yard to the other. They were all dirty and torn: panties, shirts, jeans; Paulette didn't care; she just wanted them off the clothesline. Mom wept.

One day, we all went out into the yard to check on Paulette, but she was nowhere in sight. Over against the wall was her doghouse, but no Paulette. No signs of a struggle. We began to come up with some theories as to where she might have gone or what happened to her. Vicki, thinking conspiracy speculated, "Maybe she was dognapped." I thought something more obvious had taken place and said, "I think she climbed on top of her doghouse and jumped over the wall." Timmy was more in line with my thinking and commented, "I think she wan away." "Me too," Kathy added.

We searched the neighborhood, house to house, up and down the street. No Paulette. Dad didn't give any theories of his own and strangely didn't help in the all out search, but he did think my theory was a strong possibility. Mom was mum. Very suspicious. It would be years later that we would try the "pet" thing again, and although the results would be different, they would have some excitement of their own (the next attempt would be with cats and there would be plenty of them).

Bringing home the lizard was just one of many times we captured small creatures and brought them home for scientific observation. One such creature was the red ant, one of the most common species of ant, known scientifically as *Myrmica ruginodis*. Colonies from 100 to 300 ants can be found under stones and paving as well as in gardens and rotting tree trunks. Their sting is the piercing type and can be quite painful, as each of us would find out. Capturing the ant was easy, but keeping them alive was much more of a challenge.

We had seen numerous advertisements for ant farms in comic books, magazines, bubble gum packages, etc. In the ads, the ants were pictured in a normal-sized aquarium, and the neat thing was that with the sides of the aquarium all glass, you could see the ant tunnels and the ants moving to and fro throughout. We couldn't quite afford the ant farms advertised, but felt we could make our own. After all, we had the ants, we had the dirt, and all we needed was a container to put them in. After searching around the garage with no luck, I asked, "Mommy, do we have an extra aquarium around here?" Her response seemed a little short. "No, and what do you want it for anyway?" "We're going to make an ant farm," I informed her. "Not in the house you aren't."

We always received great support when we came up with our ideas and schemes. Since we didn't have an aquarium, we would have to improvise. The best we could come up with was an empty pickle jar, approximately thirty-two ounces. Not an aquarium, but not bad.

In order to catch ants, all you needed was a small stick, a twig would do, and a container to put them in. The house on the corner of the block didn't have any grass, just dirt for a yard. The dirt was really as much sand as it was dirt, but it was the perfect home for the red ants. At the edge of the sidewalk, we would find little mounds of dirt with a hole in the middle and ants coming and going, carrying various bundles with them. Ants are amazing, and the objects they carried were often two to three times larger than they were. Some of the objects were food, little pieces of bread or other consumables, and some were materials such as sticks and rocks to be used for who knew what. Once the ants were spotted, we would take our jar, now filled with dirt, and the sticks, and squat down in a circle around the ant hill. The stick would be placed on the ground in front of the ant, and the ant would climb on the stick. Then the stick would be placed into the jar and shaken until the ant fell off, and once on the new dirt surface, the ant would run around in circles (I guess they got confused, what with being removed from their normal habitat and dropped into a jar). After we had captured a couple of dozen ants, we headed home.

In the process of catching the ants, we sometimes got a bit too close, and the ant came in contact with a body part, usually a finger, and the result was quite exhilarating. "Mommy, an ant stung my finguh!" Timmy cried as he ran into the house. Mom was quite helpful and replied, "Timmy, ants don't sting, they bite." "Thanks for the entomowogy wesson Mommy." Timmy had expected much more than science.

Once the jar of ants and dirt arrived home, we had to figure out how to keep the ants alive. We assumed they needed air, but if we left the lid off the jar, they would crawl out and then we'd have ants all over the house and our ant farm would face foreclosure. So we took the lid, a hammer, and a 16-penny nail and punctured a number of holes in the lid to allow an airflow (we didn't realize it at the time, but the ants could climb out through the air holes). We also had to figure out what to feed the ants. After watching a few Yogi Bear cartoons, we learned that ants eat picnic food and sweets, especially sugar. We went to the sugar bowl and poured a bunch of sugar into the jar, a large pile of it. For days, we watched the ant farm, hoping to see tunnels and ants moving in and out, but all we found were dead ants (probably from being gorged on sugar) or escaped ants running around the floor of the house. All that work and preparation and no resemblance to the ant farms advertised in the magazines. Talk about overselling and under delivering! We grew impatient and moved on.

Our favorite insects were found right outside our bedroom window. There were two bushes next to the house that had white blossoms that emitted a pungent odor that could be smelled from quite a distance. Buzzing around these bushes was a type of bee that we named H-bees (we named the bushes bee bushes, for obvious reasons). If you look very closely at the abdomen of these bees, you will notice dark black markings in the shape of an H, thus the name.

We discovered something very interesting about these H-bees; we could catch them with our hands and not get stung! Observing us around the bushes in the front yard Mom was curious and asked, "What are you kids doing? Get away from those bees; you're going to get stung." Timmy was proud to let her know, "H-bees don't sting, Mommy." "Well, okay. You kids have fun catching bees with your hands."

Like the ants, we had jars that we stuffed with twigs and leaves (creating a natural habitat was an important part of this exercise) and a set of holes were poked into the lid for airflow. Once we caught the bee, we unscrewed the lid with one hand and threw the bee into the jar, quickly screwing the lid back on. Not only was there a nice visual, but the sound emanating through the holes in the lid of the jar was neat. As bees were added, the sound grew louder. Shaking the jar would aggravate the bees, and the buzzing sound would grow in volume.

Sometimes, while tossing the bee in the jar and trying to screw the lid on to prevent escape, a bee would be caught mid-escape and cut in half by the lid. Good thing there were plenty of bees on our bee bushes. Other than the flowers on the bushes, we couldn't think of anything else that the bees would eat, so the blossoms had to do.

One day, while catching the bees in our hands (it wasn't beyond us to shake the bee in our closed hand to get them stirred up a bit prior to throwing them into the jar), something strange happened. Running into the house I cried, "Mommy, a bee just stung me!" Acting nonchalant about the incident, Mom said, "I thought you said that H-bees didn't sting." "H-bees do sting!" I cried, not getting the humor or casual reaction from Mom.

This reminds me of the old joke about the dog. This from Inspector Jacque Clouseau:

> "Does your dog bite?" Inspector Clouseau of *The Pink Panther* fame asks the hotel clerk as he sees a dog at his feet. "No," the clerk responds. Clouseau bends over to pet the dog and has his sleeve ripped off. "I thought you said your dog doesn't bite!" he remarks angrily. Replies the clerk, "That's not my dog."

Our version would go like this: "Do your bees sting?" Mom asks. I reply, "H-bees don't sting." A few seconds later I run into the house crying, "Waaahhh!" "I thought you said H-bees didn't sting." "That wasn't an H-bee," I wail.

One of two things happened: H-bees did indeed sting, or I had failed to identify the H-bee marking on its back and grabbed an impostor bee. Apparently, the insect we identified as H-bees were in reality not a bee at all. The common name is drone fly, *Eristalis tenax*, and children call them H-bees. They do not sting and are harmless, but we didn't know that, so from that day on, all bees were caught with a jar (with jar in left hand and lid in right hand, we would lower the jar over the flower that held the bee and close the lid and jar over it) and not by hand. As much as the four of us studied insects growing up, you might conclude that one of us would have become an entomology professor.

THE SOWER WENT OUT TO SOW

In Matthew 13, Jesus teaches a parable that some refer to as the parable of the seed and others refer to as the parable of the soils. I refer to it as both. Here is the parable: "And He spoke many things to them in parables, saying, 'Behold, the sower went out to sow: and as he sowed, some seeds fell beside the road, and the birds came and ate them up. And others fell upon the rocky places, where they did not have much soil; and immediately they sprang up, because they had no depth of soil. But when the sun had risen, they were scorched; and because they had no root, they withered away. And others fell among the thorns, and the thorns came up and choked them out. And others fell on the good soil, and yielded a crop, some a hundredfold, some sixty, and some thirty. He who has ears, let him hear.'"

God is in the business of planting seed (his word), and the effect it has depends on the soil (each person's heart) on which it lands. God pursues those whom he has chosen (Jonah and Paul are good examples) and each person responds as they will. The Bay family was being pursued by God, although they didn't realize it at the time. Seeds were being planted, and each heart was at different stages of fertility.

I mentioned in a couple of other chapters that we were a secular family (heathens for sure) that did not attend church (Sunday mornings were reserved for championship wrestling and roller derby). In fact, I don't even remember going to church on Christmas and Easter, as lukewarm Christians tend to do. However, God has his ways of planting seed when it isn't so obvious.

Mom, from time to time, needed to free herself from the four little minions that we were, if only for a little while. She took advantage of a movie matinee once in a while, but that could become pretty expensive if utilized on a regular basis. I imagine Mom talking to herself thus, "I wonder where I can drop these kids? I definitely need a break, if only for a few hours. The movie is out, I've overdone that one. Where can I find somewhere really cheap, or better yet free? Somewhere that the kids can't do too much harm and where there's adult supervision. Hmmm? I remember reading a sign on the front lawn of the church down the street; something about Vacation Bible School. It's worth a try."

So Mom dropped the four of us off at the church. Each night that week, we were at the church for two to three hours. They must have done this VBS thing before because they sure knew how to keep us kids busy. There were kids of all ages, playing games outside, doing crafts inside, singing songs, and eating cookies and drinking Kool-Aid. There were even stories that we heard every night about God and miracles and Jesus and other men and women from the Bible. We didn't have a Bible in our house, so all of these stories were new to us.

Each night, there was time set aside for us to do a craft. The particular craft that I not only enjoyed making, but also enjoyed giving to Mom, was a chicken made of corn. A plywood board was covered with burlap, and on the burlap was an outline of a chicken. We were all given a number of corn pieces in various colors to glue to the burlap, with each color filling in a particular part of the chicken (yellow corn for the beak, etc.). The project was not completed in one sitting, so we had time to work on our chicken each night we were there. When I brought my masterpiece home, Mom was obviously overjoyed. With pride beaming from my face I said, "Mom, look what I made at Vacation Bible School!" "That's very nice, son. You must have worked hard on it. What is it supposed to be?" A little taken aback by the question, I answered, "A chicken, of course. It's for you." Mom tried to sound grateful and said, "Oh. Thank you so much." Noticing the chicken being set aside I blurted out, "You're supposed to hang it. It has a pull tab from one of Dad's beer cans on the back to hang it up with. Where are you going to hang it?" Caught off guard, Mom stuttered, "Uh, I'll uh, hanging it right here in the kitchen. Right behind the door."

I was very proud of that chicken until pieces of corn began to fall off, one after the other. Eventually, it came off the wall and ended up somewhere, I'm not sure.

Another part of each evening involved going outside behind the church and playing games. After the tedious craft work, the kids were a little restless. There was a field of grass behind the church that allowed us all to run around chasing each other, burning off pent-up energy. Once the volunteers had settled us down, we played two games that I enjoyed.

The first game was called "Red Light, Green Light." All the kids lined up behind an imaginary line, and an adult stood about thirty paces out into the field. When the adult said "green light," you could run, but when she said "red light," you had to immediately stop. The idea was to see who would pass the volunteer first and be declared the winner. Of course, there was a little cheating going on: when the volunteer said "red light," it took some of us a few extra steps to come to a complete stop (those extra steps could mean the difference between winning and losing).

The other outdoor game was called "Lemonade, Lemonade, What's Your Trade?" This game was much like charades. Each child was given a specific profession (fireman, teacher, janitor, truck driver, etc.) and through body actions, you had to get the others to guess which profession you were. This was hard! How do you pantomime a teacher? I much preferred the physical game, "Red Light, Green Light."

One of my favorite parts of the evening involved snack time. I loved the cookies: chocolate chip and oatmeal raisin cookies, and the Kool-Aid was refreshing after running around the yard in the hot summer sun. After snack time, we were ushered off into separate classrooms and taught Bible lessons and different songs.

The classrooms faced an open area, similar to a courtyard that was full of numerous varieties of foliage, with a fountain in the center (like all fountains there were coins visible at the bottom). They were aligned in a square with a walkway between the classrooms and the courtyard area. A skylight allowed sunshine to stream down on the plants. It was all pretty.

Eventually, we were all led to a large auditorium where we sang songs, prayed, and listened to a couple of men as they encouraged the entire group with inspiring words (during the inspiring words portion, I either fell asleep or was distracted by some other kid down the row behind me). I particularly enjoyed the singing.

Every night was fun, and each following day, we asked Mom if we could go back again. There wasn't any resistance on Mom's part. Not only did she gain some alone time, but we always came home worn out, which made us more pliant and easier to put to bed.

After VBS was completed, one of the volunteers approached the four of us and asked if we would like to come to her house and learn more about Jesus and the Bible. We told her that we wanted to go home first and ask our Mom. Our spokesperson, Vicki, asked, "Mommy, a lady from VBS asked if the four of us can go over to her house to learn about Jesus. Can we go?" "What is the lady's name?" Mom replied. Vicki hadn't bothered with that bit of information. "I don't know." Mom pressed for more, "Where does she live?" Again, not real sure, Vicki answered, "She said she lives up the street, just a few blocks from our house." That was good enough for Mom who said, "Okay. You can go."

I don't need to tell you that this would never happen today. In fact, both Mom and the lady would be arrested. Seeds were being sown despite the obstacles.

When we arrived at the lady's house, she took the four of us into the front living room where she had a number of folding chairs lined up in a classroom fashion (it was similar to a Sunday school class although it wasn't Sunday). There were a handful of other kids already seated; I think they were her children. She seemed delighted that we had come. At the front of the class were an easel and a felt board on which representations of people and animals were laid out to tell Bible stories. We sang one song that still plays in my head to this day.

> Good news, good news, Christ died for me.
> Good news, good news, he set me free.

That's all I remember of the lyrics, but it was such a wonderful melody that I found myself singing it over and over. The actual second line in the song was different than what I remember, but I have a tendency to make up lines in songs either because I wasn't paying attention to the original or I have a natural writing talent that just can't be held at bay.

The lady was very nice and also fed us cookies and Kool-Aid (cookies and Kool-Aid must have been in the curriculum), but there was something a little bit strange going on in her back bedroom. Kids would leave the main session and disappear behind the door of the back bedroom where they gave confessions in order to be saved. When they came out, they were given a treat (due to the treats being dispersed, several kids double dipped with numerous "confessions"). The lady approached the four of us. "Would you children like to come back with me to the bedroom and make your confessions? When you're done with that, I have some treats for you." Vicki was a bit suspicious and coyly replied,

"Not until I talk to Mommy and Daddy." Timmy was stubborn and said, "I don't want to." Kathy adamantly stated "No."

I also rejected the offer (the fear of what was behind that closed door did play into my decision), running out the door and straight home. At this point in my life, my "soil" was not quite ready for this (the soil of my heart was like the soil at the Bonneville Salt Flats; salty, hard, crusty, and dry. No vegetation grows there), but there would be a time.

At this point, the family still wasn't churchgoing, but from time to time, the four of us would wander off to church on a Sunday morning, Mom and Dad sleeping in. One of these Sundays turned out to be significant for Vicki. This particular day, Vicki went to church by herself (Timmy, Kathy, and myself must have been watching roller derby) and ended up on the front row of the church, sitting alone.

The preacher started telling the story of Jesus being baptized and the accompanying affirmation from the Father, "This is my beloved Son in whom I am well pleased." The emphasis in this sermon was the obedience of Jesus to his Father. Vicki's take on obedience was learned from scripture examples. Peter, looking out into the night called out, "Lord, if it is you, command me to come to you on the water." Jesus replied, "Come." Peter got out of the boat and walked on the water and came toward Jesus. In another example, Jesus had instructed John the Baptist to baptize Him and John was in an argumentative mood when he replied, "I have need to be baptized by you, and do you come to me?" Jesus patiently corrected John, "Permit it at this time, for in this way it is fitting for us to fulfill all righteousness." Then John baptized Jesus.

Vicki heard this from God, "Vicki, get up and get baptized."

For Vicki, it was all about obedience. There was much she didn't understand: sin and redemption, buried and raised to walk again, grace and being covered by Jesus's blood, but she did understand obeying God. When the preacher made the altar call, Vicki got up alone and went forward to be baptized. This church had a tradition that the actual baptism would be held at a later date, Easter Sunday.

When she came home with the good news, Dad wasn't all that pleased (maybe he felt that he should have been consulted prior to such a big decision). Nevertheless, the baptism went on as planned, and Mom and Dad were in the audience at the church. As Vicki came up out of the water, she was so proud that she wanted everyone in the audience to see her and stood out in front basking in the attention, but because of the additional baptisms going on, the preacher gently brushed her aside and went on to the next individual.

Apparently Vicki's "soil" was similar to the kind that is found in Illinois and other Midwestern crop states: dark, moist, and rich with nutrients. The seed had taken root. One Bay down, five more to go. God was not done planting seed. There would be more to come.

LEAVING LA

(THERE'S NO PLACE LIKE HOME... CLICK, CLICK, CLICK)

In the movie *The Wizard of Oz*, Dorothy was quite sure that getting out of Kansas would solve all of her problems. After all, life on the farm and the boredom that accompanies it, especially for a teenage girl, was more than Dorothy could stand. She needed to get away, find a new life, one of adventure and opportunity. When she and Toto, the dog, arrived in Oz, all of her dreams and aspirations seemed to be coming true. Oz was full of adventure and opportunity as well as danger and many strange people and creatures. Her trip was culminated in the Emerald City, a glamorous and glorious place to be sure. Unfortunately, she realized not long after she had arrived, that the real place she wanted to be was home, with all of her friends and family. There's no place like home, indeed.

Mom and Dad, like Dorothy and Toto (Mom did resemble Dorothy in that she was very pretty and could sing like a bird, whereas Dad did not resemble Toto at all; his bite was much worse than his bark, unlike Toto who was a vociferous barker, but not much in the biting department. Miss Gulch would probably argue that last point, but who believes the Wicked Witch of the West anyway?), decided that they too wanted to "get out of

Kansas" for a new life and opportunity that they didn't see in their current circumstance.

When Mom and Dad were married in the mid-1950s, the economy in Missouri was stagnant, and all of the opportunities for jobs were in California (the Land of Oz) and specifically Los Angeles (the Emerald City). They decided to leave the boredom and go to where the adventure was.

What wasn't to like in LA? There were mountains, beaches, forests, deserts, swimming pools, and movie stars! Dad had a great new job, and the money was good and steady. Mom had all of the fresh fruits and vegetables she could ever dream of and plenty of warm sunshine. We, the little heathens, had the neighborhood and all of the fun that accompanied it. All the while, underneath the surface, Dad was secretly longing to go home: home to family, friends, and roots. Little did we know, but a plot was underway, and only one person would be excited about the eventual outcome.

At the end of the school year, for me the fourth grade, we were all excited about another summer and all the neighborhood adventure that would surely follow. Baseball was on the agenda and more trips to the public pool were in the offing. Then the rumors started. Vicki pulled me aside one day and said, "I heard Mommy say that Daddy said we were moving." Feeling left out I responded, "Daddy didn't tell me." "He didn't tell me either. Maybe he's going to tell us all at once."

Dad wasn't one for formalities, so we never had family meetings like some households do. I don't believe Dad intended for us to find out this way, it just happened. Once the rumors started, it was hard to stop them, and the issue had to be addressed. Dad finally got us all together and told us what was on his mind. "Kids, we're moving." He was blunt. Not really grasping the finality of moving, I said "Where are we going?" Vicki wasn't pleased and commented, "I don't care where we're going, I'm not going! All my friends are here." Dad explained further, "We're moving back to Missouri. Your mother and I were born there and most of our families still live there." Timmy was clueless and asked, "Wheh is Missouwi?" Kathy too didn't understand moving and she wanted to know, "Can Sandy come with us?"

By this time, Dad realized that he had a pressure cooker on his hands and decided to sweeten the pot so that we would all look at this in a positive light. After all, we had never lived anywhere else and this was quite a shock to us. Dad further explained the advantages of going to Missouri. "Kids, Missouri is a wonderful place. You'll get to see Grandma Nina and Grandma and Grandpa Bell." Timmy was still unaware of Missouri and asked, "Ah theh oceans theh?" Dad, trying to spin things positively, told us "No, there aren't any oceans, but there are plenty of creeks, rivers, and lakes." Kathy was still concerned about her friend when she asked, "Will Sandy be theh?" Again, Dad had to be positive and answered Kathy, "No, but you'll be able to make many new friends." Still angry at the idea, Vicki said "You could promise me the world and I'm still not going. I'm staying here." I think she believed that she could stay behind. This time Dad directed his comments to Vicki and promised, "Kids, we're going to live on a farm and you all are going to have your own horses. We'll go fishing all the time and swimming in the lakes and rivers. It will be a lot of fun!"

Dad finally turned Vicki with the horses. I was sold once I heard we were going to live on a farm (Dad fully intended to fulfill these promises once we got to Missouri, but before that happened, there were a few details to work out, like where he was going to work). Once Vicki and I were on board, the two little ones fell in line. Mom wasn't too thrilled about leaving the fruit and vegetable mecca that southern California was, but she had learned to go with the flow and did her best to remain positive about the move. During the big meeting, a date was never mentioned for the move, and we never thought to ask. Once the meeting was over, we went back to playing like we normally did.

Russell and I were playing in his front yard one sunny summer morning (it couldn't have been too early, Russell had to have his beauty sleep after all) when I noticed him staring down the street toward my house. "Ronnie, what's that big U-haul truck doing in your driveway?" Not getting the memo, I was a little surprised myself and answered, "Huh? I guess there *is* a U-haul in my driveway." Russell was curious and excited and suggested, "Let's go down there and see what's going on." As if I didn't know what was going on I agreed and said, "Yeah. Let's see what's going on down there at my house."

As we stood in the yard watching the loading of the U-haul, it never dawned on me the finality of it all. We were moving and not coming back. The four of us had grown-up in this house, in this neighborhood. We had never moved before. Oddly, I didn't feel sad until I saw that Russell and some of the other guys in the neighborhood were sad. I felt sorry for them.

To my detriment, what I did next I regret to this day. For some reason, I had the "going-away present" thing all mixed up. When someone is going away, they are usually given gifts as a token of appreciation and to wish them the best in their new endeavors. I, on the other hand, decided that I was the one that needed to give a gift to those that were staying. The only thing of real value that I had was my baseball card collection. I ran in the house and grabbed my shoebox full of cards, about a thousand in all, and gave it to Russell and Mark. Why, oh why did I do that? I was one goofy kid. The value of those cards today.

When the truck was finally loaded, jam-packed, it was time for all of us to go. I noticed a tear in Dad's eye and didn't find out until later that it wasn't because he was sad to leave. There were things that had to be left behind that wouldn't fit in the truck, and one of those things was Dad's roll-top desk (the one that Timmy fell out of bed and hit his head on). That desk was a beautiful desk, the nicest piece of furniture in the house, and today would be worth quite a bit of money.

Timmy and I climbed up into the U-haul with Dad, while Vicki and Kathy jumped into the 1962 Ford Galaxie 500 with Mom (throughout the trip, the boys and girls would trade places). As we pulled out of the driveway and into the street, all four of us had friends to wave good-bye to. We would never see them again, at least all of them but Russell, his little sister Sandy, and his mom and dad (they came out to Missouri to visit a few years later). It only took me a few seconds to forget the old neighborhood and focus on the adventure right in front of us.

The drive to Missouri would cover over 1,600 miles. The Ford was good to go except one minor detail: it didn't have an air conditioner. We were going to travel 1,600 miles across the hottest, most barren land in the entire country, in summer no less, without an air conditioner! Who in their right mind would take on such an endeavor under these conditions? My dad. To his credit, Dad did have a plan.

At this stage of technological advancement, there was an apparatus available that, in the event one didn't have an air conditioner, would serve as an adequate substitute. It was called a car cooler. The car cooler was designed to mount on the window of an automobile for the purpose of cooling the car. The apparatus was filled with water and the water evaporation was what cooled the air. These devices, prior to the air conditioner being standard on most cars, were popular in low humidity places like California, Arizona, New Mexico and Texas.

With nothing to compare it to (we never experienced an air conditioner in any of our cars), I suppose it was a relief. Being sprayed in the face with a squirt gun would be a relief while traveling through the 120 degree Mojave Desert. Unfortunately, the U-haul was not equipped with either of these options, and the warm desert air flowing into the cab of the truck would have to do.

Dad, the old truck driver, had this trip mapped out to the mile. When Dad picked up the truck, the U-haul man estimated the total miles based on the normal route and with it the accompanying charges associated with the miles. Dad had other ideas, and not only would he take another route, he was determined to do it in far less miles. First stop on the trip would be at Uncle Wendell's place in Ehrenberg, Arizona, right on the Colorado River (Dad's special route was I-10 to Phoenix and then old Highway 60 the rest of the way to Springfield, Missouri.). Dad surely knew that this was an adventurous kid's dream; we would be in the middle of the desert, which is always great for exploration, and along a major river. To top it off, Uncle Wendell had a small store with candy and pop. Wow! Great idea, Dad.

The trip from our home to Uncle Wendell's was 220 miles and would take approximately four hours (the U-haul had a governor installed and would only top out at fifty-five miles per hour). It wasn't a stop designed out of necessity, but was more of a planned family visit. Because Timmy and I were in the truck with Dad, and Kathy and Vicki were in the car without Ronnie and Timmy, the usual shenanigans that accompanied our travel ("Kathy touched me," "Wonnie's on my side of the seat," "Timmy's sticking his finger an inch from my nose, but not officially touching me") were muted. Since there was an advantage to being in the car with Mom (air cooler), occasionally one of the kids in the car could be seen taunting those in the U-haul by sticking out their tongues and laughing.

As we were finally leaving LA for the last time, there was an incident that brought out the best in Dad. Some knucklehead in a car was in traffic and cut off Mom. Dad saw the entire incident from the U-haul following behind. Dad was livid. He yelled out the window, waved his fist in the air, honked his horn, whatever he could do to let the guy know that if he could get this vehicle to go faster than fifty-five miles per hour, he would catch up with him and teach him a lesson.

This incident reminds me of a situation between Mom, Dad, and me when I was a teenager. I was pretty cocky and obnoxious as a teenager, and when Dad wasn't around, I was often disrespectful to Mom. One particular day, I was at the top of my obnoxious game and Mom couldn't take any more. She broke down in tears, and at that point, I knew there would be trouble ahead when Dad came home. Once Mom had filled him in on the day's activities, he surprised me by calling me into his office (the living room). I could tell that this was going to be a serious conversation because he muted the television show he was watching. "Ronnie, you know how much you care for Julie and what you would do to someone if they mistreated her?" Not sure where this was going, I answered hesitantly, "Yeah." "Well, son, your mother is my girlfriend, just like Julie is yours. If you ever make your mother cry again, you will have me to deal with." Not taking long to get the point I responded, "Okay."

One sure thing about Dad: you didn't mess with him or those that belonged to him. The guy in the other vehicle finally disappeared over the horizon, and we continued on our journey across the Mojave Desert, (Vicki, Kathy, and Mom as cool as cucumbers; Ronnie, Timmy, and Dad as hot as the desert sun) soon to be at Uncle Wendell's home.

We arrived in Ehrenberg and pulled into Uncle Wendell's convenience store parking lot. His home was behind the small store, and a couple of gas pumps stood out front. Even though it was just off the main highway, it wasn't very busy. Inside, the store was equipped with all of the basics that a person would need: bread, milk, canned goods, chips, some health and beauty items, and the two things that interested us the most, candy and pop. Over in the corner was a metal pop cooler with a sliding lid on the top and a bottle opener on the front left side. Coca Cola was written in large script on the front and sides. Not being shy

I asked, "Uncle Wendell, can we have a pop?" Before he could answer, Timmy added, "Uncuh Wenduwh, can we have some candy?" Uncle Wendell gave us the answer we didn't want to hear, "You kids have to ask your dad and lunch comes first."

Somehow, I knew he would say that. After lunch and after much whining and nagging, we got a pop (ice-cold pop out of a bottle is quite refreshing, especially in the desert) and a pick of one candy each. Apple Stix for me.

We had the river or the desert to explore. Which would it be? Our answer came quickly when Dad said we were going out to the desert, and we could watch him and Uncle Wendell shoot their shotguns. This sounded really neat to me. Number 1: we would be in the desert, and number 2: I had never seen or heard a gun before. I was so excited that I could barely sit still on the way out there.

Back in the "old" neighborhood (funny how four to five hours changes a person's perspective), we had been exposed to a few desert creatures. One day, Mark came down the street carrying a small box in his hand. Mark proudly said, "I bet you guys can't guess what I have in this box. Not in a million years." "I don't know," Russell correctly answered. "I wonder what it is?" Timmy spoke for the rest of us. I was a little less impressed and offered, "A million years is a long time. What's in the box?"

As we all gathered around, Mark made sure to open the box very slowly to heighten the suspense and attention he was getting. Once the lid was off the box, we were able to see a rattler, minus the rattlesnake. Mark allowed us to hold it, and we were amazed that if you shook the rattle, it sounded like it did when the rattlesnake was angry. This was big. "Where did you get it?" I asked finally impressed. "What happened to the snake?" Timmy wanted to know. Mark proudly answered, "My dad shot it with his gun."

All of a sudden, Mark had just risen to the top of the "my dad is better than your dad argument." At least, he was having his moment in the sun. All boys should experience that feeling. His glory only lasted a few minutes when he was called back home, and it was quite evident from the body language that the rattle was never meant to be shown to the neighbor kids, let alone handled by them.

A neighbor down the street called all of us to his backyard to see his new pet. In the yard was a wooden box with sand, gravel, and rocks laid out on the bottom (much fancier than our cardboard lizard box). We were directed to the box to see his prize. Staring down into the box of debris, Timmy asked, "Wheh is it?" Vicki was stumped too and said, "All I see are rocks, sand, and gravel." Kathy was not sure either and queried, "What ah we supposed to be looking at?" I couldn't see anything and commented, "This is boring."

The neighbor kid leaned into the box with a stick in hand, and as he poked the rock in the back corner of the box, the rock jumped forward a few inches. We all jumped back, startled for the moment. He proceeded to give us a lesson on horny toads. We had always heard about them, but this was our first experience up close. Interesting creatures.

Other than the cactus in our backyard and a few stories about the danger of scorpions and how they liked to hide in your shoes and if you were stung you could die, we didn't have any other reference points for the desert experience except the rattlesnake rattle and horny toad.

Dad and Uncle Wendell were shooting bottles with their shotguns, and for a moment, I was pretty engaged. The loud noise of the shotgun scared me, but the exploding bottles and cans made it worthwhile. Soon, I began to wander around looking under and behind rocks for rattlesnakes, horny toads, scorpions, black widow spiders, tarantulas, coyotes, and any other creature or animal that I could think of. All of nature must have been warned we were coming because I did a lot of looking and absolutely didn't see anything. How disappointing.

I began to daydream about riding my horse across the desert, taking my Bowie knife to the base of a cactus when thirst began to overtake me, shooting a rattlesnake with my six-shooter, and cooking the thick chunks of meat over an open fire. As the Apaches began to surround me, I made my way down the dry riverbed and escaped into the mountains. Awakened from my dreaming I heard dad, "Kids, get in the car. We're done out here."

My daydream would have to wait for another day.

After a few minutes at Uncle Wendell's house, we became bored and needed to expend some energy (our energy was unlimited), so Mom told us to go outside and try not to get lost. We headed down to the Colorado River to explore. The four of us found and wandered down a dirt road that ran parallel with the river, but the river itself was a hundred yards away. Between us and the river was a lot of swamp and mud, so exploring the actual river was not an option. We followed the road a little farther and came upon what looked like an old camp area. As we dug around in the assorted trash and junk left behind, we discovered some old cans. The cans were rusty, but had never been opened. We shook them just to make sure and became excited as to what they might contain. Our imaginations began to be stirred and Vicki said, "I wonder if these cans belonged to some cowboys that were passing through here a long time ago?" I became excited and added, "Yeah, look at the tops of these cans. They don't make them like this anymore." "I wonder what food is in these cans," Vicki said. Being the cowboy expert, at least in my mind, I answered, "I'll bet that they contain beans and stew. That's what cowboys used to eat." Vicki came up with the idea, "Let's open one and see what's inside." Agreeable Kathy said, "Okay," but Timmy wasn't sure and asked, "How ah we going to open up these cans?" Timmy asked a great question, but I was already thinking ahead when I said,

"Maybe if we get them open we can cook whatever's in them over a campfire!"

Opening the cans did present a dilemma: we didn't even have a pocketknife between us. Finally after staring at the cans for quite some time, Vicki came up with the idea of finding a larger rock with a pointed end that could be used as a can opener substitute. After looking around on the ground, we found a couple of rocks that would serve the purpose. The cans were set on the ground, and we proceeded to strike the top of the can with the rock until we succeeded in opening the can, juice raining around us once we broke through. We poured out the ingredients, but couldn't identify the substance. A rusty brown liquid was all that came out of the can. It didn't smell like food, at least from what we could tell in our limited research.

This confirmed our theory: these cans had to be really old and were surely in the possession of some cowboys nearly one hundred years ago. But what happened to the cowboys? Why did they leave these valuable foodstuffs behind? The obvious answer: Indians. They could have been killed or they ran away, but either way, we now had the cans of food. We didn't get too far in our speculation when we noticed some adults approaching us from the other end of the road. We decided it was getting late, and we needed to get back to Uncle Wendell's house.

That night was a good night for sleep. We were extremely worn out, and with minds racing, we fell into a deep sleep, the perfect sleep for dreams. Dreams of Indians and cowboys, campfires and beans and rattlesnakes and scorpions. The next morning, Dad was his usual subtle self in waking us. Pounding the door to our room, Dad's voice boomed, "Kids, get up. We have a long drive ahead of us. Let's go."

It was the boys turn to ride in the car with Mom and the air cooler while the girls would ride with Dad in the truck. Most of the trip was through desert terrain, with a few mountains to traverse along the way. All of the scenery was interesting to me because I had never seen it before. There were tumbleweeds blowing across the road with an occasional sandstorm thrown in from time to time. Flat desert would quickly change to rocky mountains. My eyes remained glued to the windows as I tried to take it all in.

Dad, always the big kid, tried to make it a fun trip for us whenever he could. In the mountain stretches, it was a challenge for the U-haul to climb to the top, but once at the apex, the downhill was a breeze. When it came time for the downhill, Dad would put the truck into neutral and coast down the hill. For some reason, we thought this was extremely exciting. The engine would be relatively silent, and the only sound we heard was the wind whistling through the windows. It seemed like we were going much faster in neutral than the truck could go under power (with the governor limiting its speed to fifty-five miles per hour, I'm sure that coasting down the mountain road would allow the truck to exceed that number substantially).

Before long, we were out of Arizona and into New Mexico. Somehow, we got off Dad's travel plans and ended up between Las Cruces and Alamogordo where we stopped in the White Sands National Monument. This was a great opportunity for us to get out of the car and burn some energy. The white sand dunes were magnificent. They looked like pictures of the Sahara Desert and stretched as far as the eye could see. We climbed up to the top of one of the sand mountains alongside the road. We played in the sand for a while, and then it was back in the vehicles again (boys and girls flip-flopping).

It didn't take Dad long to get us back on track. He was determined to get a refund at the U-haul dealer once the journey was over. There is one mystery from this trip that has been debated within the family for years. Why did Dad choose a route that took us away from the Grand Canyon, which we all wanted to see, and then turn around and go off track to see the White Sands National Monument? No one knows the answer except Dad, and he hasn't supplied one to date. Our theory is that he was set on proving the U-haul guy wrong on the total miles for the trip (after all, Dad was the professional truck driver) and the route near the Grand Canyon would not allow him to win the debate and get his refund. It's a crying shame. I still haven't seen the Grand Canyon to this day. White sand hills were neat, but no giant hole in the ground.

The remainder of the trip was relatively uneventful, save for the normal potty breaks and back and forth between the four of us. In the bigger scheme of things, we were pretty well behaved. Separating us in two different vehicles paid dividends, and I'm sure Mom and Dad were a little surprised at their fortune.

After three days of driving, we finally arrived in Springfield, Missouri, and Grandpa and Grandma Bell's house. It was late in the evening, and they were expecting us. Because of the late hour and the fact that we were all dead tired, the usual greetings and introductions were quick and concise. Off to bed we went. The next day, Dad unloaded all of our stuff into Grandpa's garage and returned the truck (and received a refund for going far under the miles allowed for the trip). At this point, Dad didn't have a job, and we didn't have anywhere to live. I'm sure there was a feeling of consternation in the grandparents. That first night, lying next to each other in bed, Grandpa turned to Grandma and said, "Sugar babe, I'm not sure how long I can take these kids in our house (It had only been one day, but Grandpa had heard the rumors). I know we want to help, but he doesn't have a job and they don't have a place to live. What if this takes weeks or months?" Grandma answered sarcastically, "She's your daughter. What do you want to do, move?"

The Bay family had arrived in the Show Me state. Although California left us with many memories and adventures, Missouri was going to present far more opportunities than we could ever imagine. We had a lot to show the state, and the state had a lot to show us. After eleven years in the Land of Oz, Dorothy and Toto had finally made it home. Home to family and friends and to places of familiarity. There truly is "no place like home."